JAPANESE PILGRIMAGE

Oliver Statler

Original
published by Pan Books

Permission to quote from the following works is gratefully acknowledged:

The Confessions of Lady Nijō, translated by Karen Brazell, copyright © 1973 by Karen Brazell. Reprinted by permission of Doubleday Publishing Co., Anchor Press.
Heike Monogatari, translated by A. L. Sadler and originally published in two instalments of the *Transactions of the Asiatic Society of Japan*, copyright 1918 and 1921 by the Asiatic Society of Japan.
Hōgen Monogatari, translated by William R. Wilson, copyright ©1971 by *Monumenta Nipponica*, Sophia University of Tokyo, Japan.
"The Japanese Mission to China, 801–806" by Robert Borgen, published in the Spring 1982 issue of the journal *Monumenta Nipponica*, copyright © 1982 by *Monumenta Nipponica*, Sophia University of Tokyo, Japan.
Kūkai by Yoshito S. Hakeda. Copyright © 1972 by Columbia University Press.
Mirror for the Moon by Saigyō, translated by William R. LaFleur, copyright © 1978 by William R. LaFleur. Reprinted by permission of New Directions Publishing Corporation.
Religions of the East by Joseph M. Kitagawa, copyright © 1960 by W. L. Jenkins, reprinted by permission of The Westminster Press. The passage quoted makes reference to *The Way to Nivana*, by L. de la Vallée Poussin (Cambridge University Press, 1917) and *Philosophy of the Buddha*, by A. J. Bahm (Harper & Brothers, 1958).
Some Prefer Nettles, by Junichirō Tanizaki, translated by Edward G. Seidensticker, copyright © 1955 by Alfred A. Knopf, Inc.
"Songs on the Buddha's Foot-Prints," translated by D. L. Philippi, from *Nihonbunka-Kenkyujo-Kiyo* No. 2, March 1958, copyright © 1958 by*Nihonbunka-Kenkyujo-Kiyo*, Kokugahin University, Tokyo, Japan.
Sources of the Japanese Tradition, compiled by Tsunoda, de Bary and Keene, copyright © 1958 by Columbia University Press.
Ugetsu Monogatari by Ueda Akinari, translated by Leon Zolbrod, Vancouver, University of British Columbia Press, copyright © 1979. Reprinted by permission of University of British Columbia Press.
The maps on pages 17 and 18 are by Denise DeVone.

First published in Great Britain 1984 by Pan Books Ltd,
Cavaye Place, London SW10 9PG
© Oliver Statler 1983
Casebound ISBN 0 330 28376 6
Paperback ISBN 0 330 28375 8
Printed and bound in Great Britain by
Richard Clay (The Chaucer Press) Ltd, Bungay, Suffolk

TO JOSEPH M. KITAGAWA

CONTENTS

LIST OF ILLUSTRATIONS

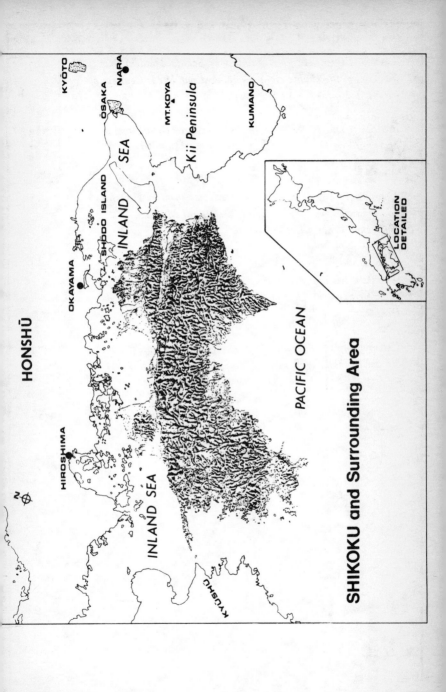

SHIKOKU and Surrounding Area

HONSHŪ

KYŌTO
NARA
ŌSAKA
MT. KŌYA
Kii Peninsula
KUMANO

INLAND SEA

SHŌDŌ ISLAND

OKAYAMA

HIROSHIMA

N

KYŪSHŪ

INLAND SEA

PACIFIC OCEAN

LOCATION DETAILED

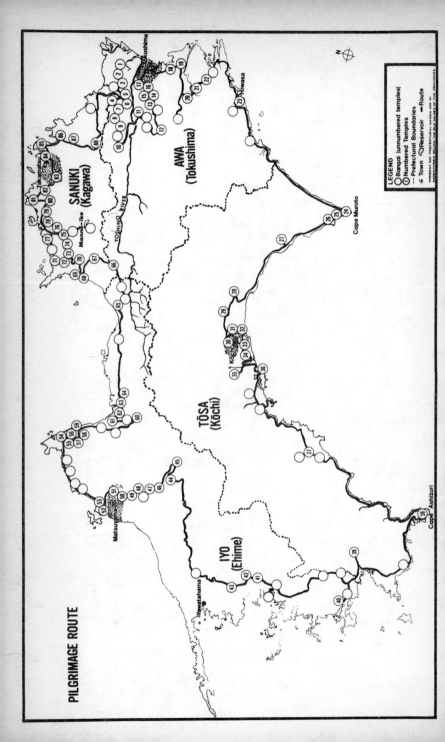

I
Master

1 This is where one begins. On this mountaintop, at the holiest spot of this sprawling complex of temples, in the shadow of these towering cedars, one stands before the tomb of the saint whose life and legacy inspire the pilgrimage. Here one asks his blessing, his guidance and protection, *his company,* on the pilgrimage to come.

I linger here as I always do. Before me is the ancient tomb, deep in the shadow of the trees; behind me a great hall where thousands of lanterns crowd the ceiling to dim recesses, each flickering light testimony to a prayer and an offering, where priests sell talismans and perform the fire service to burn away the sins of man.

I watch the worshipers stream by. They light their candles and their sticks of incense, adding them to banks of flame and urns that issue clouds of scented smoke. They come singly, in families, and in tour groups marshaled by an amplified guide. The groups worship on cue and move out obediently but most of the others linger. A priest beseeches the saint's intercession for a petitioner who stands beside him. A young woman who has been bowed at the rail retreats and sags to a bench, her face streaked with tears. She sits tensed and anguished until an older woman, a stranger, moves to her and comforts her. "The saint will help you. He will. He will." Presently they move together to stand again before the tomb. The old woman's voice rings out as they chant a litany of homage. The girl's voice, faint at first, becomes stronger and her back straightens.

He was born in 774. In the spring of 835 he announced the day that his life would end. He had journeyed to Kyoto to lead a festival of prayer at the imperial palace, he had bade farewell to the emperor and the two retired emperors, he had returned here to Mount Koya, to the monastic center he had founded in 816; banks of snow still lay in the shade of the temples he had built. He had chosen this spot to be buried. He made his will and named those who would succeed to large responsibilities. A disciple, an imperial prince who once was destined for the throne, painted his portrait. The saint himself completed it by brushing in the eyes. And on the next day, the appointed day, he passed out of this life.

As a priest he bore the name of Kukai but he is best known as Kobo Daishi, a title conferred by the imperial court posthumously, in 921. *Kobo* means "to spread widely the Buddhist teachings"; *Daishi* means "great teacher" or "great master," but considering the connotations it is probably more accurate to be less literal and translate it as "saint." He was neither the first nor the last to be canonized as Daishi but the Japanese have a saying, "Kobo stole the title of Daishi"—which is to say that when one speaks of *the* Daishi there is no question whom one means.

The eminent historian Sir George Sansom called him the greatest figure in the history of Japanese religion, a judgment I do not quarrel with. As the founder of Shingon, a major sect, he is a giant figure in the naturalization of Buddhism, in molding it to flourish in Japan. He is one of his country's great scholars: a poet, a calligrapher, an artist, an educator, a social worker, and, among other things, a first-rate civil engineer.

It is faith in the Daishi that has always sent the pilgrim forth, set him on the long route that encircles the island of Shikoku, fourth largest of the Japanese islands. The journey is almost a thousand miles: if walked—and for centuries there was no way to go but to walk—it takes about two months.

One moves along sandy beaches and jagged rocky coasts, through farmlands and villages and cities, goes deep into rugged mountains. Along the way are eighty-eight Buddhist temples, numbered in sequence, clockwise. This is the Pilgrimage to the Eighty-eight Sacred Places of Shikoku.

Kobo Daishi was born on Shikoku, and after his conversion to Buddhism he returned often to his home island for ascetic practice

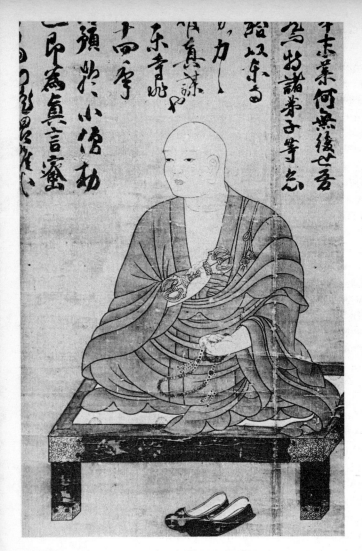

Kobo Daishi *(detail from a copy of the original painting)*

in remote places in its mountains. It is believed that the pilgrimage follows a trail that he trod.

More than that, the pilgrim believes that he walks with the Daishi at his side. Some say that though Kobo Daishi left this life he did not die, that he lies uncorrupted in this tomb under these ancient trees, awaiting the coming of the future Buddha who will signal the salvation of the world. Whether or not one holds to this belief, it is a fundamental tenet of the pilgrimage that the pilgrim walks with the Daishi—to some, quite literally; to others, in spirit. The motto of the pilgrimage is "We Two—Pilgrims Together," the Daishi and I.

I shiver, feeling the chill as this early spring afternoon wanes. I bow once more, ask that he be with me, ask that my pilgrimage may be a worthy one.

I move around the hall to the front. Before descending its steps I look down the mile-long path that disappears under the cedars, as the tops of the cedars themselves disappear in mist. Some of those trees were standing when the Daishi founded this mountain sanctuary more than a millennium ago.

Walking this path is walking through history. Stretching on both sides is the greatest cemetery of Japan. Mighty names crowd one another. These may not be their only graves, I know, for in Japan one may have many graves—it is enough to bury a lock of hair, a bit of ashes—but they are here because it was important to be here, on Koya, this Buddhist mountain, close to Kobo Daishi.

Massive tombstones, geometric towers mossy with age; clean fragrant air, a sense of great peace: I walk in deepening shade toward the temple where I lodge, the temple among the hundred up here that I call mine. Tomorrow I will go down from this holy mountain, cross the wide strait to Shikoku, and take myself to Temple Number One.

The cemetery on Mount Koya *(a print by Hiratsuka)*

2 Temple Number One: * when I made my first pilgrimage I was puzzled and I asked the priest, why is this particular temple Number One? Wouldn't it be more logical to begin at Kobo Daishi's birthplace? The very first guidebooks for the pilgrimage, more than three centuries ago, told pilgrims to start there, yet that temple is numbered Seventy-five.

The priest told me of a tradition that pilgrims should begin by visiting the Daishi's tomb on Mount Koya, as I have done. Coming

---

* Besides numbers, all the temples of course have names; they are given in the table beginning on page 329.

down from Koya and crossing over to Shikoku, they arrived near here. And so, when the temples acquired numbers, this became One.

Yet I know that people have always done the sensible thing: if they lived on Shikoku they started from home; if they came from another island they started at the port where they landed, and that might be on the opposite side of Shikoku.

It was, and is, entirely proper that they should do so. For this pilgrimage has no goal in the usual sense, no holy of holies to which one journeys and, after celebration in worship, returns home. This pilgrimage is essentially a circle: a circle has no beginning and no end. And so it is not at all important where one begins. What is important is that one go all the way around and return to one's starting point. One must close the circle.

The lane that leads from the town's main street to the temple gate is lined with pilgrims' inns and pilgrims' shops. Nowadays the temple seems like an adjunct to the town, at its periphery. But the temple came first; to serve those who flocked to it the town grew up at its gate. Many Japanese towns began that way.

The gate makes that history manifest. It dominates the block as it once dominated the town. It is monumental, two-storied, capped by a massive, flaring tile roof that culminates in dolphins who flip their tails as if in greeting. The gate is a symbol, summoning one from the secular world to the sacred precincts within.

Menacing giants flank the passageway: the rampant figures of the guardian deities who protect the temple glare down in warning to the insincere. For all their threatening stance these gods inspire worship; here as at other temples straw sandals are tied to the screens around their alcoves, offered by pilgrims with prayers for a safe journey, or by local people for relief from suffering in feet or legs—there is no mistaking the strength of those huge limbs or the solidity with which those feet are planted.

It is said—at least it was said in the old days—that when a pilgrim passes through the gate of his first temple he commits himself to completing his pilgrimage even at the risk of death along the way. His white robe testifies to that: in Japan white is

Temple One *(a painting by Sakata)*

the color of death. Moving through the gate of Number One I too feel a sense of commitment. Now I am a *henro*—a pilgrim to the Eighty-eight Sacred Places of Shikoku.

Straight ahead, a long stone walk leads to the main hall. On my left, open all around but under a roof, the stone ablution basin holds water for symbolic purification; there are bamboo dippers so that I may rinse my mouth, colorful towels left by groups of henro so that I may dry my hands. Farther along is the bell tower; I may if I wish—and I do wish—grasp the rope, pull back the heavy timber, and swing it forward to strike the bell, announcing my arrival to the temple deities and to Kobo Daishi. Deeper in the temple is a pagoda, a two-story structure distinctive to Kobo Daishi's kind of Buddhism, the first story square, the second story round; with the sculptures it houses it symbolizes the universe. On my right, beside a pool that is as much for fire fighting as for beauty, stands a tall bronze statue of the Daishi in the garb of a pilgrim, an appropriate figure for the first temple. Past him, at the end of a walkway to the right, is one of the essentials of a pilgrimage temple, the hall enshrining the Daishi. Beyond and behind the Daishi Hall are the temple office, the quarters for the priest and his family, and the big rooms where a couple of hundred henro can be lodged.

This is the traditional season for beginning the pilgrimage; there are numbers of henro about. I make my way to the main hall, light a candle, offer sticks of incense, and climb the steps to the wide veranda sheltered by the projecting roof. Gratefully I ease my pack off my back and step forward to bow in worship.

My mind goes back to the day some years ago when I began my first pilgrimage, and to the early morning service that began the day. I was traveling with a young priest; he joined the temple's priest at the altar so that I was the only one in attendance. It was a gray, rainy dawn. There was the soft early light, the murmur of the rain, the music of the liturgy that reminds me of a Gregorian chant. And there were the pigeons flying freely in and out of the open-fronted hall, their coos and the whir of their wings making accents like the priest's bell and drum. A temple is home to many pigeons. They are drawn by the rice that some people still leave as their offering, though most now drop a coin or two into the big grate-covered offertory box.

Worship here is as the individual chooses. A devout and knowing Buddhist may go through a whole litany. Some kneel in silent prayer, some pray very audibly. But one phrase constantly recurs to the lips of any henro: *Namu Daishi Henjo Kongo*. It is not easy to translate: "I put my faith in the great teacher who brings light to all the people, Universal Adamantine Illuminator." Or more simply, "Homage to Kobo Daishi, who impels our quest, who guides and acccompanies us." We Two—Pilgrims Together.

I take up my pack and move to the Daishi Hall. There is a special warmth in the prayers said to the Daishi. "Namu Daishi Henjo Kongo."

Beyond a bridging archway I find the priest and his wife. We exchange greetings—we are old friends now—and I introduce my

The Daishi as a
pilgrim *(a print by an
unknown artist)*

companion. He and I are shown to the room where we will sleep,
and a bit later we pour ourselves tea and sit with the doors slid
open to a handsome garden.

To go by myself would be lonely, and there is a tradition
against it because in the old days if accident or illness befell a lone
henro there would have been no one to look after him—or her, for
there have always been many women pilgrims. This spring I will
undertake the pilgrimage with a young man who has just graduated from college (the Japanese school year begins in April and
ends in March). He is free to go because unlike most of his class-
mates, who have already started working for some big corporation—the bigger the better, it is generally considered—he is going to
the United States to work for two years at a school for retarded

children, and it will be several weeks before his visa comes through.

I considered carefully before I asked him to join me. First, he is robust though not big (his sport is judo) and I think he will enjoy the hard walking and climbing. Then, in contrast to most of his peers, he is interested in his country's culture, and the pilgrimage is a deep plunge into that culture. Finally, we like each other and that is a good way to begin; I hope we can say as much when we end. His name is Morikawa Nobuo (in Japanese style, which places surnames first).

I have my equipment from previous pilgrimages but Morikawa must be outfitted, so we go to the temple's shop. He gets a white robe like mine, about hip-length. Traditionally henro have dressed all in white but for practical reasons we will wear ordinary slacks and hiking shoes.

He gets a stole, a purple band of cloth to wear over his shoulders, embroidered to announce that he started his pilgrimage at Number One (technically it is the stole that is a priest's vestment of office, his flowing robes are merely clothing; our abbreviated stoles mark us as laymen engaged in religious exercise). He gets a sedge hat, woven nowadays of straw, round, shaped like an inverted bowl, about a foot and a half in diameter. Its ancient design is really very practical, I have discovered: it shades the eyes, it is cool on the head, and when its vinyl cover is stretched over it—a modern extra to compensate for the fact that neither the material nor the weaving is up to old standards—it makes an effective rain hat. He gets a rosary of a hundred and eight prayer beads. We each get a bell of brass to hang from the belt; I have not carried one before but this time I want to. A bell calls one to prayer and is a reminder of impermanence: its quickly fading sound is like human life— "changing, inconstant, unstable," predestined to be transitory.

He gets an album filled with doubled sheets of fine paper. The pages are blank now but at each temple he will present this book and on a fresh page his visit will be certified with vermilion stamps and calligraphy in black ink. I have mine: one carries the same album for life; the temples add stamps over and beside the old impressions. Count the stamps and you will know how many times a henro has made the pilgrimage.

Album leaf inscribed
at Temple Seventy-five
*(calligraphy in black ink,
stamps in vermilion)*

He gets a supply of name-slips and a pouch to carry them in. Printed on the slips are the name of the pilgrimage and a likeness of Kobo Daishi based on that last portrait painted by his prince-disciple. At every altar where we worship we will leave a slip on which we have written name, age, home address, and date. Thus henro testify to their prayers and presumably sublimate man's deep-seated urge to commit graffiti. Yet many temple walls bear names and dates historically valuable because they are centuries old.

Most important, Morikawa selects a sturdy staff. It is the henro's one essential. He leans on it often, especially in the mountains; he is grateful for its support. But beyond that, it symbolizes Kobo Daishi. It embodies the faith at the heart of the pilgrimage, that the Daishi travels at the side of every pilgrim. And so the henro treats it reverently. When he stops for the night, his first act, before he looks to his own needs, is to wash the base of his staff, to wash the dust of travel from Kobo Daishi's feet as was necessary in the days of straw sandals. And in the room where he sleeps he puts the staff in the place of honor. On not only the staff but on much of the rest of our equipment—hat, album, name-slips and the pouch to carry them in—are the words *Dogyo Ninin:* "We Two— Pilgrims Together."

The hat bears other writing. Four lines of a very Buddhist poem radiate from the crown in the four directions:

> *For the benighted the illusions of the world.*
> *For the enlightened the knowledge that all is vanity.*
> *In the beginning there was no east and west—*
> *Where then is there a north and south?*

A bit enigmatic, Morikawa and I agree, but taken to heart they should help a henro to throw off the concerns of his worldly life, the impedimenta of day-to-day existence that hinder his struggle toward the essentials. On the front of the hat, in one of the quadrants formed by the poem, is a symbol of that effort, the Sanskrit letter *A,* the mother of sounds, signifying the vow to attain enlightenment. That is what the pilgrimage is all about but there is no use trying to define enlightenment. It is a state of grace that no one has been able to describe—not those who have attained it and certainly not those like Morikawa and me, who are struggling toward it. (Pushed to the ultimate degree, enlightenment is synonymous with Buddhahood: the name Buddha means the "Enlightened One." The two of us dare not aspire to that.)

One thing remains to be brushed on Morikawa's hat and staff—his name—and we go to the priest and ask him to do that.

I like this priest: relaxed and informal without shedding dignity, lean and pleasant face, eyes friendly yet appraising. He has seen thousands of henro set out for almost as many reasons. He blesses them all.

He invites us to bathe before the rush begins. The temple tonight will lodge 120 henro. I feel for the priest's wife: 120 dinners to be cooked and served, 120 beds to be laid on the mats, 120 breakfasts and 120 box lunches to be ready at dawn.

After dinner it seems like a good idea to meet some of our fellow henro (all but we are traveling by chartered bus). We introduce ourselves to four elderly men who are chatting together. This has been their first day on the road and they are getting acquainted. They tell us that their group comes from all over Japan; seven out of ten are women and most of them are widows as most of the men are widowers. When I remark that all look healthy despite their advancing years they counter by saying they have already learned of three women who are praying for recovery from illness.

I ask what Buddhist sects they represent and find that each of the four is a member of a different sect and none belongs to Kobo Daishi's Shingon. This, they assure me, should cause no surprise: all Buddhists can unite in worshiping Kobo Daishi—well, almost all. The pilgrimage is nonsectarian.

One of them has with him the album carried by his grandfather when he twice made the pilgrimage, in 1903 and 1905; "My father did the pilgrimage too, and I hope my son will." Another says he really wanted to take two months and do it on foot, but his children raised a fuss, saying they would worry about him, so he joined the bus group. A third shows a little bag that hangs from his neck. It holds his wife's ashes. "She died almost a hundred days ago," he says. At whatever temple they stay on that important day of mourning he will ask the priest to perform a memorial service. He smiles: "I feel that I am traveling with her."

They are tired and looking forward to bed. "Remember," one calls after us as we say good night, "all Buddhists join in revering Kobo Daishi."

3 It is a chill, gray, rainy morning as we set out. The pilgrimage begets two views of rain: it is the henro's torment; it is part of the henro's training and he should thank the Daishi for providing it. We take such comfort as we can from the latter.

April is likely to be a wet month but it became a traditional time to begin the pilgrimage because in the old days it was a hiatus for farmers, a slack period before the winter wheat could be harvested and the rice seedlings transplanted to the same fields after they were flooded, plowed, and worked to hospitable mud. Nowadays with diversified farming, truck gardening and fruit growing, a farmer has no slack time, but late March and early April still call forth a spring tide of henro.

Our first two days we shall be walking straight inland, up the valley of Shikoku's biggest river, the Yoshino. On our right when the clouds lift we glimpse the serried mountains that hem the valley on this side. On our left across the river are ranged the mountains we must penetrate after we leave the valley; I know those peaks are there but now they are lost in mist.

The temples are irregularly spaced along the pilgrimage route but they lie close together in this valley, a clear indication that it was an ancient center of population. Walking this road I get the feeling that men have lived here a long time. And so they have: there are prehistoric graves in the foothills. How many dozens of generations, I wonder, have sculpted these paddy fields, maintained the ridges between them, manured and watered and tilled this soil? This is an aged landscape yet always renascent. Cherry trees are about to blossom, winter-blooming camellias still offer splashes of pink and red, and a rusty metal building is a glowing background for the velvety white flowes of a tulip tree. We pass fields yellow with the blossoms of rape, grown for its delicate oil, fields purple with clover, and beds lush with the tender green of rice seedlings.

Another crop flourishes here and everywhere along the pilgrimage route. Legends about the wonders that the Daishi wrought are found all over Japan, including areas he could not possibly have visited in his lifetime, but nowhere do they cluster as thickly as along the road that henro travel.

We begin to encounter them at Temple Two. (Temple One purveys no legends, perhaps because as its priest once said to me, "Its position as Number One is sufficient unto itself.") At the second temple we find an ancient cedar said to have been planted by the Daishi; people call it the Longevity Cedar and say that if you pray pressing your hands to it you will be granted long life. Offerings of coins, hundreds of them, are stuck into its tough old bark.

Nearby a statue of the Daishi celebrates another legend. There once was a woman of Osaka who had been afflicted with miscarriage after miscarriage so that she had never been able to bear a child. Becoming pregnant again, she set out on the pilgrimage. Here at Temple Two labor pains set in, and then Kobo Daishi appeared and helped her give birth to a healthy baby. And if you demur, as I did, that she hadn't walked very far, the priest will correct you: she had walked in reverse order, counterclockwise, so she had nearly completed her pilgrimage. Since then pregnant women have prayed here for safe and easy delivery, and one whose prayer was answered contributed this statue.

At Temple Three the Daishi is said to have found that the local people suffered from a lack of good water; he thrust his staff into the ground and brought forth a spring. This is one of the legends found most frequently throughout Japan, sometimes featuring another saintly figure but most often Kobo Daishi. It testifies to the concern about water that has always dogged the inhabitants of these islands: they get goodly amounts of rain but it runs quickly off the steep slopes into the sea. Many of the pilgrimage temples have a legend about the Daishi's bringing forth a spring or digging a well in one night or taming an unruly river. Temple Six, not far ahead, was founded when he opened a hot spring with curative powers; he built a bath for the people and beside it he erected a chapel that grew into the temple.

Though such tales interest me I keep searching for the flesh-and-blood Daishi, the man who lived from 774 to 835. It is not easy to find him—he is so buried under legend—but I keep trying.

To take my mind off the rain, which now is trickling down my back, I make another effort.

Over the range of mountains on our right is the fourth province of our pilgrimage; as we walk through it we will be moving back toward Number One, nearing the end of our journey. Deep into that province, where the mountains give way to the plain along the shores of the Inland Sea, is Temple Seventy-five: it marks the site of his family home. Six or seven weeks from now, if all goes well, Morikawa and I will be approaching it and the temples that cluster about it, once subtemples, now independent. At them we will begin to encounter the reverent legends that have grown up around his childhood.

The setting for one of them is a precipitous mountain; thrusting sharply up from the plain, its rugged form rises sixteen hundred feet. It is said that at the age of seven the Boy Daishi climbed to its summit and threw himself from the peak, crying: "If I am called to save the people, save me, O Buddha! If I am not, let me die!" And there appeared a company of angels who caught the boy in their robes and carried him back to the top.

We will climb that peak. Half an hour on a steep path bordered by stone images representing the eighty-eight temples will bring us to the sanctuary that originally was Temple Seventy-three: the main hall bears a crest formed by a triad of outstretched wings; the bell tower stands against the wind, anchored to the mountain by chains. Two centuries ago new buildings were built in the valley below and the temple was moved down there to make it more accessible, but on the height just above us is its reason for being. Our path continues to a cliff hung with chains to help climbers; hand over hand we pull ourselves up. On the windswept summit there is room for a stone altar and a statue of the Child Daishi, but mostly there is a sense of nothing at our feet. The plain below is a geometric abstraction. Beyond it, the haze over the Inland Sea is clotted with islands. Of course this peak would pull an energetic boy. The more so because it was noted as one of those sacred places where wandering holy men practiced austerities, where they sought to draw into themselves the magical power attributed to the mountains.

Nearer Temple Seventy-five we will come to a crossroads chapel enshrining side by side the Child Daishi and the deity Jizo, guardian of children. We are told the boy used to play here, making mud images of the Buddha. I flinch from the notion of so saintly a child and am more moved by a grave where they say he buried his dog. I like the garden: it is a playground with swings and slides.

I remember Seventy-five from earlier visits: big, as it should be; imposing, as it should be; standing where his home stood. I try to visualize that house of twelve centuries ago: low, with open galleries all around but probably a dim interior, the patrician house of a landowner and aristocrat—a provincial aristocrat but an aristocrat nevertheless. Beyond a spacious garden there would be a wall of wattles and clay.

I see a small boy standing by the gate, watching his father's peasants as they trudge out to work their plots of land or bring home on their backs a fardel of twigs and sticks for firewood. That is an everyday scene but the boy's eyes open wide when on occasion a holy man appears. He retreats to a safer distance but his attention is riveted on the gaunt and ragged figure with wild eyes who stands there at the gate, holding out a begging bowl and bawling a strange mumbo jumbo until one of the servants comes hurrying with a cupful of barley, which causes the stranger to change his cry to one that the servant says is thanks and a blessing on the house and those who live in it.

Not knowing exactly what a blessing is but feeling more important for having received one, the boy resumes his station at the gate and wonders at the homage the peasants give this stranger, greater even and somehow different from the deference they show his father's bailiff or even his father. Next day a servant tells him that the holy man can cure sickness and rout ghosts and that she herself slipped out at night to receive treatment for the pains she suffers. Holy men go deep into the mountains, she says, to hidden places where they talk with the gods and learn secrets that enable them to work magic and to see into the future.

When he is bigger he roams the countryside and climbs nearby mountains, especially that challenging sharp peak, pulling himself handhold to handhold—there were no chains then—to the dizzying ledge where holy men communicate with the gods. He wonders how they do it. On his knees with his eyes closed he presses his palms together and tries to commune, but the only message he hears is the whistling of the wind.

I have been imagining what his boyhood was like; we have so few facts. He was born in 774 to a family named Saeki. The Saeki were a branch of the great Otomo clan, whose antecedents stretched back to mythological times. When the Sun Goddess sent her heavenly grandchild earthward to rule the Japanese islands, the ancestor of the Otomo put on his back a heavenly quiver, girt on his heavenly sword, took up his heavenly bow, grasped heavenly arrows, and proceeded in front of the heavenly grandchild: Otomo means "great escort." All of which signifies that the Otomo very early allied themselves with the clan that became the imperial line and that they distinguished themselves as warriors. They had ample chance to prove themselves, for the myths tell us that it took four generations of fighting to push from the island of Kyushu to the heartland where present-day Kyoto, Nara, and Osaka stand, and there establish the heavenly grandchild's great-grandson as the first emperor of Japan. That first emperor's greatest general was an Otomo.

But as the chronicles point out, the Otomo were more than generals: they "fought at the same time both for their Emperor and to rescue the people from misery"; they were "learned ministers and enlightened assistants"; they "propounded the policy and divine Japan flourished." Very likely their daughters married emperors, for imperial edicts call them near kindred. There were periods when they dominated the court and, there being no law of succession, themselves settled the inevitable brawls by deciding which prince would be emperor, following which they assumed the post of Great Minister and conducted affairs. (Early in the game, surely by the sixth century, Japanese emperors slipped into the pattern of reigning without ruling.)

As late as 749 they were singled out in an imperial edict: "Further, ye men of the house of Otomo and Saeki . . . [who] in serving the Sovereign House have no regard for aught else and . . . have always said, 'We will not die peacefully, we will die by the side of our King. If we go to the sea our bodies shall steep in the water. If we go to the mountains over our corpses the grass shall grow.' Wherefore We employ you, in Our reign as in the reigns of Our Distant Sovereign Ancestors, to be Our bodyguard."

Yet by 774, when the child was born, the Otomo were no longer dominant. They had been thrust aside by the descendants of other clans, though they were still prominent at court. Three relatives—two cousins of his father and an uncle on his mother's side—held high positions as scholars and administrators in the bureaucracy. As it became evident that the boy was gifted, it was natural to assume that he would follow them into government service, the most respected profession of the times.

But the times were not peaceful. It was only two centuries since the beginning of serious effort to remodel a loose federation of tribes into a real nation, an effort in which China had been taken as the model and Buddhism utilized as a unifying force. Nationhood was as yet far from achieved; troubles menaced everywhere. In the northeast there were frequent uprisings by "barbarians"— any tribe that had not yet bowed to the central power; again and again military expeditions had to be mounted and sent against them. Further depleting the treasury, there had been a rash of temple building, including a monastery and a nunnery in each province and a great headquarters temple at Nara.

Crushing taxes, military conscription, and levies of forced labor had exhausted the common people; many abandoned the land and wandered homeless. At any real distance from the capital, local chieftains still flouted the emperor's government, disregarding its commands and paying it no taxes. The throne itself was shaky. The attempt by a scheming priest to make himself emperor led to a decision in 784 to move the capital from Nara, where it was too much subject to the influence of powerful monasteries. Events following that decision shook the Otomo-Saeki clan.

Two officials were placed in charge of building a splendid new capital. One was a member of the powerful Fujiwara family and the other was the head of the Saeki family, a man who had made a reputation on construction projects. They could not have been a congenial team, since the Fujiwara, as imperial counselor, had just blocked a significant advancement in rank for the Saeki—a promotion that had been urged by the crown prince. Within months the Fujiwara man was murdered; the assassin was an Otomo who promptly implicated the late head of the Otomo, a greatly respected administrator and poet, Otomo Yakamochi. Yakamochi had died about a month earlier so he could not defend himself, but perhaps he could not have successfully done so anyway because he had vehemently opposed moving the capital. He was posthumously stripped of his titles, his son was exiled, and punishment fell heavy on other members of his family.

But that was not all. The Saeki codirector of construction was suspected of being involved in the plot, and so was his patron, the crown prince, a brother of the emperor. Both were banished; the prince, perhaps to protest his innocence and perhaps because he expected to be murdered anyway, starved himself to death on his way to exile.

These events took place when the boy who would become the Daishi was eleven years old. His immediate family was not punished but the disgraced head of the Saeki was his father's cousin and the whole family was under a cloud. The Otomo-Saeki name was no longer bright.

That was the way it was when the fourteen-year-old was sent up to the new capital to study with his maternal uncle, who began his serious education in the Chinese classics. The boy had a good teacher; his uncle was a distinguished Confucian scholar and tutor to one of the emperor's sons.

In 791, when he was seventeen, he entered the university at the capital, the highest educational institution in the country, open only to the sons of aristocratic families. Its purpose was to train officials for the government; its curriculum, following the Chinese pattern, was Confucianist, with emphasis on principles of government, history, poetry, and filial piety—which by natural extension encompassed loyalty to one's master, one's ruler.

"I studied diligently," he wrote later, but it must have been difficult to concentrate. The unfinished capital was in turmoil. In the aftermath of the murder and ensuing banishments, the empress had died, the emperor's son had fallen into an illness that neither physicians nor necromancers could cure, calamity had followed calamity. All were ascribed to the vengeful spirit of the dead crown prince. The site seemed to have been cursed from the beginning and a search was already on for another place to locate the government. (When they found it, it became Kyoto.)

His personal life seemed just as precarious. A year earlier his Saeki relative had died in exile, still in disgrace. The young man was forced to reflect on how fleeting was glory in this world, how transient were riches and an emperor's favor and life itself. As for a career in government he bore a stained name and the high-placed relatives who might have helped him had been wiped out. The works he was assigned to study—pronouncements of Chinese sages on virtuous emperors and counselors—had a bitter taste to him. He had reason to be depressed and disturbed. In the words of his earliest biographer, probably one of his disciples, "he constantly told himself . . . that what he was learning was only dregs derived from the men of old. They benefited him little at that time; how much less would they benefit him after death when his body had decayed? He then thought it essential to learn the ultimate truth."

He had already begun to read Buddhist scriptures and he had met an impressive Buddhist monk—not one of those associated with the rich and busy temples of Nara, not one who spent his time performing ceremonies for the government or wealthy patrons, but one of the few who had turned away from the pomp of the great temples to build retreats in the mountains where they practiced meditation. And so he was drawn to Buddhism not by study of abstruse doctrine in the temples but by the experience of meditation in the natural grandeur of the mountains.

He pondered his life and he left the university.

It was not an easy decision. He was turning his back on the

tradition of government service that his family had followed since mythic times. He was breaking with all they stood for, and he was not permitted to do this without pain. Although his Otomo forebears had fought to introduce the Buddha to Japan, it is clear that the Daishi's own family had not embraced Buddhism; they honored the native spirits of Shinto and lived by their ancestral code of fealty to the emperor.

He not only abandoned his heritage and his birthright but he did it in a way that to his family was outrageous. Yet it was a way fitting to one reared on Shikoku with its dark mountains, the sacred places within them, the wandering holy men who sought them out. As a boy he had seen them; now he became one of them. He turned to the mountains.

When he came back to Shikoku he surely went first to face his family. When he was twenty-four he was still trying to explain to them. "What has induced me to write this," he set down in the preface to his first major work, is "the opposition of my relatives to my becoming a Buddhist. . . . My teachers and relatives opposed my entering the priesthood." Though the body of the work is cast in the form of fiction, the central character, a mendicant Buddhist, is certainly himself, and he makes us feel the storm of protest that he faced and the anguish that it cost him.

The mendicant is lectured by his teacher: "The most excellent virtues of man are filial piety and loyalty. . . . Your parents are still living and there is also a lord in the country whom you can serve. Why do you not serve your parents and your lord? You have meaninglessly sunk into the ranks of beggars. . . . You put your ancestors to shame; your name will remain noxious to later generations. . . . Your relatives, out of embarrassment, will feel like crawling into the earth because of you. Even strangers, on seeing you, pretend they have not seen you."

And the mendicant answers: "I understand your meaning well. . . . My heart is about to burst from being unable to forget these duties. . . . This thought penetrates my skin and bone. . . . I feel ashamed and sad." But he argues that there is a transcending virtue, that of conforming to the "right way."

His years from eighteen to thirty-one were filled by a long

search for the "right way." Periods of intense study of Buddhist texts at temples alternated with periods of meditation in the mountains. He did not always travel alone; sometimes he went with others like himself, unordained lay seekers after the mystery at the heart of things. In that first work he pictured an ascetic who was surely himself: "Not being obliged to his father or elder brothers and having no contact with his relatives he wandered throughout the country like duckweed floating on water or dry grass blown by the wind. . . .

"His shaven head was like a round tray of copper, and his ashen face like an earthenware pot. He was haggard and small; his legs were long like those of a heron standing near a pond; and his sinewy short neck resembled that of a turtle in the mud." He carried an "often-mended begging bowl," a "broken water jug," and "a pilgrim's staff with the ring at the top missing"; "the rosary in his right hand with its 108 beads hung like a horse's girth, he wore sandals of straw, not of leather; . . . yet he enjoyed life in nature, brushing aside the snow to sleep, using his arms for a pillow. The blue sky was the ceiling of his hut and the clouds hanging over the mountains were his curtains; he did not need to worry about where he lived or where he slept. In summer he opened his neckband in a relaxed mood and delighted in the gentle breezes as though he were a great king, but in winter he watched the fire with his neck drawn into his shoulders. If he had enough horse chestnuts and bitter vegetables to last ten days, he was lucky. His bare shoulders showed through his paper robe and clothes padded with grass cloth. He was, however, quite satisfied with what was given him. . . . Though his appearance was laughable, his deep-rooted will could not be taken away from him. . . . He . . . applied himself diligently to the realization of Buddhism."

4 The third day of our pilgrimage: Morikawa predicted better weather and he was right. The skies have cleared, it's a sunny, mild morning, and there is joy in walking. We pass stands of mulberry bushes, signifying silkworm culture, and under long tunnels of plastic, young tobacco plants are being conned into fast growth. From sheds near the road cows moo at us in a chatty, matronly way; most households have just one, with maybe a calf beside her. There are yards filled with slate-blue rocks, much prized in landscape gardening all over Japan; dug from the riverbed, they sit disordered now, all shapes and sizes, waiting the eye of the connoisseur who will find one of them to be exactly what is wanted in the prospect he envisions.

A television antenna sprouts from every house but the shape of the roofs says old-fashioned thatch, though the thatch has been covered with a skin of sheet metal—easier to maintain, and there is still that thick blanket beneath to keep these sturdy old houses warmer in winter and cooler in summer. With sheet metal has come color. There are sky-blue roofs and umber ones and some of black. A friend with an eye sharper than mine discerned a correlation between the color of the roof and the importance of the house. Blue and brown cover the houses of ordinary farmers, but a black roof is the sign of a family of substance, of a former headman or a landowning village elder. Such a heritage is not forgotten in this landscape.

Rounding a curve in the road, we enter the village that has grown up below Number Ten. The temple is out of sight on the wooded height above us. It is the last of the temples in this valley; it is the first of the temples we must climb to reach. Up till now we have been walking an ancient local pilgrimage, older than the eighty-eight-temple pilgrimage and incorporated into it when it took form. The goal of the ancient pilgrimage was this mountain because the people of the valley have long regarded it as the home of the souls of their dead.

All over the world men have gazed on mountains in awe and reverence. Their peaks are where heaven and earth meet. They are homes of the gods or places where the gods descend when called upon in prayer. One thinks of Sinai and Olympus, but nowhere have mountains entered more deeply into life and faith than in Japan, perhaps because it has so many of them.

The ancient Japanese drew no hard line between their gods and their ancestors. Ancestors became spirits—occasionally malevolent but usually benign—who watched over the family in a continuing relationship with those living and those yet unborn. Spirits regarded so intimately had to have a residence. Prehistoric Japanese had only vague notions of an afterlife; it was somehow a continuation of this existence. They peopled their mountains with their dead.

Buddhism when it came from China did nothing to diminish this reverence for ancestors; it made old beliefs stronger and more complex. This mountain became a Buddhist mountain. Now the dead are remembered in Buddhist ways.

Through the open fronts of the village shops we glimpse traditional artisans at work. This place has a virtual monopoly on the production of hanging scrolls picturing Kobo Daishi; they are retailed here and wholesaled all over Japan. We stop at a shop with a fine display of them and all manner of religious articles. The owner, a round and genial little man, places cushions for us and pours tea, all the while inviting us to leave our packs with him while we make our way up to the temple and to rest awhile before we tackle the climb—generations of henro have called it heart pounding.

The cheaper scrolls, he tells us, are printed from copper plates; the more expensive ones are painted. Alas, craftsmen are getting scarce. He employs three painters. Repeating the same design again and again, each man works swiftly, two paintings at a time, adding strokes to one while the other dries. Still, with the increasing number of henro it's difficult to keep up with the demand.

He views benignly the new breed of henro who travel by bus or car. They have money to spend and they don't mind buying things heavy to carry. He chuckles: some try to bargain but they don't succeed—a man can't expect divine favor from a sacred article after he's knocked down its price. It's only that bus henro are held to such a tight schedule they don't have time to sit and chat. He pours us more tea.

Finally we rouse ourselves and start up. The shops end, there are a couple of farmhouses and noisy chickens, then the temple's gate at the foot of the forested mountain and behind it the first long flight of stone steps.

Halfway up is an altar where one must pause: a spring (credited to the Daishi, of course), a stone basin into which it flows, images of Kannon and Jizo, two of Buddhism's friendliest deities, and heaped before them, long thin strips of wood, each bearing the name of someone who has died. We pray here. We dip water from the basin and pour it over the statues, for in washing them we cleanse ourselves. We wet the strips of wood in benediction to the departed souls, to erase their sins and calm their spirits.

It's true: our hearts are pounding when we reach the main hall. Inside at a high desk sits the old gentleman who inscribes albums. The priest of this temple is a schoolteacher; I have never met him. It was this old man with wispy chin whiskers from whom three years ago I heard the temple's legend. He had been listening to a baseball game on his transistor radio but he obligingly turned down the volume and told the story.

When as a young man Kobo Daishi wandered Shikoku in his search for the highest truth in Buddhism, he found at the foot of this mountain a hut and a lovely young woman weaving cloth. The girl, as warm-hearted as she was beautiful, gave him food during the seven days he did ascetic practice on the mountain. On the seventh day he asked if he might have some cloth for new leggings and wristlets. The girl willingly gave him what he asked for and cut another long piece of her finest weaving to make him a new robe. Grateful and curious, he asked how she came to be at this lonely spot and she told him her story.

At the imperial court her mother had been a lady-in-waiting, her father a young officer of the guard. He became involved in one of the cabals that swirled around the throne, was found out and exiled. Her mother was left pregnant. Knowing that she was suspect because of her affair with a conspirator, she feared that if her child were a boy he would be killed, and so for six months she went daily to Kyoto's great Kiyomizu Temple to pray that she might give birth to a girl. She prayed to Kannon, the Buddhist embodiment of compassion. Her prayers were answered.

Seven years later Kannon came to her in a dream to tell her that she and her daughter were in mortal danger and that they should flee to Shikoku. They came to this place. Later, as the mother lay dying, she told her daughter all this, told her she was heaven-sent by Kannon, told her she should worship Kannon with all her heart.

This story so moved the Daishi that he began at once to carve an image of Kannon. He observed the strictest ritual, bowing three times before each cut of his blade into the sacred wood. When the statue was finished the girl begged him to ordain her a nun and so he cut her hair and administered the rites. As he did, a violet cloud descended from the sky and heavenly music was heard all about and in that instant the girl attained Buddhahood and was transformed into an image of Kannon. Kobo Daishi ascended the mountain, founded this temple, enshrined both images, and called the temple Kirihata-ji—*kiri* means "cut" and *hata* means "cloth"— "Cut-Cloth Temple."

This is one of the loveliest temple legends of them all. It dramatizes the heart of Kobo Daishi's Shingon, the belief that mortal man—even woman, to whom the Buddhism of the Daishi's time was not prepared to grant equality—can attain enlightenment, can aspire to Buddhahood in this life. A Japanese writer has called this the love story of Kobo Daishi's youth. A conventional priest might find his remark impertinent but there would be agreement that man, who has within him the seed of Buddha, is also flesh and blood. Shingon, like the original Buddhism of the historical Buddha, focuses on this life, not on the hereafter.

Descending, we pause at the Daishi's spring. Facing the altar is an old woman, her hands pressed tightly together in prayer. "I am eighty-four years old, Daishi-sama, and I am so grateful to be here, to be able to come here again." She says it again and again. When she turns, tears are streaming down her cheeks.

We exchange name-slips with her, as henro do who meet along the way. She is from across the Inland Sea and she is certain this is the last time she can make the pilgrimage. She had not expected this chance, for she has no family left, but some neighbors invited her to join them. At this point she could climb no farther and, waiting here for her companions to come down again, she has been pouring out her gratitude. We tell her truthfully that she looks very healthy despite her eighty-four years. "I am quite ready to die at any time," she answers. "I ask only to be buried along the pilgrimage route."

We cross the wide gravelly bed of the Yoshino River and head into the foothills to Temple Eleven. There we spend the night, resting our blisters for the daylong climb up into the mountains to Number Twelve.

It is a long climb. Sometimes the old path is gentle underfoot, sometimes rough and steep. We pass through tangled copses and stands of tall cedars, plumb valleys, and file along ridges from which the mountains fall away on either side to rise again in ranges green and blue as far as the eye can see. We find gravestones a century or two old. Most bear no name, just HENRO and a date; this trail has taken its toll.

It is late afternoon when we break into the temple's clearing. The highest peak of the range looms before us. Far below are the valley and its people. In the same instant we both start to say the same thing: surely up here the vexations of life down there must fall away.

Twelve is the first real mountain temple of the pilgrimage: high in the mountains, deep in the mountains, of the mountains. The Japanese have always revered their mountains. In this country the universal emotions that mountains stir—the sense of beauty, mystery, awe—became the singular Japanese blending of god and man, nature and art. And so the mountain temples of the pil-

The steps leading to Temple Twelve *(a painting by Kawabata)*

grimage have a special character and significance. We sense that here, in the compound of the temple, and yet we know that we have not reached the locus of this mountain's secret. Temple Twelve's legends center on its innermost sanctuary. We are tired, our legs have climbed today as far as they want to, but still we must reach that inner altar on the peak. We announce our arrival, shed our packs, and ask the priest about the path up.

It is hard going. Three-quarters of a mile takes us three-quarters of an hour. We know we are close when we find a stone image and a sign: women must go no farther; they will worship from here. On this mountain an ancient taboo is still maintained. (Mount Koya's prohibition against women was lifted a hundred years ago.) We push on, sometimes skirting precipice, sometimes buffeted by sudden gusts. But the vistas—gaunt old trees, cloud-swept ranges, patchwork valley shrunk below: Morikawa says it is like moving through a Chinese landscape painting.

At last the altar. Here by a small stone sanctuary, braced against the cold blast sweeping over the peak, I try to focus on that mystical figure out of the cloudy past who is enshrined here, for he is one of the spiritual ancestors of the wandering ascetic that the young Daishi became.

He is called En the Ascetic. He was of a family called En, traditional diviners and healers who served as priests to the god of one of Japan's most sacred mountains. They were therefore priests in the native religion of Japan, the ancient feelings of awe in the face of nature that we call Shinto.

A century before En the Ascetic was born in 634 the old beliefs his ancestors had lived by were challenged by the power of Buddha. Traveling from China by way of Korea, Buddhism was part of the great Chinese wave—including writing and new ways of government—that transformed Japan. A king of Korea recommended the new religion fervently: "This doctrine is among all doctrines the most excellent. It can create religious merit and retribution without measure and without bounds. Imagine a man in possession of treasures to his heart's content, so that he might satisfy all his wishes. Thus it is with this wonderful doctrine. Every prayer is fulfilled and none is wanting." The chronicles say that the emperor leaped for joy when he heard all this but Buddhism's entry was not quite that smooth. First there was conflict, which raged around the emperor, who was, after all, the high priest of Shinto. Then came accommodation.

To shamans like En it was no great problem. Since Buddhism was a more powerful magic they adopted it. In former times they invoked the gods, the *kami*, of Shinto. They still did, but now in their pantheon it was Buddha who was sovereign. It was Buddha, the supreme miracle worker, they called upon as they tramped the countryside, healers and diviners to the common people. It was not orthodox Buddhism they brought. They took what they perceived of it and grafted it onto their heritage of Shinto, creating a heady mix dyed with the mystery of the mountains they had always looked to as the source of their power. Nor did orthodox Buddhism compete with them, for the priests of the temples clustered around the capital had no time for the common people: they were preoccupied with ministering to the nobility and with buttressing Buddhism's position as a state religion. It was not until En the Ascetic attracted a great following that, outraged, they had him "banished to a far-away place" because "he led the people astray by weird arts." Pardoned after three years, and unrepentant, he wandered into western Japan still carrying the new religion to the countryside. And so very quickly after Buddhism's arrival in Japan he and mystics like him began to naturalize it, adapting it to Japanese ways of thinking and feeling, making it the people's religion.

Legend says that sometime in his life he came here. That they say he climbed this peak shows how Buddhism had altered the ancient native beliefs about the mountains. For Japanese scholars say that the old ideas of the mountain as a sacred place prohibited men from trespassing to the heights; they worshiped from below. It was Buddhism that led to the climbing of sacred mountains to perform religious rituals and to undergo the austere disciplines, mental and physical, that brought superhuman powers.

En the Ascetic is important to henro—and therefore Temple Twelve is a key temple of the pilgrimage—because he represents something deep and elemental in Japanese Buddhism, the strong current of mountain asceticism. This is the Buddhism not of priests presiding over incense-filled temples but of wandering holy men, of saintly laymen whose altars are the peaks. It is just such a wandering ascetic that Kobo Daishi became when he turned to the mountains.

But there is another great current in Japanese Buddhism and here on this windswept peak it too asserts itself. Far below but insistent to the eye is the valley with its motley of cultivated fields, its villages and towns and distant city. Though the people gaze up toward the mountains they live down there. That other great current is a tradition of service to the people.

It is typified by another of the Daishi's precursors, a priest named Gyogi, who lived from 668 to 749. He was better trained in Buddhism than En but still was unordained, a lay priest, a maverick, and a thorn in the side of the establishment. Like En he had charisma. Even a hostile observer, writing about him and his disciples, had to admit that.

"They collect a great number of people at a spot in the hills east of the capital, where they preach dubious words which only confuse everyone. At times as many as ten thousand flock there to listen. . . . Such individuals are clearly guilty of breaking the law."

The charges are reminiscent of those flung against En but the "dubious words" that Gyogi preached were the fundamental Buddhist doctrine of cause and effect, that every thought, every deed, every utterance will produce an effect in the future. Evil breeds evil, good breeds good: this is the law called Karma.

And so Gyogi preached of "sin and happiness." He would erect an altar and conduct a service in the open. "Everywhere people flocked to him, leaving nobody in the towns, struggling with each other in their eagerness to worship him." He urged them to action that would atone for the sins they had committed in this and previous existences.

Action to Gyogi was not an abstraction. He led an army of holy men who went among the common people, organizing them to build roads and bridges, dams to impound ponds for irrigation, dikes to tame flood waters—these to make life easier; to make life brighter Gyogi and his followers founded temples that were much more than places of worship: they housed libraries that were centers of learning, dispensaries where simple medicines were given to the sick, almshouses where the poor were fed and clothed. Most of Gyogi's disciples worked at the age-old problem of raising money but others were civil engineers, carpenters, metalers, sculptors, painters. The people gave what tiny offerings they could and they gave the strength of their arms and backs. The contribution of each was small but the aggregate was great.

Gyogi's monumental achievement was the Great Buddha at Nara. The emperor ordered its construction but it soon became evident that neither the government nor the temples at Nara had the resources to accomplish it. In 743 the emperor entrusted the project to Gyogi and we must believe there was no alternative, for the priests of Nara had no love for this man. It was a colossal task: to cast a bronze sculpture weighing more than four hundred and fifty tons, a seated figure fifty-three feet tall on a lotus pedestal sixty-eight feet in diameter. Image and base had to be slowly built up, small section by section. Six years saw repeated failures but no stopping. In 749 it was completed, a towering image glowing in a vast hall. Gyogi's campaign workers had raised the money to pay for it; Gyogi's artisans, many of them Korean, had solved the technical problems of creating it. The emperor gave Gyogi a title and the people revered him but the priests never ordained him. Incidentally—no, not incidentally at all—more than a third of the eighty-eight temples claim Gyogi as founder. They would be hard put to document the claim but the tribute is genuine.

Part of the genius of Kobo Daishi was that he spanned both worlds: the world of meditation and austerity in the mountains, the world of action and service on the plains. Morikawa and I, as we slowly descend, find ourselves telling each other that we feel his presence on this mountain. The legends that bring him here are hard to evaluate but there is also this to be considered: the temple is dedicated to the deity Kokuzo. Kokuzo is called the deity of space because his wisdom is as vast as space itself. He has never been as popular as Kannon, who personifies mercy, or Yakushi, the god of healing, or Amida, who promises rebirth in the Pure Land in the West, but he was the deity the Daishi called upon in his struggle to attain enlightenment. When he joined a group of monks in the mountains near Nara, the type of meditation that they practiced and he learned was based on invoking Kokuzo. By coincidence, Kokuzo was his guardian deity: he was born in the Year of the Tiger and according to Japanese calendrical lore Kokuzo watches over those born in that cyclical year. Perhaps that strengthened his devotion to this deity. Only two other temples among the eighty-eight are dedicated to Kokuzo, and their links to the Daishi are certified. In his writings he speaks of the places where they stand; they were places of crisis in his life. Legend, only legend, says he came here.

Later we talk with the priest about the temple's legends. The first has it that when En the Ascetic came here he found the mountain devastated by a great poisonous snake whose weapon was fire. En subdued the serpent, rendered it harmless. The sanctuary to which we climbed memorializes his victory.

A century later Kobo Daishi came to this mountain where Temple Twelve now stands. He found that En's spell had lost its power; the fiery serpent was again ravaging and destroying. It was the Daishi, calling on Kokuzo, who finally extinguished the devil fire for all time. It was he who founded the temple and carved its central image: Kokuzo.

I write it in my notebook, consider it, and am puzzled. What does it mean, I ask, and the priest interprets it. In the dim past the people of the valley were gripped by a primitive cult of fear: they worshiped the mountain, they worshiped the spirit of the mountain, but the spirit was evil, a venomous great serpent. En quelled the serpent but his magic did not last. Then Kobo Daishi came, bringing true Buddhism. The serpent fought savagely but it was vanquished. The Daishi ended a snake cult. The people were freed from mythic superstition to follow the path of Buddha.

There are other, similar stories. There are no foxes on Shikoku and people say that the Daishi banished them. A folklorist is likely to deduce that Buddhism eradicated a cult of fox worship. Buddhism was stronger,

In the evening the priest performs a fire service, a *goma,* for the henro lodging at the temple tonight. The goma is one of the great rituals of Shingon; always I am caught up in its drama. The priest sits at a special altar with a fire basin at its center. Intoning the supplication, he kindles the fire and feeds it with a hundred and eight sticks of wood. They represent the hundred and eight illusions of the soul, but the number is an abstraction: the sins of man, the illusions he is heir to, are infinite. The priest chants. He strikes drums and gongs and bells. He adds incense, oils, and green leaves, which spit and snap. The flames leap high.

I have seen several priests perform the goma. Each stamps his personality on it as he must: it is not only a service conducted for the worshipers but an intense inner experience for the priest. The abbot of the temple where I lodge on Mount Koya is a scholar and a perfectionist; he brings to the goma precision and grace within passionate concentration. The priest here at Twelve reflects the traditions of this temple: he evokes beliefs before Buddhism, holy men to whom the mountains were home. In his intensity there is something wild: the sticks of firewood are jumbled, the thrown leaves do not always fall in the fire. His little son, four years old perhaps, scampers about the altar retrieving those that miss and adding them to the flames. There is nothing unseemly in this: a child cannot be irreverent.

The last stick of wood is placed in the fire; the flames die down; the priest finishes the liturgy and rises to leave. At the doorway he turns and invites us, if we wish, to rub the smoke from the dying fire on those parts of our body that need help. Then he is gone. Is his leaving a gesture of disdain for an old superstition? If so it is lost on us. We all cluster about the fire, catch the smoke in our hands, and rub it on our legs, knees, backs, and, in obligatory modesty, on our heads.

In the morning we leave Temple Twelve, start down the mountain. We come to a roadside chapel, a great cedar, a gravestone, and the legend of how the pilgrimage began.

The story is that of the first pilgrim, Emon Saburo. It is the story of a rich and greedy man who refused to give alms when the Daishi appeared at his gate, but who then, chastened and remorseful, set out to find the Daishi and beg forgiveness. Worn out from circling Shikoku again and again, near death, struggling up this path in bitter cold, he finally met the Daishi here. Here the Daishi gave him absolution as he died, buried him, and planted his staff beside the grave. The staff grew into the cedar that shades us. (Actually, says a man passing by, this tree is the second generation.)

This is the primary legend of the pilgrimage. It points to the basic concept of the pilgrimage, that the henro travels always with the Daishi, for it is implied that Kobo Daishi guided Emon Saburo all through his grueling quest. And it emphasizes that the pilgrimage was originated by a layman, not a priest, attesting to the popular nature of Kobo Daishi worship and of the pilgrimage. It goes to the heart of the common man's religion, a religion of faith and piety uncluttered by doctrine.

We continue down the mountain.

5

The life of the Daishi: legend and fact—where does one end and the other begin?

It is our sixth day of walking and we are approaching one of the unnumbered temples of the pilgrimage, a *bangai*. I have learned that most of the bangai are as much a part of the pilgrimage as the temples that bear a number, though by some accident of history they were not included among the eighty-eight.

Buildings rise among hills backed by blue mountains. The long lane, climbing and curving, is lined with cherry trees and on this warm and sunny afternoon they are a froth of pink against a dark forest. It is Sunday; the holiday has come when the blossoms are at their best and it looks as if half the population of the city— the prefectural capital, not far away by car—are partying here. We pick our way through automobiles and picnickers, revelers from great-grandparents to toddlers. From a point where cars are barred, the lane is lined with stalls: cotton candy, red balloons shaped like octopuses, Kewpie dolls; saké and beer and soft drinks; sweet-bean buns and hot dogs. We climb to where we can see over the bank on our left: an irrigation pond of deep green, dozens of boats, spirited rowers (there will be sore muscles in the city tomorrow). At the temple people are queuing for a glimpse of its treasures.

It's a joyous day but surely the wrong one for us; surely the priest is too occupied to see us. We pray at the altars and take our albums to the open windows of the office for inscription. And would it be possible to talk with the priest on such a busy day? Just for a few minutes?

Moments later we are invited in. We take off our boots (how discolored and sweaty our heavy socks!) and are led inside, around to the back, and into a serenely handsome room thrown open to the garden. Here the hubbub is shut out, there is only quiet and beauty: almost at our feet a pool of lazing golden carp, a stone bridge crossing it to paths that wander up a hillside sculptured with rocks and bushes; a stone pagoda about the height of a man is the focus to which the eye returns.

A priest appears to welcome us. He pours fine tea, puts cakes and fruit before us. He urges us to eat, saying that today the temple has been flooded with gifts of food. He introduces himself as the head priest's assistant, his adopted son and son-in-law, and he tells us that the festival is managed by the temple's support association. What a happy way to make money—no wonder the temple looks prosperous.

An older man appears: obviously he is the head priest. I know that today dozens of guests and supporters important to the temple are visitors and we apologize for taking him away from them, but he makes us feel as though we are the honored guests. "Very few henro come here anymore," he says.

He talks while the younger man keeps our teacups filled. "This temple was a school for the nobility. It is where Kobo Daishi studied as a child, from the years when he was eight or nine until he went up to the university at the capital. By that time he had a very sound understanding of Buddhism. Here he was also taught the other requisites, including of course calligraphy."

In Japan calligraphy is a fine art and the Daishi is acknowledged to be one of the greatest calligraphers ever. The priest calls for and gives each of us a reproduction of calligraphy that he says the young Daishi did here. It is a fluent brushing of the *Iroha*.

Among the brilliant achievements credited to Kobo Daishi is the invention of *kana:* forty-seven symbols, each representing a syllable such as *sa, to,* or *mu.* Given these symbols, with a couple of modifying marks that, for example, change *ha* to *ba* or *pa,* one can write Japanese phonetically. Once kana was created no longer was it necessary to learn thousands of complex Chinese characters—for the Japanese, who had no writing system when Chinese culture came to their islands, had taken over the Chinese way of writing, the only one known to them, even though Japanese and Chinese were totally different languages and the Chinese writing system was singularly unsuited to writing Japanese. (This particular borrowing has fittingly been called the greatest disaster in Japanese history.)

Kana democratized literacy in Japan. Reading and writing were no longer reserved to scholars and aristocrats who could spend years acquiring an expensive education. For centuries kana was the common people's way of writing. For centuries it was also a woman's way of writing, even if she was highborn, for women were not considered to have the intellect necessary to wrestle with Chinese. And so it was that in the tenth, eleventh, and twelfth centuries a coterie of court ladies wrote in phonetic script some of the gems of Japanese literature, including the world's first great novel, *The Tale of Genji*.

The Iroha, which the priest has placed in our hands, is a way of writing kana in a sequence that uses all the symbols and repeats none, and that makes a poem and thus a memory aid. The poem is strongly Buddhist: "The flowers, however fragrantly blooming, are doomed to wither. Who in this world can hope to live forever? The remotest mountain pass of existence is crossed today! Awaking from a dream so evanescent, I am no more subject to intoxication." A Western scholar condensed it for impatient foreigners this way: "All is transitory in this fleeting world. Let me escape from its illusions and vanities."

The Buddhist flavor of the Iroha is just one indication; certainly it was priests, and very likely Shingon priests, who developed kana. First, they were among the most learned men of their society; second, they had to study Sanskrit in order to read many of the Buddhist scriptures and since Sanskrit is written phonetically they were aware of what could be done; and third, they had to communicate with the common people. But modern scholars do not believe that kana was achieved in Kobo Daishi's lifetime (though he sparked much that was accomplished by those who followed him).

And so when we are handed this handsome version of the

Iroha and told that he brushed it as a child I feel that we have passed into the realm of legend. This does not lessen the warmth I feel toward this priest and this beautiful and well-loved temple; nor does the knowledge that scholars believe he lived at home until he went up to the capital. Actually, I tell myself, very little is known about his early years. It is at least within the realm of possibility that he came here to school; along old traffic routes it would have been less than three days' walk from his home. I take another sip of tea and let my eyes rest on the garden. I would like to believe that the Boy Daishi walked those paths. Here and now, I will believe it.

Shadows are creeping across the garden. We try to thank our hosts and we take our leave. The festival is still in full swing.

On the seventh day of our pilgrimage we go through the noisy city of Tokushima and cross a coastal plain to a pine-clad hill and the deep quiet of Temple Eighteen. Its legend says that it was founded by Gyogi and was flourishing when as a young monk Kobo Daishi came here to train; that his mother journeyed from home to visit him; that as usual at a monastery no women were admitted and she was turned back at the gate, whereupon the Daishi began a twenty-one-day ritual to break that rule, and succeeded. They say she stayed here with her son for some time, that here she became a nun. A monument in the compound marks the spot where they buried her worldly clothes and her hair, cut when she was tonsured.

It would be good to believe that his mother at least, among his family, was reconciled to his becoming a Buddhist. But even if we have no sure evidence of that, we recognize that here is another story which testifies to his regard for women and his assertion, in an age which thought otherwise, that they as well as men could attain Buddhahood.

In the evening we talk with the priest. The temple's income has never been enough to keep it in repair and to support his family, and so he has taught in the local high school. Now his son, who will someday take over as priest, has graduated from the uni-

Temple Eighteen *(a painting by Sakata)*

versity on Mount Koya and is settled in a position with the city government; the father is eager to retire from teaching and give full time to the priesthood. He wanted to retire at the end of the school year just completed but he was persuaded to teach one more year. He seems a little tired, a little wistful. Teaching is an honorable profession but it is not his chosen profession. He wants to devote the rest of his life to religious training.

6 Temple Twenty-one stands atop Mount Tairyu. It is one of the few places along the pilgrimage route where we know that we stand where the Daishi stood, for by his own testimony he came to this mountain.

He followed the trace of others who had searched out this place for sacred rites. Like them he must have ascended the valley of the river we crossed this afternoon—rivers furnished the easiest routes to the interior—and then, finding the same tumbling mountain stream we climbed beside, followed its rocky course upward. It brought him to the huts of some woodcutters. They pointed out the way to the summit, or perhaps one of them guided him; it is recorded that he moved up here, no doubt with their help, the Shinto shrine he found at their hamlet; it still stands in the temple compound.

He had meditated at many remote places, following the prescribed ritual for invoking his guardian deity, Kokuzo, and for attaining Kokuzo's boundless blessing. So far he had not succeeded. Now he would try on this mountain.

Following the rules, he had painted a full moon on a pure white cloth and in the center of this moon he had painted in golden color the image of Kokuzo, taller than the length of his own forearm, seated upon a lotus flower with his right foot on his left knee and his left foot under his right knee. On Kokuzo's crown were images of the Buddhas. His left hand held a white lotus flower with a slight tint of red and on this lotus lay a pearl emitting yellow rays. His right hand was open, palm forward and fingers down, in the gesture of fulfilling the vow—the historical Buddha's original vow to strive for the salvation of all beings.

In the early morning of his first day on this mountaintop the Daishi purified himself by washing in the clear water of a spring. In a place beneath the cedars that was level and clean of brush he placed the altar he had carried on his back. He had made it of fragrant sandalwood; it stood exactly four fingers high. Above the altar he hung the painting of Kokuzo with its face to the west so that he himself would face east, but for the moment he covered the image with a white cloth. After again washing, he prepared the five kinds of offerings: incense made from white sandalwood, the flowers of the season (it was spring, as it is now, and the flowers were buttercups and violets), incense made from camphorwood, pure water and fresh food (the herbs of the mountain), and small lamps whose flames would be fed by delicate oil crushed from seeds. He placed all these near the altar.

At the spring he repeatedly washed his hands. Then he made the special gesture for Kokuzo by extending the fingers of his right hand and bending the middle finger to his thumb as though he were pinching incense, and with his hand in this position he spoke the mantra, the mystic syllables for invoking Kokuzo, and from his palm drank the spring's pure water. Holding his hand in the same position he collected more water in his palm and sprinkled it over his body from the crown of his head to the soles of his feet; each dip of the water he made powerful by three incantations of Kokuzo's mantra. In this manner he purified himself inside and out.

Thereupon he went to the altar. He sat facing the image in the same posture as the image and he took away the cloth covering it. He raised his right hand, again making the gesture of Kokuzo; he touched the crown of his head, his right shoulder, his left shoulder, his heart, and his throat, each time with one incantation of the mantra.

He "bound the region": as though putting walls around himself or marking off the ritual site with rope he threw the gesture in the ten directions, reciting the mantra seven times as he did so, holding his body perfectly steady.

Then he closed his eyes and meditated. He envisioned Kokuzo and, making prescribed gestures, he recited the mantra twenty-five times and beckoned to invite the deity. He recited the mantra three times as he visualized a lotus flower rising to form a seat, and he thought: "May the Deity come to sit upon this lotus." Forthwith he opened his eyes, made Kokuzo's gesture, and recited the mantra three times. He thought: "Now the Deity has come here. The power of the mantra is not my power. I wish only that the Venerable One may reside here for a short time."

Then he made the offerings he had prepared, reciting the mantra once as he offered each, and thinking about the purity and fragrance of the incense and flowers and the radiance of the flames, produced as they were by the felicitous wisdom of all the Buddhas. He made the gesture and spoke the mantra and then he meditated, making the offerings again in meditation.

He closed his eyes, steadily reciting the mantra, carefully counting the number of times with the beads of his rosary, his hand held in the proper gesture. He contemplated the Full Moon Kokuzo. He thought: "Over the Deity's heart there is a full moon." The mantra appeared in the moon, written in gold, and then it flowed out from the moon, streamed down upon the crown of his head, entered his head, came out of his mouth, and returned to enter the deity's feet, and as it did so the syllables spontaneously uttered themselves as a report to the deity. So the characters meditated upon kept coming and going continually without interruption, turning like a wheel.

When his body and mind grew tired he stopped breathing for a little while, opened his eyes, and bowed in worship. Then he resumed breathing, resumed counting, resumed meditation. There came a moment, deep in meditation, when the boundary between him and the deity disappeared, he no longer seemed to be imitating Kokuzo, he and Kokuzo were one, and the mantra endlessly rotated through one body.

Gradually he diminished his meditation, slowly returning to the state in which he had begun. Having ceased to meditate, he made the gesture and recited the mantra three times, thinking as he did so: "I pray only for benevolence and compassion, charity and liberality in giving alms and offerings, and joy in fulfilling these meritorious actions."

He performed these lengthy devotions once during the day and once during the night, leaving himself little time for rest or sleep. He performed them each time exactly as he had done them the first time. His nightly devotions ended as the night drew to a close. He searched the eastern sky for a bright star and to it uttered a final prayer that he might develop a compassionate heart. Between devotions he underwent a rite of repentance, throwing himself down before the altar with the full force of his body, prostrating himself with his head, his arms, and his knees to the ground.

All that he did in his devotions—the recitation of the mantra, the precise gestures, the thoughts, the visions, and the prayers—constituted a minutely regulated drama, performed exactly as prescribed in the text, a drama in which, by imitating the deity he worshiped, he aspired to become like that deity, to take on the deity's virtues and strengths: to become one with Kokuzo. Many of the syllables he recited were meaningless, but they were syllables linked to Kokuzo and they created resonances within his mind and body. The gestures he made were Kokuzo's gestures. Was all this entwined with magic? Of course; he lived in an age that believed in magic (and there is magic in every religion). But imitation, emulation, identification—these are steps we all take in one way or another as we are molded or mold ourselves.

The text he had found at Nara stated that in a period of worship the mantra should be spoken one million times, neither more nor less. "In that work," the young man later wrote, "it is stated that if one recites the mantra one million times according to the proper method, one will be able to memorize passages and understand the meaning of any scripture." "To memorize passages" . . . how important that must have seemed to him (later in life men marveled at his phenomenal memory). He had not been raised a Buddhist; he had a sense of coming to it late in his young life, with much catching-up to do. Faced with the vast canon of Buddhist scriptures—not a single Bible but hundreds of volumes—

he ached to read and retain them all, to comprehend them, to find in them the "right way" he was searching for.

"Believing what the Buddha says to be true, I recited the mantra incessantly, as if I were rubbing one piece of wood against another to make fire, all the while earnestly hoping. I climbed Mount Tairyu in Awa Province. . . . The valley reverberated to the sound of my voice."

It took him fifty days to chant the mantra one million times. For fifty days, or perhaps twice fifty, without regard for rain or cold, he acted out the drama on this mountain. Yet here he failed. He did not achieve the breakthrough that he sought. An early biographer, embellishing the Daishi's firsthand report, tells us that he did receive encouragement, that he beheld the flashing sword of Kokuzo come flying toward him. Perhaps he did: there is no telling what visions he beheld as with fasting and austerities he drove himself to the limit on this mountain. Perhaps that sword pointed the way. From here he went southwest to the great promontory that juts like a blade into the Pacific Ocean and at the very tip he tried again. "I . . . meditated at Muroto Cape in Tosa." And there he succeeded.

A few days from now Morikawa and I will reach that cape. We will have left Awa, the first province of our pilgrimage, and entered the second of Shikoku's four provinces, Tosa. . . .

For three days we walk along Tosa's bleak and craggy ramparts against the open Pacific. From the highway hacked into the cliff we look down on black rocks savaged for ages by a violent sea. The old path clung to the shoreline. There is no trace of it on today's maps but we wonder if some vestige remains. It was not an easy path; in the wash of waves the traveler scrambled over rocks that were "jumping stones, bucking stones, tumbling stones." Late in our third day of walking above the booming ocean, as we near the tip of the cape, we pass hundreds of stone statues of Jizo. Jizo is not only the guardian deity of children; he also stands between this world and the next to rescue souls on their way to hell. His images

"Jumping stones, bucking stones, tumbling stones": the perilous path
along Tosa's rocky shore (*detail from a book illustration by Shugetsu*)

have been placed here and prayed to in memory of sailors and
fishermen lost at sea.

"The sea is often stormy around Muroto," the priest of the
temple on the height above has said. "There are any number of
legends about sailors saved from the rocks by a vision of Kobo
Daishi. The danger isn't as great as it was when boats were frailer
but many of the temple's members are fishermen; they go out on
long voyages after tuna or whales, and some of them don't come
back.

"Many of the typhoons that hit Japan hit Muroto first, at
their most violent. They have battered the temple for twelve centuries; one of the major duties of the priest and the people is to
repair the damage. During World War II the B-29 bombers used
the cape as a landmark and then flew to their targets. When they
attacked the prefectural capital I watched through my telescope as
the city burned. The horror of that night is still with me." And
with a wry smile: "Muroto sticks out like a hook and it catches

trouble. . . . But all that aside, this place is sacred because it was here that the young Daishi set his life's course."

Just short of the tip of the cape we reach the caves where many believe that the Daishi invoked Kokuzo. "He chose to get close to the sea, not to worship from the crest," the priest says. "The caves open to the southeast so that from them he could have seen Venus at dawn." For Venus is considered a manifestation of Kokuzo. Affirming that in meditation at this cape he at last broke through to enlightenment, he wrote: "The planet Venus appeared in the sky."

A massive rock, clutched by the roots of a banyan tree (Muroto is subtropical, brushed by the warm Black Current out of the South Pacific) separates grottoes large enough to give refuge from the wind and rain. Within, it is strangely hushed: the pounding of the breakers is muffled. All about are stones piled up by people who have carefully balanced one upon another as evidence of prayers offered.

Was it in this cave the young monk achieved enlightenment? Was it here he pledged his life? "From that time on, I despised fame and wealth and longed for a life in the midst of nature. Whenever I saw articles of luxury—light furs, well-fed horses, swift vehicles—I felt sad, knowing that, being transient as lightning, they too would fade away. Whenever I saw a cripple or a beggar, I lamented and wondered what had caused him to spend his days in such a miserable state. Seeing these piteous conditions encouraged me to renounce the world. Can anyone now break my determination? No, just as there is no one who can stop the wind."

> *Muroto:*
> *The voice of Buddha*
> *Is heard—*
> *Yet day in, day out,*
> *Winds roar and waves surge.*

. . . winds and waves: the vicissitudes of life; despite them the voice of Buddha is within us if we but listen. He was insisting on that, as henceforth he always would.

A path rises steep to the temple above; its compound spreads over the flat crown of the promontory. We have climbed away from the sound of the ocean: at the main hall it is shady and still. We lower our packs and pray. This is the third and last temple where Kokuzo is enshrined. Here is memorialized the Daishi's enlightenment.

We leave the cover of the trees, walk to the tip of the headland, stand with the wind in our faces. Before us is the open Pacific, the limitless horizon. Suddenly I feel that I am standing where he stood when, having achieved enlightenment, he took the name he used for the rest of his life: Kukai. It joins the *Ku* of Kokuzo, meaning "sky," and *kai,* meaning "sea." It images this sweep of view. It is a prayer for compassion as wide as the sky and as deep as the sea.

It is here that fully, finally committed to Buddhism, the young monk began the transition to great master. And to the sainthood and immortality signified by his posthumous title, Kobo Daishi.

There were still long years of difficult search ahead. He was not satisfied with the Buddhism he found in Japan. Later in life he reminisced: "Three vehicles, five vehicles, a dozen scriptures—there were so many ways for me to seek the essence of Buddhism, but still my mind had doubts which could not be resolved. I beseeched all the Buddhas of the three worlds and the ten directions to show me not the disparity but the unity of the teachings. . . . Not knowing the way, I cried many times at the crossroad." He was rewarded at last when he found the scripture, the sutra, that presents the Buddha Dainichi—presents Dainichi as idealizing the truth of the universe, as the Buddha who *is* the universe and who, residing in the heart of every being, reveals the mysteries by which one may discover one's own pure mind of enlightenment. Dainichi was the central figure of the new kind of Buddhism he had been seeking, the central Buddha of the Shingon doctrine he would embrace and enhance. But the sutra that he found contained difficult passages that no one could interpret. To find a master who could transmit its secrets to him he would have to go to China, and that is what he

Cape Muroto *(a print by Hasui)*

set himself to do. He said he wanted to study there for twenty years.

During the preceding two centuries the Japanese had sent almost twenty embassies to China. Scholarly aristocrats and Buddhist monks escorted a cargo of what the Chinese were pleased to call tribute and the Japanese considered a bargain, for if the fragile little ships were lucky enough to get there and back they returned with gifts far richer than those sent and, more important, the envoys brought back precious knowledge to enrich life in Japan. The Chinese also bestowed honors—empty honors, but they confirmed Japan's place as a civilized nation in a China-centered world.

Still, it was not a voyage to be undertaken lightly. Japanese knowledge of navigation was primitive and so were their ships: they had to be rowed much of the time because, having no keel, they could sail only before the wind. The risks were so great that, in the words of Yoshito S. Hakeda, the Daishi's modern biographer, "whenever the government announced plans to send an envoy to the Chinese court, officials of the middle or lower ranks were thrown into a frenzy for fear they might be sent. Some had to be punished for evading government orders, and others became exhausted from mental strain even before embarking."

Despite the danger, the emperor and the court, now that they were settled in the new capital we call Kyoto, began in 801 to plan another embassy, for it had been twenty years since the previous mission had returned. It took two years to build the four ships that were needed and to collect the splendid gifts. On a spring day in 803 they set out from the port now named Osaka. Two days later, while they were still in the usually placid Inland Sea, they were hit by a violent storm. One of the ships managed to continue to Kyushu. The three others limped back to their home port. The mission had to be put off for a year in order to make repairs.

It was this postponement that made it possible for the Daishi to go. Perhaps he had not been included earlier because, wandering in the mountains, he was not even aware that the embassy was being planned. Perhaps his family was in such bad odor that an earlier request had foundered. But given the delay he was able to obtain consent; there has been much speculation over the circumstances. Was his proficiency in Chinese now more persuasive?—for among those drowned in the storm was a sorely missed professor of classics. Did his uncle, the tutor to the imperial prince, exert influence on behalf of his wayward nephew? Or was the emperor trying to make amends for his harsh treatment of the Otomo and Saeki men some years earlier? Whatever the reasons, permission seems to have come at almost the last moment: he was ordained a monk—a necessary qualification he had not bothered with previously—just days before the ships reembarked. He was fortunate—it was more than thirty years before the government undertook another mission to China. He sailed on the ambassador's ship.

The three ships joined the fourth that had been waiting in Kyushu, and together they sailed into the China Sea in the late summer of 804. Chinese or Korean sailors would have known better; the Japanese had not yet learned: they sailed at the beginning of the typhoon season and when the monsoon winds were dead against them. On their second night at sea a storm struck. Two of the ships were blown back to Japan; Ships One and Two were separated but each continued on its way. Ship Two, carrying a notable priest named Saicho, older than the Daishi and a favorite of the emperor, drifted for two months but did reach China and, considering the navigational problems, not overly far from the fleet's target, the mouth of the Yangtze River. Ship One, with the ambassador and the Daishi, was thirty-four days at sea but landed three hundred miles south of its goal, at a little port where no Japanese envoy had appeared before and this one was not welcome. After two months of frustration they were sent to another port, the provincial capital, but that was not the end of their difficulties. The governor of the province was new and unaccustomed to Japanese idiosyncrasy. The Japanese followed Chinese protocol only so far: they were willing to bring "tribute," they were even willing to label themselves barbarians, but they were not willing to acknowledge the emperor of China as their sovereign and to pledge fealty to him. The lack of such an obsequious message led the governor to conclude that they were not an official embassy but merely traders trying to evade a tax on their merchandise. He announced he would seek instructions from the capital, more than a thousand miles away, and meanwhile he refused to let the party land. He ordered their ship moored in an unhealthful swamp and kept it under surveillance.

They were saved from a long and painful wait by an appeal that Kobo Daishi wrote for the ambassador. His Chinese was elegant and his argument was persuasive.

He began by observing "that under the sage rule of the great T'ang dynasty, the frost and dew come in their proper seasons. . . . The imperial virtue spreads throughout the universe. . . . Because in Japan the natural phenomena are harmonious and well ordered, we know that a sage emperor surely rules in China. Therefore, we cut the timber that grows on great peaks to make boats and send the best of our officialdom to visit your vermilion court."

He described the perilous voyage. "A fierce storm struck us, . . . ripping our sail and breaking our rudder. Great waves tossed our small boat. . . . We cringed before the terrible wind, terrified that the great waves might wash us away. . . . We drifted north and south, and saw nothing but the blue of sky and sea. . . . Our water was exhausted; our crew fatigued. . . . How can words describe our plight!"

Then he got to the matter at hand. "Whereas the eight northern barbarians gather like clouds to grovel before the imperial palace, and the seven western tribes flock together like mist to kowtow at the royal court, the great T'ang dynasty has always given Japanese envoys special treatment as respected guests of state. . . . How could we be discussed even on the same day as those insignificant barbarians? Moreover, it is the very nature of inscriptions or credentials to contain lies and fabrications. In a land of honest and unaffected people, what need is there for such documents?

"But now, the officials of this province are emphasizing documents and doubting our honesty. They are inspecting our boat and listing its goods, both official and private. To be sure, this is both legal and proper as the duty of conscientious officials. On the other hand, we have just arrived from afar with the weariness of our journey and the hardships of our voyage still heavy on our hearts. Yet we have not been able to gratify ourselves with the succor of the wine of imperial virtue. The restrictions placed upon us leave us in despair, unable to rest. . . .

"Humbly we beg to be received with the benevolence granted visitors from afar. . . . Be indulgent of our customs. . . . We humbly beg to be treated in the usual way. Filled with awe, we thus petition you."

The governor had glanced at the ambassador's own messages and tossed them away but he was impressed by the Daishi's calligraphy and his mastery of Chinese. He immediately ordered that the Japanese should be made comfortable and treated well. If the ambassador did not earlier esteem the Daishi's scholarship, he did now.

Clearance finally arrived and the party made the fifty-day journey to the Chinese capital, Ch'ang-an. They reached it in late 804, about six months after sailing from Japan, and were settled into a government residence. During the ambassador's three months at the capital he chose to keep in his official party the man who had proved invaluable, and so the Daishi was able to savor the brilliance of the city: almost two million people, the greatest metropolis in the world, symbol of the glory of China. The Japanese sensed that the T'ang dynasty was tottering toward its ruin, but China was still the strongest, richest, most civilized country on the globe, ruler of the largest empire yet amassed. Ch'ang-an thronged with foreigners: embassies from all over Asia; traders from the far reaches of the continent, the Middle East, the southern seas; missionaries Buddhist, Nestorian, and Moslem; soldiers, adventurers, minstrels. To the Japanese the city was breathtakingly cosmopolitan, and there was an added fascination: it had been the model for the capital at Nara, for the short-lived interim capital, and for the new capital now being built, the city today called Kyoto.

Buddhism flourished in Ch'ang-an. There were sixty-four temples for monks and twenty-seven for nuns and, of special interest to the Daishi, there was a strongly felt new current from India. Called Esoteric Buddhism, it was the kind of Buddhism he had experienced in his meditation on Kokuzo and in the sutra on the Buddha Dainichi.

On the same day that the ambassador started home, the Daishi moved to an eminent Buddhist temple to take up the studies he had come for. Here at last he met the patriarch of Esoteric Buddhism, Hui-ko. With the insight born of enlightenment the aging master at once recognized the young Japanese as the successor he had been waiting for: "He smiled with pleasure and joyfully said, 'I knew that you would come! I have waited such a long time. What pleasure it gives me to look upon you today at last! My life is drawing to an end, and until you came there was no one to whom I could transmit the teachings.' "

Hui-ko had been holding on to life until his successor should appear. Now he passed on all that he had to offer, as one would "pour water from one jar into another." The Daishi showed amazing facility; his years of study and lonely meditation had brought him further than he knew; within three months he was given the final ordination as master. At the age of thirty-two he became the eighth patriarch of Esoteric Buddhism.

Near death, Hui-ko bequeathed to the Daishi the ritual implements he had inherited from his master and told him to return to Japan and propagate the teachings there. "When you first arrived, I feared I did not have enough time left to teach you everything, but now I have completed teaching you, and the work of copying the sutras and making the images has also been finished. Hasten back to your country, offer these things to the court, and spread the teachings throughout your country to increase the happiness of the people. Then the land will know peace, and people everywhere will be content. In that way you will return thanks to the Buddha and to your teacher. That is also the way to show your devotion to your country and to your family. My disciple I-ming will carry on the teachings here. Your task is to transmit them to the Eastern Land. Do your best! Do your best!"

It was the Daishi who wrote the epitaph for his master's tomb. Under the gaze of his fellow disciples and of scholars at the capital, he "moistened his inkstone with his tears" and produced a composition and calligraphy that proved him worthy. Then, one of the two ships that had been blown back to Japan having at last reached China (the other ended wrecked on a desolate island), he applied for permission to return home on it. In about two years he had learned Sanskrit; he had met Indian masters living in Ch'ang-an and with them had studied Buddhism as it existed in India; he had studied poetry and calligraphy with eminent Chinese; he had even learned such little essentials as how to make a writing brush of badgers' hair—all while becoming the eighth patriarch of Esoteric Buddhism.

Back on the island of Kyushu late in 806, thirty months after he had set out from it, he sent a memorial to the emperor. He reported on what he had achieved as a government-sponsored scholar, listing all the sutras and religious objects he had brought back, explaining their significance, summarizing the Esoteric Buddhist tradition, and telling how he had succeeded to Hui-ko. And then he waited. Religion was a function of the state and strictly controlled by it. Without authorization he could not propagate his teachings; he could not even take up residence in a temple.

He was asking a great deal: permission to establish a new school of Buddhism, implying that it was superior to those already entrenched. Without court sanction he was powerless. There was no reply to his memorial. He was not even told to proceed to the capital; he had to wait on Kyushu. He waited for three years.

He himself is silent concerning that trying period, but some reasons for the court's cold treatment can be adduced. There was a new emperor; the emperor who had sent him to China had died, and one of his sons had ascended the throne. At this time the new emperor was not an ardent Buddhist and what enthusiasm he had was directed toward Saicho, the distinguished priest who had gone to China at the same time as the Daishi but had returned much earlier. Having brought back some texts and ritual implements of Esoteric Buddhism, Saicho was considered an authority on the subject. A challenge from a younger man who had little reputation in Japan was not received kindly.

There was more. Not long after the Daishi returned, the new emperor's reign was rocked by a conspiracy, real or trumped up: a younger half brother was accused of plotting to seize the throne; imprisoned in a temple, he and his mother committed suicide. It was that prince whom Kobo Daishi's uncle had tutored—the same uncle who had tutored and perhaps sponsored the Daishi. The uncle fled to Shikoku; his nephew could scarcely have been welcome in the capital.

However, after an ill-starred reign of four years the emperor abdicated in favor of his full brother, who became the Emperor Saga. At once the climate changed; Saga became the Daishi's patron and friend and welcomed him to the capital.

This was the new capital. It would be called Kyoto, a gem among cities, but in 809 it was just fifteen years old, lively and new. It still rang with the sounds of saw and hammer but much had been accomplished in the few years he had been away. The naked saplings he had seen planted had grown to trees; along the broad central avenue willows danced in the breeze and glittered in the sun as mounted attendants, handsome every one, escorted the ornate ox-drawn carriages of court ladies—each lady hidden behind damask curtains save for the artfully draped display of her sleeves, the heavy outer robe and the dozen underrobes of silk layered to show the wearer's exquisite sense of color.

This was the capital that for the next four centuries would be home to an aristocracy who measured taste and sensibility by the elegance of one's dress and scent and handwriting, who kept the sword subordinate to the writing brush, and who yet managed to govern the nation without recourse to war and to bequeath a dazzling legacy of art and architecture, prose and poetry, and a memory of how civilized man can be.

In this new capital the Daishi was acknowledged as the master of Esoteric Buddhism. Emperor and subjects sought him out. To-ji, a state temple still unfinished but crucial in the plan of the city, was given to him to complete as he wished and make his headquarters.

In 816 he asked Saga to give him Mount Koya—a place he had discovered during his ascetic wanderings—as the site for a monastic center. His petition stressed the importance of meditation. "Students of meditation . . . are treasures of the nation; they are like bridges for the people." Yet in Japan, "It is regrettable that only a few priests practice meditation in high mountains, in deep forests, in wide canyons, and in secluded caves. This is because the teaching of meditation has not been transmitted, nor has a suitable place been allocated for the practice of meditation.

"According to the meditation sutras, meditation should be practiced preferably on a flat area deep in the mountains. When young, I . . . often walked through mountainous areas and crossed many rivers. There is a quiet, open place called Koya located two days' walk to the west from a point that is one day's walk south from Yoshino. . . . High peaks surround Koya in all four directions; no human tracks, still less trails, are to be seen there. I should like to clear the wilderness in order to build a monastery there for the practice of meditation, for the benefit of the nation and of those who desire to discipline themselves. . . ."

Mount Koya was promptly granted to him. For the rest of his life he spent as much time there as he could, planning the architecture to harmonize with the setting and with Shingon doctrine, soliciting money and materials for construction, and, of course, meditating. It was his spiritual home; letters and poems prove how much he loved it.

But he was not permitted to spend his life on the mountain. The emperor wanted his companionship; the court wanted his participation in state rituals; he wanted to secure the future of Shingon. He wrote voluminously, developing and communicating his doctrine. He lived to see Shingon firmly established.

He was much more than a transmitter of what he had found in China. Only in Japan did Shingon emerge as an independent sect and it bears his stamp. It is optimistic. Its essence is the conviction that man can attain Buddhahood "in this very existence"—not after traditional Buddhism's countless cycles of birth, rebirth, and misery, but, with faith and practice, in the here and now. He leveled barriers that had been insuperable: "male or female, of high or low birth," with faith and practice all have the "great capacity."

This is not the place to recite his achievements, but one must be noted. In the capital, near his headquarters at To-ji, he founded the first school in Japan open to the poor as well as the rich, the lowly born as well as the aristocracy. He argued that commoners as well as nobility had a contribution to make. "It has never been possible to produce a delicious dish out of one flavor or a beautiful melody out of one tone."

First of all he had to educate his teachers. Addressing the lay teachers, because he feared they might be more inclined to prejudice than the monks, he wrote: "If young, uneducated children wish to learn how to read and write, teachers, if genuine, should instruct them in a spirit of deep compassion. . . . 'The beings in the triple world are my children,' announced the Buddha. And there is a beautiful saying of Confucius that 'all within the four seas are brothers.' Do honor to these teachings!"

He gave free meals to both students and teachers—a necessity so that poor children could attend, and just as necessary to attract humble teachers who would be willing to cooperate in this radical innovation. And for his schoolchildren he compiled a dictionary, the oldest extant in Japan.

As he neared the end of his life he retired to Koya. At midnight on the twenty-first day of the Third Month of 835—by the Gregorian calendar, April 22—he breathed his last.

One of his disciples sent a report to the temple in China where he had met his master, Hui-ko: ". . . In the Third Month [of 835] his fuel became exhausted and his fire was extinguished. He was sixty-two years old. Alas! Mount Koya turned gray; the clouds and trees appeared sad. The emperor in sorrow hastily sent a messenger to convey his condolences. The disciples wept as if they had lost their parents. Alas! We feel in our hearts as if we had swallowed fire, and our tears gush forth like fountains. Being unable to die, we are guarding the place where he passed away. . . ."

II
Savior

7 At Cape Muroto, Tosa's coastline changes radically. The eastern verge, down which we have traveled, is a harsh scarp of black rock. After one rounds Muroto the coast sweeps for two hundred miles in a lopsided crescent of sandy shores that end at another rocky cape. This crescent is scalloped with shallow curves. Stitched along the first of these are three temples—Twenty-four, Twenty-five, and Twenty-six—all of which are considered to be at Muroto. The familiar names that the local people have given them take for granted that they form a group: Twenty-four is East Temple, Twenty-six is West Temple, and Twenty-five, in the fishing town between them, is Port Temple. The three are inextricably linked, all having been founded because it was at Muroto that the Daishi achieved enlightenment.

East Temple rises on the crest of the promontory where he invoked Kokuzo but it is argued that he could not have lived there, that it was too formidable, that he found more hospitable surroundings on the hill where West Temple now stands; on the walk there, seven miles or so, the site of Port Temple would have been a convenient place to rest.

On the other hand, there are those who say that the rocky point below West Temple is the place where wandering holy men trained in the Daishi's time, so it must have been there that he practiced, not at the cape—a theory that puts West Temple at the heart of things.

As we walk toward it, Morikawa notices posters and calls them to my attention. They herald West Temple's annual ceremonies on the anniversary of the Daishi's death. It seems an incredible bit of luck that without knowing, we made a reservation to stay at the temple on the eve of that day. Morikawa says now he understands why, when he phoned, the wife at the temple seemed hesitant about accepting us: they will be busy and we must take care not to get in the way.

It isn't easy. We arrive early, learn that the priest is away for the day. A group of women are at work in the big kitchen preparing food for the two hundred or more who will sit down to tomorrow's feast; other members are at other chores. One of them comes at once to greet us. She has a face that evokes every loving grandmother. She wants us to know how pleased she is that we are here and she wants to bring us some lunch. To avoid being a distraction we go down to the town.

The priest returns in the late afternoon and despite the demands on him he seeks us out. He has age and dignity, mellow authority. "The salient thing about this temple," he begins, "is the historical record that Kobo Daishi trained here." Then, as background for the service that will be held tonight, he relates the temple legend. "When the Daishi came here he found that monstrous beings, creatures of corruption, dwelled on this height; a huge camphor tree was their lair. The Daishi overpowered them and to commemorate having banished their evil he carved his own image on the trunk of the tree. After he returned from China and achieved fame he asked the emperor's support in building temples where he had trained as a young monk. In this place he removed the image he had carved into the tree, cut down the tree and from its timber built a chapel, and in the chapel he placed the image. That image can be shown only one day a year, on the Daishi's anniversary. It will be revealed tonight and displayed until tomorrow evening."

It has grown dark and we are called to supper. We join the members who have been working all day (they will stay the night) as they sit with the priest and his family. We are given a preview of what is to come tomorrow, old-fashioned dishes native to Tosa that strangers like us could never experience save on an occasion like this. Unlike most henro of times past, I like Tosa and one of the reasons is Tosa food.

Later we are summoned by the priest's son and assistant. With him and the members we walk the long gravel path through the darkness to where the lights glow in the Daishi Hall. It is the oldest building on this hill, dating from 1486. Fire destroyed the rest of the temple in 1899: I am sure it was this building and its revered image that they fought to save and did. As we mount the steps and enter, a feeling of age carries us out of the present into an ancient timelessness.

Six priests attend, in formal robes. The head priest takes his place before the altar, his son close at hand. The others are ranged at the side of the altar. Invocations are made and then they chant a sutra I find very beautiful. Under its music are the low tones of the priest as he recites the mystic formula obligatory when this image is revealed, a secret petition and dedication that has been transmitted orally from priest to successor. As the liturgy draws to a close, while all in the chapel chant, "Namu Daishi Henjo Kongo," the priest and his son move to the inner altar, mount the steps, open the cabinet.

The priest turns and speaks to his people, very simply. He talks of this once-a-year chance to meet Kobo Daishi. He says that he has the Daishi's blessing to transfer to us all, and he urges each of us to pray here, tonight, for what is closest to heart. He introduces the two of us as henro who have come to be with them on this occasion.

One of the priests escorts Morikawa and me to the inner altar so that we may view the image. We kneel and pray; the words tumble out: "Namu Daishi Henjo Kongo." . . . I can see it clearly now. It is much fuller than a relief carving, almost in the round but not quite cut away from the wood of the tree, which forms a background. Age has blackened it but someone, long ago and reverently, whitened the face to indicate nobility. As sculpture it is simple and naïve: it would be called primitive. Its appeal is direct and I am stirred. It is the figure of a young monk, still a seeker. Ahead are the great achievements, the remolding of Japanese religion, the everlasting impress on Japanese civilization, the momentous journey to final rest on Mount Koya one thousand, one hundred, and thirty-six years ago this day.

The priest's son walks back to the residence with us and in the study prepares that special treat, tea from the first picking of the

The old Daishi Hall at Temple Twenty-six *(a painting by Sakata)*

new crop. He tells us that the major sutra we heard tonight, the one that moved me so, is the scripture that in Shingon is chanted for the dead, adding that, as is fitting in Shingon, it emphasizes the enlightenment to be achieved in this life. Optimistic and heartening, it affirms the joy of love.

We are back in our room when he brings me a gift from the elderly lady who came to talk with us this morning: a henro's white robe on the back of which she has printed a portrait of the Daishi from a wood block that belongs to the temple—a gift to cherish.

Next morning the priest somehow finds time to escort us to the temple's treasure house for a private viewing. He unlocks a steel door and reveals an astonishing collection. "Many of these things belonged to the Daishi," he tells us. "They are here because he gave them to one of his most beloved disciples, the holy priest Chiko, who, after the Daishi's death, came here to live out the rest of his life. He is buried here."

First to catch the eye is a portable set of altar instruments, made to nest together and fit in a wooden case that a priest could carry on his back. The utensils are small but every essential is included, exquisitely crafted as such things must be in Shingon, light, delicate, of thin polished brass. They were made in China. The assumption is that the Daishi brought them when he came home. Another set is a copy made in Japan, supposedly on the Daishi's order, a little larger, a little heavier.

We are shown treasure after treasure: sculpture, paintings, prints, bells, sutras. It would take weeks to become passingly familiar with all that is here. What the priest is most excited about he cannot show us: ten scrolls encompassing the two basic scriptures of Shingon. They had always been listed among the temple treasures, "never to be taken from the temple precincts," but a few years ago, when a special government committee investigated the cultural assets of the eighty-eight temples, these scrolls came to light for what they are: a single set with the same calligraphy, paper, and covers, made not later than the second half of the ninth century. They are probably the earliest copies of these sutras made in Japan, transcribed from those that the Daishi brought from

China, but much research remains to be done and it is not impossible that they *are* the scrolls he brought back. They were found to be in excellent condition but some restoration was deemed desirable and they have been in Kyoto for that work. They will be returned to the temple next week.

It is clear that the priest believes—perhaps because he so wants to believe—that these scrolls are the very ones the Daishi carried with him from China. "He had mastered one of the sutras here in Japan but the other had not been brought here yet. The two realms are complementary, inseparable, incomplete without each other. You know that Shingon centers on the Buddha Dainichi. The sutra that the Daishi found at a temple in Nara reveals that aspect of Dainichi which is mercy—Buddha reaching down to save man. The other, which he had to go to China to find, reveals that aspect of Dainichi which is wisdom—the diamond-hard wisdom that cuts through illusion, the wisdom that enables man to strive upward toward Buddhahood.

"Buddha descending in mercy, creatures ascending in wisdom: two aspects of the whole. You can understand why he had to find that second sutra. But he learned much more in China. Until then the sutras had only been *recited* in Japan. He learned the liturgy, the indispensable services and ceremonies, and he carried back the indispensable instruments. Then and only then, having learned all that the seventh patriarch, Hui-ko, could teach him, could he formulate his doctrine of Shingon.

"You can appreciate the crucial position that the Wisdom Sutra occupied in his life, in the development of his thought. It is central to his insistence that man can achieve Buddhahood in this existence." He shoots a look at us from under white brows. "It is wisdom that impels henro to make the pilgrimage."

As he locks the doors he points out that the treasures we have seen are a clue to the origin of the pilgrimage. Priest Chiko was not alone in seeking out the places on Shikoku where the Daishi had trained. Other disciples came also and many followed them. Within a century or two a phrase, "the remote places of Shikoku," was in common use; quite clearly it meant the spots associated with the Daishi. A book written in the early twelfth century by a retired emperor quotes a monk's testimony: "In our training we carried garlic and a priest's stole over our shoulders and in clothes quite tattered from wear we traveled to the remote places of Shikoku"—Cape Muroto of Tosa was mentioned as a place especially to be sought out.

And so pilgrimage to Shikoku began early, with the Daishi's contemporaries, his immediate disciples. And surely for a time most of the pilgrims who sought out places associated with the Daishi were priests of the Shingon sect that the Daishi had founded. But then older traditions asserted themselves. The Daishi had blazed few new trails in his ascetic practice on Shikoku. He had naturally sought out spots already marked as holy, places that—long before Buddhism came to Japan—had been transfigured because it was believed that the gods dwelled there, places where man could be transfigured by the presence of the gods. Buddhism did not negate these places: it gave new reasons for their being sacred.

But this Buddhism was not the Buddhism of the great temples around the capital. Since the beginning there had been two kinds of Buddhism in Japan. One was officially sanctioned and government controlled. In Japan religion and the state had never been separate; they were part of the same function. Religion was the foundation of government: the emperor was emperor because he was chief priest to the Sun Goddess, the Shinto deity who was not only worshiped by the imperial clan but had become the guardian deity for the whole country. When Buddhism crossed the strait from the continent to Japan it was welcomed, after initial resistance, because it was considered an even more powerful magic than Shinto. It was adopted not to replace Shinto but to supplement it, and it was adopted on the same basis as Shinto: that it would protect the nation, that it would become an arm of the government. Therefore Buddhist temples and Buddhist priests were authorized by the government, regulated by the government, given official rank by the government, and called upon to assist and bolster the government.

When the country needed rain, Buddhist temples conducted elaborate services to pray for rain. If a vengeful spirit struck down ministers of the government or menaced the land with earthquake, fire, or flood, Buddhism was called upon to tranquilize that spirit. If a lady of the nobility experienced difficult childbirth, Buddhist priests were called in to exorcise the evil spirits who had possessed her. None of these services had anything to do with Buddhist doctrine. No matter: in a superstitious age men called on the strongest magic available to them.

Yet from the beginning there were mavericks and rebels who either chose to stay outside the government-regulated hierarchies or were refused admittance because they were nonconformist or unschooled. Some turned their backs on the great temples because they were bustling places, occupied with official concerns. They went to the mountains, to lonely quiet places deep among the peaks, fitting for ascetic practice. And because they fled the environs of the capital for the countryside, they were the evangelists who carried Buddhism to the common people; they filled the void left by the temples and the hierarchies, who were too involved with the government and the aristocracy to concern themselves with ordinary folk. These rebels and mavericks shaped a whole other kind of Buddhism, outside of government control. They were the unordained holy men.

Kobo Daishi began as one of them while he searched for his "right way." When he found it and founded Shingon he preempted the establishment: he succeeded in having his creed, his temples, and his hierarchy accepted as an official arm of the government. He was one of the rare ones who moved from one realm of Japanese Buddhism to the other and left his mark on both.

Holy men like those whose steps the Daishi had followed never stopped coming to Shikoku. And they continued to be lay priests, unordained, outside the hierarchy. Only now they followed the Daishi's steps. Now they came in the Daishi's name and they made the Daishi's monastic center on Mount Koya their home base. They were called the holy men of Koya.

The beginnings of this can be traced to 994. In that year Koya was swept by fire. The monastery was devastated. No hermitages remained to live in so most of the priests left, moving to other mountain temples or into the capital. The few who stayed lived not on the mountain but at its base, and they climbed to the peak only on special days during the year. People generally considered that Koya was finished. The governor of the province, whose duty it was to protect and sustain the monastery, instead seized its manors, its rich rice lands, the endowment bequeathed by the pious. Since the monastery had ceased to exist, the governor declared, its manors were forfeit. What's more, when one of the priests drew up a petition to initiate a campaign for contributions to rebuild, the governor refused to forward the document to the imperial government for approval. Such a campaign would be futile, he said, and moreover, soliciting within the home province, which he governed, would drain away the wealth of the district to no purpose.

But he could not prevent a priest with the necessary connections at the court from making a direct appeal to the head of the government, the regent. "The peaks piercing the clouds were founded on a single fistful of soil, the deep waves were amassed from single drops of water," the priest's petition began, paraphrasing the Daishi's appeal when he was building Koya. Rebuilding Koya would require "the united power of many people . . . from His Imperial Majesty . . . to the denizens of the cities. . . . For how else can we hope to pile up hundreds and thousands of timbers?"

This was not a rhetorical question. The sizable contributions that could be obtained from a few wealthy patrons would be nowhere near enough. Beyond that were needed the offerings of multitudes; their individual gifts might be tiny but collectively they could rebuild Koya.

The regent gave his approval and support and the campaign was officially opened. But winning over the regent and conducting a countrywide campaign were two quite different problems. What was needed now was a leader in the tradition of Gyogi, who had achieved the Great Buddha at Nara, or of the Daishi himself, who had proved to be a virtuoso campaigner when he built Koya. What was needed was a man who could inspire an army of holy men and send them out over the whole country to convince the masses that they should contribute their handfuls of rice, their cups of oil.

The holy men had already begun to gather. They recognized

a need and an opportunity: whenever an important Buddhist temple or Shinto shrine faced a major rebuilding job, they rallied. In that tradition older than Gyogi they were the campaign workers; that was the way they lived.

And then a leader appeared. He was a priest named Joyo, an ordained priest impressive in his learning and his saintliness but one who knew what it was to be a holy man: he had chastened himself as a mountain ascetic and he had journeyed the provinces seeking contributions. At the age of sixty, or some say sixty-two, Joyo climbed Koya to live there the rest of his life. The holy men embraced him as their own. It was he who inspired and organized their gathering army.

Tradition says that Joyo had ardently prayed for the sight of his dead mother and father dwelling in paradise. Then in a dream he beheld a vision of Kannon—Kannon clad as a pilgrim, holding a pilgrim's staff—who told him that to see what he had prayed for he should go to Koya, for Koya was paradise here on earth.

That was the belief that impassioned the holy men. The Daishi's mountain, his monastery for the practice of meditation, had become, like the mountain of Temple Ten, like so many other mountains in Japan, home to the souls of the dead. But more than that, it was the next world revealed in this world; it was a certain gateway to paradise.

The regent himself validated this belief when he journeyed to Koya in 1019. At the place where his ancestors were buried he dedicated a temple and a hermitage for which he had given the money. As he lighted the eternal flame that burns there yet, he prayed that "all those whose bones are buried on this mountain . . . from the days of the past throughout the future shall be assured of entry into paradise and the salvation of Buddhism." So began the practice of bringing to the mountain the ashes of the dead, and since that meant making an offering and establishing an everlasting tie, the monastery was rebuilt and became prosperous.

The holy men of Koya fanned out over the country. They ministered to all, but most of them were of the common people and they went to the common people; there where the need was greatest they brought spiritual solace and practical help, they recited incantations and built bridges. Above all, they assured entry into paradise by carrying back to the sacred mountain the ashes of the dead. They made Koya "the burial place for all Japan."

The holy men are nameless, almost all of them. They were neither learned nor ordained and they left few records. But they did leave a rich and still vital legacy. Every henro is in their debt.

8 He could see the crossroads now. A good thing, for it had been a wearying day: a farewell mass at the last village, one more round of the houses to say a final blessing and collect a few late offerings, the steep rocky path up the mountain, and then finding that body near the summit. For an instant he had been tempted to avert his eyes, pretend he had not seen it—how many others passing this way had done so?—but his conscience would not let him. And so he had lifted the pannier from his back, tried to find the spot where the shifting breeze carried the least stench, and, composing himself, fingered his beads as he said the prayer for the dead—perhaps a bit hastily, skipping here and there, but not enough (he was certain) to anguish the spirit of the dead man. Surely that spirit must be grateful for rescue from the tortures of hell, grateful at the prospect of burial in the sacred soil of Koya, and grateful for the promise that flowed from burial there, near the Daishi's resting place, the promise of entry into Amida's paradise of the next world, the Pure Land in the West.

Crows and small beasts had picked some of the bones clean, and he was thankful for that. He had collected what dry wood he could find, kindled a fire with his flint, and using stout twigs as tongs placed a few small bones in the flames. With a fallen branch he had scraped a shallow trench and consigned the rest of the body to the grave. It was when he had replaced the earth over it, smoothed and tamped it down, that suddenly he had felt the tears flow down his face, and, overcome at the thought of the transiency of things, he had sunk to his knees beside the freshly turned sod and poured out his heart in prayer. For he knew that he might someday fall at the roadside. Would anyone carry his bones to Koya?

When his sobs subsided, when he had composed himself, he had picked bits of bone and ash from the dying flames and added them to those in an almost full bamboo tube in his pannier, said a final short prayer, put on his wide hat of cypress bark from the holy mountain, and hitched up his black robe to free his legs for the descent. In the gloom of the forest he had picked his way over the tumbled rocks of a washed-out trail. Where the slope began to level, the path broke into the open. Below him lay the crossroads, the clustered houses of the village, the pattern of the paddy fields that meted out the valley floor. A few minutes later he knew he had been spotted. He could see three men setting out to meet him. In the lead he was certain he recognized the figure of the headman, in whose house he had always been made welcome. How long had he been coming to this village, fifteen years? The headman would know.

Of one thing he was certain: from this village he would head back to Koya. He had been too long on the road. His muscles ached, fatigue had crept into his bones, but that he knew would pass, given a few easy days. More important, he was drained in spirit. He had said too many prayers, led too many masses, exorcised too many wild and baleful spirits. He had been too long in the world. He was beginning to be obsessed with desire for a woman.

He was not a priest: he was a layman and he had sworn no monastic vows, but he had chosen to become a holy man and a holy man should forswear sex. Ever since the day he had walked out of his house and shop to make his way to Koya he had been celibate. He never thought of his wife; she was a slattern and he despised her. He felt no concern for his son, the one child who had survived out of the many born to them; he seemed to have inherited his mother's unruly nature and, anyway, he was then fifteen and old enough to run the shop if he ever could. He felt no yearning toward his family but sometimes, in the villages on his circuit, he would see a woman so desirable that she would set him to trembling while he conducted a service. It was worst of all when that woman was part of the household where he was guest—wife or daughter—and almost unbearable when her eyes told him that given the slightest encouragement she would creep to his bed that night while the rest of the family slept. At this next, this last village, happily, the torment would be minimal: the headman possessed a wife and two daughters—unless the young women had been married off—who were quite remarkably ugly. He smiled a little.

But he wanted to be out of temptation's way. He longed for the sanctity of Koya, for its pine-scented air, for its valleys that were utterly quiet save for the birds that sang of the Three Treasures of Buddhism, "Bup-po-so, Bup-po-so." He longed for the company of others like himself, for days of chorusing homage to the Daishi and to Amida Buddha, for the sight of Joyo and the spur of Joyo's faith and fervor. Joyo would speak of revelation and of the holy ground they stood on, of the bliss to come and of the hard task they meanwhile faced, of the great halls that must rise again to thrust their golden finials toward Koya's sky. Joyo would praise him for the contributions he brought and inspire him to do more. And when his allotted time on the mountain was over he would return to the world and his campaigning, fresh and eager. But now he was tired.

The villagers were within hailing distance now, hurrying to greet him. He pulled himself a little more erect.

Later, seated in the place of honor at the headman's hearth, he listened to the catalog of misfortunes to which he must attend. Seven had died since his last visit; their anxious families had awaited his return to chant the sacred formulas that would atone for sins, that would assuage the troubled souls, releasing them from the bondage of this life, from their troubling presence still among the living, formulas that would guide them on their passage to the next world. Greatest boon of all, he would carry their ashes to Koya, he would inter them in that sacred soil near the Daishi, and so he would assure their rebirth in paradise. It was agreed that he would conduct a mass for the dead next morning, which all the village would attend.

The headman and the two elders, those who had met him, now exchanged uneasy glances; instinctively the holy man knew that this village was troubled and he tensed, wondering what burden would be laid on him. Haltingly, which was unusual for him, the headman explained. There was a family in the village that was accursed. One of the dead had been its head, a strong, stout fellow who had never been ill till he toppled over as he worked his land; he had spoken not a word after that, though he had lived several days and made guttural noises that surely emitted from the evil spirit that had seized him: his eyes never lost their terror at what he alone beheld. A few days later his widow had given birth to a baby that was unspeakably malformed, clearly the work of that same malevolence; the midwife had drowned it, of course, and so two of the dead were from the same family. There were differing ideas, the headman went on, as to the identity of the spirit that was afflicting that house. Fingers had been pointed at other villagers who might have harbored jealousy or hatred of the dead man—other villagers both dead and alive, for it was common knowledge that the obsessed soul of a living person, without that person's being aware, could wander off to wreak vengeance. There had been gossip—ugly gossip, the headman added vehemently, and the holy man realized that the headman had been a target of that gossip and he understood why this village leader, who had always been so self-assured, today seemed hesitant and distracted. The headman paused, seemingly unable to continue, and one of the elders concluded: the villagers looked to the holy man to identify the vengeful spirit and pacify it. The holy man did not answer. He had a feeling that it was unfair of them to present him with such a problem when his spirit was so depleted. But there was no escape. He must resolve their mystery or lose their faith in him, and, yes, the news of failure if he failed would travel swiftly to other villages. He said nothing but he bowed in acquiescence.

Relieved to have passed their trouble to him, the village leaders quickly listed routine matters, the usual incantations he had always performed. It was agreed that after the evening meal he would conduct a service to open his stay with them.

From his pannier he unpacked his picture scroll and his bell— round, dish-shaped, pierced in the rim for a cord—together with the wooden mallet he struck it with. He hung the bell from his neck and followed the headman to the open space in the middle of the village. The assembled villagers squatted there, looking expectant; there was a welcome hum of greeting as they bowed. He was glad to see that a couple of them had brought hand drums. There was wood piled in the center of the area, ready to set ablaze.

He would not preach long this evening. The important thing was to raise their spirits. The headman had seen to it that a pole, forked at the top, had been planted beside the flat rock he would stand on. He hung his scroll there, still tightly rolled, and turned to face the people. He raised his arms to quiet the buzz, took a deep breath to fuse them in suspense, and then burst out, "Glory to Amida Buddha and Kobo Daishi!" There was a tentative response. He cried, "I put my faith in Amida Buddha and Kobo Daishi!" The answer was firmer. Again. He had them now. Full-voiced, they chanted together, "I put my faith in Amida Buddha and Kobo Daishi!"

He silenced them as abruptly as he had begun. Turning he pulled the cord that bound the scroll. It fell open. It was a picture of the Daishi. There was a collective gasp of reverence; foreheads touched the ground.

"I come as a messenger of Kobo Daishi!" he proclaimed, and they caught their breath and bowed again.

"I come from the Daishi's temple on Mount Koya, the home of numberless Buddhas! All who climb to its sacred heights will experience paradise on this earth! All whose bones are buried in its sacred soil—the sacred soil where the Daishi rests—they shall straightway enter paradise, Amida's paradise, the Pure Land in the West!

"The Daishi taught us this. The Daishi taught us to sing, 'Glory to Amida Buddha!'" He had them chanting again. He leaped from his rock, beckoned them to follow. Someone kindled the fire; flames flared to light their faces in the darkness. He struck his bell to set the beat; the drums took it up. With him in the lead they circled the blaze. They forgot their weariness, their lives of drudgery. Drunk on the rhythm and the melody, voices straining, bodies weaving, they circled in a frenzy of exultation, dancing, singing, "Glory to Amida Buddha! Glory to Kobo Daishi!"

They danced and sang for an hour or more, an explosion of devotion. At last, as the fire died, he mounted the rock again and quieted them, though here and there an isolated invocation broke out. "Remember," he intoned, "remember well:

> "A far, far distant land
> Is Paradise,
> I've heard them say;
> But those who want to go
> Can reach there in a day."

There was a burst of chanting and he quieted them again. He reminded them that in the morning there would be a mass for the dead. He pressed his palms together and bowed dismissal. Slowly they dispersed.

The headman, whose mood was visibly brighter, escorted him home. "At least I have raised *his* spirits," the holy man thought, and he looked forward to bed.

He was unaware that he had made havoc of the Daishi's creed. He was no scholar; like the people he ministered to, he could not read or write. He had studied no doctrine; the devotions he recited he had learned by rote; what gave him strength was his faith.

He was one of the many who had been caught up in a powerful new current in Japanese Buddhism. Traditional Buddhism as it originated in India said that those who did not achieve a state of grace in this life were doomed to rebirth and another life of suffering—endless rebirth, endless suffering. The historical Buddha found a way to achieve that state of grace—of enlightenment; he made it his mission to lead men to it. But Buddhism, like the Hinduism from which it emerged, remained deeply pessimistic: for ordinary mortals enlightenment was almost beyond achieving.

The Japanese are an optimistic people. In Japan, over the centuries, Buddhism was transformed into an optimistic creed. Kobo Daishi's contribution to this was his insistence that man—and woman too, for whom earlier Buddhism held out no hope—had within him the seed of Buddha; by hard practice following strict precepts anyone could find and nurture that seed, could manifest his innate Buddha nature—could achieve enlightenment.

About a century after the Daishi some priests pushed optimism to new heights. Hard practice, strict precepts they declared unnecessary; simple faith was enough. Their faith was in the deity Amida: one had only to call on Amida to be saved—not to achieve that state of grace called enlightenment but to be assured that after death one would be reborn in Amida's paradise, Amida's Pure Land.

There were variations on this theme. Some said that one should constantly call on Amida, to be certain that his name was on one's lips whenever death came, however unexpected. Some said that to call upon Amida once, just once, was enough. Some said that one must call upon Amida with faith. Others said that faith was unnecessary, for Amida's compassion was without limit and included a special concern for the wicked.

We are told that many eons ago there was a king who, having renounced his throne to become a monk, examined a multitude of Buddha-lands and then vowed to create his own, which would combine the excellences of all. Moreover, he vowed to bring to his Pure Land all sentient beings who would call upon him. After he passed through an infinite number of *kalpas* (a kalpa is a period defined in various ways, such as the length of time required for a celestial nymph to wear away a ten-mile cube of stone if she brushes it with her garment once every three years), during which he accumulated boundless merit, this king-turned-monk attained enlightenment and became Amida Buddha. And in accordance with his vow, anyone who invokes his name with a sincere heart can achieve rebirth in his Pure Land in the West.

One of the earliest of those who spread this gospel of Amida was a priest named Kuya, who lived from 903 till 972. His way of preaching was to sing and dance through the streets of Kyoto, striking the bell hung from his neck, invoking the deity, and calling on others to join him: "Glory to Amida Buddha!" He made up simple songs:

> He never fails
> To reach the Lotus Land of Bliss
> Who calls,
> If only once,
> The name of Amida.

Kuya was an inspiration to the holy men. He made Buddhism a joyous celebration that anyone could understand. He carried Buddhism to the common people as the holy men labored to do. He went into the countryside to build bridges and dig wells. He went into the city in the midst of plague.

Worship of Amida as Kuya taught it invigorated Japanese Buddhism. Temples and monasteries that had grown torpid since the days of their great founders were again infused with energy. Their priests were roused to reach out to the people. The new fervor swept all the religious centers of the time, including Kobo Daishi's Mount Koya.

Veneration of Amida was not new. Images of Amida stood in the temples of every sect; priests of every sect invoked Amida as they invoked other deities. Evangelism like Kuya's came not as a new creed but simply as a rousing way of worship—too rousing, complained some of Mount Koya's priests, but the monastery's holy men seized on it, following their leader Joyo. The valleys where their temples stood echoed with exultant noise. The priests put up with it. They could not know that future evangelists would

空也上人

The holy priest Kuya
(a print by an unknown artist)

preach that only Amida need be worshiped, that faith in Amida
was all men needed—that they would father new sects to rival the
established schools like Shingon.

The priests could not know that this would happen, nor did it
occur to the holy men that their message was incompatible with
the Daishi's teaching. Dainichi, not Amida, was central in the
Daishi's thought; to the Daishi, Mount Koya was a place for intense meditation, not a gateway to paradise; the Daishi had not
spoken of a paradise after death. These distinctions were beyond
the holy men. They learned the invocation to Amida and they

learned some of the invocations of the Daishi's Shingon; they used them all. They spoke not of struggle to attain enlightenment but of rebirth in the Pure Land.

It was a message suited to the age—suited to the times in which this holy man ministered to this troubled village. All over Japan people were sunk in misery. Enlightenment in this life was beyond comprehension; the promise of salvation in the next life was a ray of hope.

The song the holy man had sung to close this night's worship was one of Kuya's. To the holy man Kuya was a hero, the Daishi was a saint. How could there be contradictions between them? He stretched out on the pallet that was laid for him and fell asleep.

At the service the next morning he chanted the Shingon litany for the dead that he had been taught on Koya. This was the heart of his visit; this was why he was anxiously awaited and welcomed with relief. And so again the whole village was in attendance. The bereaved families occupied the place of honor in front. The twice-bereft widow and mother wept disconsolately; her mother-in-law at her side matched her sob for sob and managed to convey the impression that her daughter-in-law was to blame. Later in the day he must visit their home and try to penetrate the mystery of the vengeance that had descended upon them; he did not look forward to it.

The funeral mass over, he began his visits to the families of the dead. He collected the ashes, most in tubes of bamboo, although one well-to-do elder proudly handed over his wife's ashes in a vessel of pottery. The holy man could not say so, but he was unhappy about the latter: it would be heavy on his back. He promised each family that he himself would perform burial in Koya's sacred soil, near the Daishi's resting place. He assured them that the never-ceasing prayers rising from Koya's altars, that the myriad Buddhas who resided there, would usher the spirit to the bliss of Amida's Pure Land.

He did not have to ask: the people knew that an offering must accompany the remains. But he took pains to tell them how well their gifts would be used—to keep the altar lamps burning, to keep the prayers rising. The offerings were small. A piece of cloth was the largest, a cupful of rice the smallest, but he knew that in each case a sacrifice was involved and he was satisfied. To make each family feel that their contribution had meaning he quoted the Daishi when he was building Koya: "A bit of earth will make the mountain higher, a drop of water makes the ocean deeper."

He postponed until last the visit he dreaded, for there he must conduct an incantation to try to force the vengeful spirit to reveal itself. He knew it would be grueling, he was not at all sure he would be successful, and he feared the consequences of failure.

They received him with fresh wails, the dead man's widow and mother, while two small children stood wide-eyed and apprehensive in the background. It took some time for him and the village elder who had accompanied him to subdue the distraught women. They handed over the ashes of the dead man and the infant in the same bamboo. He placed it before him and asked also for a kimono that the man had worn. The widow got it and laid it before him. "His name was Hikosuke," she sobbed. The light outside was fading and the room was dim; he was glad of that, but he asked that the door be closed and secured to deepen the gloom and prevent intrusion; the elder stationed his son outside.

He lighted a stick of incense he had treasured for such an emergency, and as the scented smoke rose he closed his eyes, joined his palms, and prayed earnestly to the Daishi and to Amida, first silently, then audibly. Slowly he began to recite an incantation he had learned on Koya. He did not know the meaning of the formula he chanted but he knew it was magical. At first there were moments of panic when he was certain that nothing was going to happen; then almost imperceptibly he began to feel the hypnotic power of those resonant syllables, feel a responsive hum begin in his gut. He drifted then, unconscious of where he was, his chanting involuntary, into a whirling void, neither light nor dark, neither noisy nor quiet. He was searching, searching, but there was only the void, there were no forms, no meaning, no answers. Again he felt panic rising in him like a shrill scream, louder, louder, until it was unbearable. He clapped his hands to his ears in pain, and in that paroxysm of desperation he knew, and he knew he knew. It was clear now and slowly he unwound, the hum in him lessened, there was something like the sound of a great bell, and he found himself bent over, his palms braced against the floor, sweat dripping from his face and running down his spine, back in this hovel of a farmhouse.

The elder put an arm around his shoulders and held a cup of water to his lips. At first his eyes would not focus, but then with an exercise of will they did, and across the hearth he saw the widow and the mother, pale, silent, mesmerized.

He sat erect and straightened his robe. "It was revealed to me," he said, and in a voice flat and unemotional he recited. "Hikosuke went to the mountain to forage for firewood. A man lay there in the agony of death. He begged for help but Hikosuke was frightened and fled down the mountain. In its fury the spirit of the dead man struck down Hikosuke and the newborn child.

"There is no longer anything to fear. Crossing the mountain on my way here I found the body and cared for it. I said prayers and I will carry the ashes to Koya. The dead man's spirit is at peace."

He bowed and left the family, carrying its ashes and its offering. He trudged back to the headman's house, the elder at his side bursting to reveal that their tribulation was over, that no one in the village, least of all the headman, bore any responsibility.

He sat by the headman's hearth that evening, the focus of gratitude and admiration. He felt numb.

The next day, with the headman and all the elders, he went into the fields, invoking the gods to make them bountiful. He made the round of the other houses in the village, chanting over each hearth a prayer to prosper those who gathered there; he collected their offerings. In two houses he was asked to treat the sick; he recited a special incantation and prescribed a brew to be made from herbs found in the forest. He was received everywhere with deference; the contributions were larger than usual.

He could not, of course, carry the contributions back to Koya. Small though they were, the sum of his collections at all the villages was too much to carry on his back. Each village carried its offerings to another until they reached the "kitchen temple" at the foot of the mountain, the monastery's accounting department.

He slept one more night at the headman's house. Early the next morning he set out. He wanted to be back on Koya as quickly as possible.

9 On the twenty-sixth of November, 1140, a young captain of the guards in the elite corps of the Retired Emperor Toba, having received Toba's permission, forsook the world to become a Buddhist priest. It was not a decision he made lightly. He had considered it for months if not years. Especially it pained him to leave his wife and, some say, a four-year-old daughter and an infant son, sending them back to his wife's family with the stigma of being abandoned, rejected, by husband and father.

> *I'll never forget*
> *Her look when I said goodbye . . .*
> *Especially since,*
> *As keepsake, she set her sorrow-*
> *Filled face on the moon above.*

His action startled many at the court. His family was a branch—rather low on the tree but still a branch—of the most powerful family in Japan, the Fujiwara. By marrying their daughters into the imperial line, the Fujiwara had virtually captured the throne; commonly during these years the emperor was an infant and his Fujiwara grandfather was regent, but whether the emperor was an infant or an adult the head of the Fujiwara family ran the government. Our captain of the guards was certainly not in line to become a power in the government but he was proud of his lineage. He could trace his descent from warriors and heroes and he was devoted to the imperial family.

He was an athlete, a fine horseman and archer (and this could not be assumed from his being a captain of the guards, for we read of another captain in the guards at about this time who was unable to mount his horse, much less stay on). Loving to ride and race, spurred by competition, he excelled at polo and at kickball, a sport demanding grace as well as speed and stamina. He was a vigorous and robust young man.

He was also a poet. The atmosphere of the court was intensely literary and had been for generations. The reigning emperor loved poetry and frequently held poetry-composing parties. Good poets abounded among the nobility: a man who could not compose a creditable verse on a moment's notice was not socially acceptable. Our captain of the guards was better than that: young as he was, he was recognized as a rare talent. But he would never be invited to one of the emperor's parties. Because of the complicated structure of court ranks and privileges—because though his family had served in the capital for generations they were still regarded as a *provincial* family—he was permanently locked out of associating as an equal with the "beautiful people," the people who had access to the throne and the men who were the really fine poets of his day.

There is no doubt that this had something to do with his forsaking the world. Neither is there any doubt that he felt a genuine call to the religious life. But the fact remains that by becoming a priest he could shed his worldly status and assume a new one. As priest he could enter any home in the capital. As priest he would be welcome as a poet. As courtier his gift for poetry could never mature; as priest there would be no bounds on it. As priest he became one of Japan's great poets. When he became a priest he took the name of Saigyo.

Formalities marked his leaving the secular life: his application to the Retired Emperor Toba, its transmission through bureaucratic channels, Toba's acceptance of it. A poem shows the young man's ambivalence and pain once he had taken the step.

> So loath to lose
> What really should be loathed:
>   One's vain place in life;
> Maybe we rescue best the self
> Just by throwing it away.

No formality but tonsure marked his entering the religious life; that was as he chose it. He could have gone to almost any temple and entered its community of monks, but he did not. He did visit several temples around the capital, moving from one to another; more often living in a hut near the temple than in the temple itself, for the temples, most of them, had themselves become worldly places, catering to the court and the nobility, conducting services for the safety of the country, for good harvest, for rain, or to thwart dread portents like a flaming meteor. He found many acquaintances in the temples, for he was by no means the only one of the nobility to leave the world. The times were unsettled, men had good reason to be apprehensive about the future, and many left the capital for a temple to devote themselves to their own salvation, free of worldly responsibilities but not bereft of worldly comforts. Saigyo had to prove to himself that he could get along without the comforts, and he had not left society merely to rejoin it in another setting. He did not join a temple. He did not ask to be ordained; he did not study doctrine. He chose the other path, the other kind of Buddhism. He simply shaved his head, put on priestly robes, and *became* a priest. He became a holy man.

Staying aloof from the temples' busyness, he thrust himself into the life of a homeless mendicant. Athlete and competitor that he was, he had to put himself to the test. He had to be alone. He had to live in nature and undergo austerities.

He tested himself. He left the capital and became Saigyo in late autumn. Winter was upon him very quickly. When he was not living in a hut near a temple he went into the Yoshino mountains south of Nara for ascetic practice in their snowy, frozen recesses. Winter tested him.

> *On a mountain stream,*
> *A mandarin duck made single*
> *By loss of its mate*
> *Now floats quietly over ripples:*
> *A frame of mind I know.*

Yoshino drew him and it continued to draw him the rest of his life. Yoshino's mountains were famous as a setting for religious exercise. The most sacred of its many sacred peaks had nurtured En the Ascetic; it was said that he had planted the tens of thousands of cherry trees that made—and still make today—its slopes and valleys a brocade of bloom each spring. Kobo Daishi had practiced in Yoshino as he had practiced on Shikoku; pushing into the mountains beyond Yoshino he had found Mount Koya.

Saigyo was increasingly drawn to the Daishi as a model. Although at first he sojourned at temples of other sects he shifted to those of Shingon. He was attracted by the Daishi's insistence on practice in nature, and by the Daishi as a poet who found fulfillment in nature.

To both the Daishi and Saigyo, art and religion were one. Enlightenment could make possible the creation of art—sculpture, painting, poetry—which in itself possessed Buddhahood; in a circular flow of blessedness, contemplation of that art could bring enlightenment. The Daishi wrote that the teachings of his Buddhism were so profound that they defied expression in writing, they could baffle a novice's attempt to approach them intellectually, yet they could be revealed through a sacred painting because its images "are products of the great compassion of the Buddha; the sight of them may well enable one to attain Buddhahood. . . . Art is what reveals to us the state of perfection." Eleven centuries later André Malraux called art "a manifestation of what men are unable to see: the sacred, the supernatural, the unreal."

Saigyo said (late in life, when he was a mature artist) that composing a poem required the same state of mind as sculpting a Buddha; and that to ponder such a poem was exactly like reciting a formula such as the Daishi had used to invoke Kokuzo: the poem like the formula could lead to enlightenment.

> *The mind for truth*
> *Begins, like a stream, shallow*
> *At first, but then*
> *Adds more and more depth*
> *While gaining greater clarity.*

To push further, to both the Daishi and Saigyo nature and art and religion were one. To Saigyo nature did not exist as the creation of his god; nature was not a symbol of the Buddha, not something through which one might approach the Buddha, not an aid to comprehending the power and majesty of the Buddha—nature *was* Buddha.

Saigyo became the greatest nature poet of Japan. To Saigyo, being in nature—being alone in nature, open to it, vulnerable to it—was a religious act. To merge with nature was his ultimate goal. His poems are his acts of worship, composing them was his way of practicing Buddhism.

During the first years of his religious life, Saigyo stayed in the vicinity of the capital, the former capital of Nara, and the Yoshino mountains. Sometimes he went into the capital; he kept in touch with his old friends. He cherished their friendship; he never lost his loyalty to the people of the court. But he had another reason also: on occasion he solicited contributions from them. Since he had not joined a temple he drew no support from a temple. Instead he enlisted in the campaigns to rebuild one temple or another ravaged by time or fire. He became a holy man and a campaign worker, one of the few who could approach the nobility. He could call on his old acquaintances because he had been one of them and because his reputation as a poet was growing steadily.

In the early spring of 1147 Saigyo began his first long pilgrimage. He headed north, probably because that was where his family had originated; Fujiwara relatives there held huge tracts of land and had built a capital to rival the emperor's. He knew that in their domains he would be received hospitably. No doubt he carried some temple's commission to solicit contributions.

His journey lasted almost two years; he did not return to the capital until the close of 1148. In the next year fire again swept Mount Koya: the great pagoda and other central halls were leveled. It was then that Saigyo moved to Koya. For the next thirty years and more Kobo Daishi's monastery in the mountains would be his home while he helped raise funds to rebuild the lost structures. He was a distinguished addition to the army of workers: he was appointed manager of the campaign. For this long period of his life he was a holy man of Koya; in the history of the holy men he is one of the most eminent. Like the best of them, when he was on Koya he frequently retired in solitude to do ascetic practice. After the worldly business of raising money he had to restore his spirit.

Because he was in and out of the capital and on intimate terms with the ruling class he was witness to the tumult and disintegration of this distressing period. One of the early events shook him personally. Early in the Seventh Month of 1155 came the death of the Retired Emperor Toba, whom Saigyo had served. Retirement had not prevented Toba from controlling the imperial family. He had always had a strong dislike for his first son because he was born of a consort who had been chosen for him by his grandfather, an earlier retired emperor with a forceful personality; Toba suspected that the boy was his grandfather's son, not his own. Nevertheless when Toba chose to retire that son was his only heir and at the age of five ascended the throne as the Emperor Sutoku. As soon as his grandfather died Toba acquired some new consorts, and when a favorite among them bore him a son he quickly had the baby declared crown prince. Two years later he forced Sutoku to abdicate and installed the infant as emperor.

The child emperor died at seventeen. Established practice dictated that Sutoku's son should succeed him but Toba chose another of his own sons and made that son emperor with the name Go-Shirakawa; then he made Go-Shirakawa's son the crown prince. Sutoku's line was excluded from succession.

We do not know how Saigyo felt about this murky Elizabethan maneuvering but we do know that he felt loyalty and affection for both Toba and Sutoku. He had served Toba and it was during Sutoku's reign that he had grown up, become a man and a poet, and finally left the world for the priestly life. Sutoku, who was almost the same age as Saigyo, was a poet and a patron of poets. He created an atmosphere in which poetry thrived and Saigyo was devoted to him.

Naturally Toba's treatment left Sutoku bitter, and of course a party at the court sympathized with Sutoku and let him know that they considered him wronged—most of them had their own interests at heart as much as his, for they would profit if Sutoku's line came to power. The final indignity came when Toba died: Sutoku was refused admittance to the palace to join in the last rites for his father. Now his injuries seemed unbearable and his anger erupted. His supporters gathered and—something unheard of for centuries— mounted an armed rebellion in the heart of the capital.

Saigyo and men like him were horrified. The imperial family was split against itself; the Fujiwara family was split against itself. Saigyo had just come down from Koya to the capital, summoned by word that Toba was dying. He performed funeral services and then watched aghast as revolt erupted.

It did not last long. Sutoku's forces were few and ineptly commanded. They performed heroic feats of arms but the battle, fought at night against the flames of a burning palace, lasted only a few hours. The aftermath was as horrifying as the insurrection itself: as a shaken chronicler set down, "There was a child who cut off his father's head, there was a nephew who cut off his uncle's head, there was a younger brother who exiled his older brother, there was a woman who drowned herself in grief. These things are unnatural events in the annals of Japan." It had been nearly three hundred and fifty years—three hundred and fifty years of a gentle civilization—since the death penalty had been inflicted on a government official. Now a new age was born, an age in which men like Saigyo felt themselves aliens, an age dominated by martial emotions including, as historian George Sansom lists them, "anger, pride, rapacity, and cruelty." It began with a vengeance. Some seventy of Sutoku's supporters were executed and dozens were exiled. Sutoku, when he realized that his cause was lost, had his head shaved to indicate that he renounced all worldly ambition, and fled for sanctuary to the great Shingon temple Ninna-ji on the outskirts of the city. His younger brother was chief abbot there (from its founding until modern times Ninna-ji had an imperial prince as its superior).

Ninna-ji being Shingon, Saigyo had friends among its priests. He went there to try to see Sutoku but was told it was impossible.

"The moon was bright," he wrote; amid "unbroken gloom . . . sight of it casts me down more."

Sutoku was taken into custody and banished to Shikoku ("there was a younger brother who exiled his older brother"). He was held at a temple not far from Kobo Daishi's birthplace in the province of Sanuki. Saigyo wrote: "After Retired Emperor Sutoku had gone to Sanuki . . . not much was heard in society about poetry any longer." He wrote to a friend who was also a priest and a poet that it was a "grievous fate" to be living "just at that juncture in time when gatherings of refined poets are . . . extinct."

Saigyo now had two reasons for pilgrimage to Shikoku: to visit places associated with the Daishi and to visit Sutoku. He sent poems to the exile but unhappily he was not able to cross to Shikoku until after Sutoku's death.

Sutoku was first detained in a small hermitage belonging to the temple that is Eighty-one today; later he was more closely confined within a stockade where Seventy-nine now stands. One day he was taken out, they told him, to attend a poetry-making party. Along the way he was murdered. They kept his body in the chill waters of a spring until word came from the capital that it should be cremated. He had left instructions that without fail his bones should be carried to Mount Koya and interred there, but they took him just three miles east, to Mount Shiramine, above his first prison. "And they turned him into smoke at a place called Shiramine."

Four years later Saigyo came. "I looked for the place where the Retired Emperor had lived, but no trace of his earlier presence could be found." The buildings associated with the exile must have been deliberately razed. The court was already intensely disturbed by what they considered the workings of Sutoku's vengeful spirit. During his banishment Sutoku had devoted his time to copying the Five Great Sutras. When he had finished he sent them to the capital, using his brother the chief abbot of Ninna-ji as intermediary, with the request that they be presented at the grave of his father, Toba, or if that was impossible, sent to Koya. The Prince Abbot mediated earnestly but he had to send them back with the message that, "since the Emperor regards your guilt as heavy, not even your handwriting can be placed near the capital." Sutoku was consumed by rancor and despair. They say he bit through his tongue and in his own blood indited across the scrolls an oath to wreak vengeance in the afterlife. "Becoming the Great Devil of Japan I will disorder all under Heaven, I will trouble the Realm." Adds a chronicle: "After this, he neither cut his nails nor had his hair trimmed; leaving his appearance unsightly, he was sunk in evil meditations; it was frightful." And it was said that when he was cremated, although the wind was blowing strongly out of the north, the smoke of his burning inclined northeast toward the capital.

Saigyo's visit to Sutoku's grave quickly became embedded in the folklore of Japan. The most vivid account of it was written some six centuries later as one of a collection of tales about the supernatural; "you who pick up this book to read must by no means take the stories to be true," the author cautioned. Here is his version, much condensed. Saigyo is speaking:

> The mountain was so densely covered with oak and pine trees that it felt as dreary as if a steady drizzle of rain were falling. Then, in a small clearing among the trees I saw a high mound of earth above which three stones had been piled. The entire place was covered with brambles and vines. Sad of heart, I wondered, "Is this where the emperor rests?" I could hardly hold back my tears. "I shall honor his soul throughout the night," I vowed, and kneeling on a flat rock in front of his grave, I began softly to intone a sutra.
>
> Soon after sunset an eerie darkness filled the recesses of the mountain. An uncanny terror gripped my heart as I grieved on through the pitch-black night. Almost in a trance I heard a voice call, "Saigyo, Saigyo." I opened my eyes and peered through the darkness, where the strange form of a man loomed, tall of stature and thin as death. It was impossible to distinguish his features or the color and cut of his garments but at once I knew that I was confronted by the ghost of the Emperor Sutoku. I bowed with tears in my eyes and replied, "But why is your soul still wandering? You ought to find repose in the soul of Buddha."
>
> Sutoku gave a laugh. "It's I who've recently caused all the

trouble in the world. I will put a curse on the imperial family. I will throw the whole nation into chaos."

"I beg of you, forget past grudges. I pray and beseech you to show intelligence and return to the land of paradise and find eternal repose."

Perversely, Sutoku's ghost recites the list of enemies on whom he has inflicted horrible death and those on whom he still intends to wreak vengeance.

"Because you are so involved with the world of demons," I replied, "and ten thousand billion leagues separates you from Buddha Land, I have nothing more to say to you," and I faced him in silence.

Thereupon a tremor shook the mountains and valleys. The wind rose as if to fell the forest trees. As I watched, dumbstruck, a ball of flame flared up where his highness stood, illuminating the mountains and valleys as if it were day. In the light I could clearly see his highness's features. His face flushed crimson. His hair hung down to his knees, as tangled as a thorn bush. The pupils of his eyes were turned up, leaving only the whites exposed and his hot breath came in painful gasps. His persimmon-colored robes were filthy with soot. His fingernails and toenails had grown as long as a beast's claws. Every detail betrayed the terrifying form of a demon king. Clapping his hands in joy, his highness said, "These enemies of mine, to the last man, will perish!"

I chanted loudly, with all my heart. The ghostly flame gradually subsided, and then the emperor's form disappeared from sight. Before long the sleep-ending light of the dawn sky brought the chirruping of the morning birds. Then I chanted a section of the Wisdom Sutra in prayer for his majesty and descended the mountain. Back in my hut I pondered over the events of the night and reviewed each detail in my mind. In the facts about the persons and in the dates of the events, I could detect no mistake. What he related was as terrifying as it was mysterious.

The compendium of wretched fates that befell Sutoku's enemies was of course historically accurate: the writer had the benefit of hindsight. With the exception of Sutoku's half brother, Go-

Shirakawa, who barred the palace gate to Sutoku when their father died and who refused to accept the sutras Sutoku had copied in repentance, every notable enemy of Sutoku died in defeat and misery. Go-Shirakawa had a long life and died in bed but the years he presided over were filled with calamity for the imperial line and he was more than once humbled; though a born survivor, history's verdict on him is harsh: some call him mad and some say he was "not mad but not at all wise . . . a 'dark ruler' . . . addicted to intrigue and conspiracy."

Even before Sutoku died, apprehension or feelings of guilt had led the court to erect a Buddhist temple on the site of the battle in which his supporters went down to defeat, honoring those who lost their lives there. Then the courtiers who had been banished were called home. Seventeen years after Sutoku's death in 1181, faced with fresh disasters, they tried to pacify his spirit by giving him back his title of emperor. In spite of this, war swept the country and his enemies were crushed. In 1184 he was raised to be a Shinto god and at the battleground a shrine was dedicated to him, and still there were whirlwinds and earthquakes and no tranquillity. The efforts to placate his spirit almost literally never ceased, for never again did the imperial house control its own destiny. Envoys were sent to Shikoku to make offerings at the temples and shrines dedicated to him every year until 1868, when briefly it seemed that the imperial house would come into its own again. The assumption proved illusory.

As for Saigyo, after a visit that surely was less harrowing than the one described above, he went on to the Daishi's birthplace. The place where his family home stood is marked by the imposing Temple Seventy-five but nearby and closely associated are Seventy-four, Seventy-three, and Seventy-two. It seems clear that Saigyo stayed for a while at Seventy-two or in a hut in its precincts. In the compound grows an extraordinary pine that they say the Daishi planted. Today it is low, spreading, almost circular, and more than fifty-four feet in diameter. Rising gently to a peak in the center, it looks like a great green pilgrim's hat. One of Saigyo's much-loved poems sprang from his finding a pilgrim's hat hung from a tree in the compound (perhaps this tree) and wondering what had become of the man who wore it, reflecting on the evanescence of life. But there is a poem that moves me more and that I am quite certain he addressed to this old pine.

On seeing a tree which stood in front of my hermitage:

> *Long-living pine,*
> *Of you I ask: everlasting*
> *Mourning for me and*
> *Cover for my corpse; here is no*
> *Human to think of me when gone.*

A sharp climb up from the nearby Seventy-three is the cliff from which legend says the Child Daishi threw himself.

The climber must make an almost perpendicular ascent. . . . It is said that Kobo Daishi climbed up on this place every day to perform religious observances. Now, so that others can do devotional activities there [without falling off], a double enclosure has been put around it. Still, the dangers faced in making the climb up to that spot are really unusual. I made my way up to the top crawling on all fours.

> *Lucky to make it:*
> *Here at this point where*
> *Holy ones met once*
> *To make pledges on abrupt*
> *Precipices above it all.*

Saigyo was fifty-two years old now and renowned as a poet. His fame gave him entrée anywhere and made it that much easier for him to campaign for Koya. Although records are scanty from that long ago we catch glimpses of him: he obtained a large contribution from a daughter of Sutoku and he arranged the gift of a manor, with its rice lands and the peasants who worked them, to the temple on Koya that was the headquarters of the holy men. In a letter he wrote to that temple from the capital he reported that he had talked with the regent, the absolute ruler of the country; he had succeeded in getting Koya exempted from a tax recently levied to reconstruct a Shinto shrine, and as a measure of appreciation he asked that all the priests of Koya be assembled for a service to chant one million times a formula to insure the regent's well-being. He added that he had appealed to the regent to pay for paintings to decorate the walls of their temple and that discussions were proceeding nicely. "Owing to matters of business, I am afraid I shall be staying in Kyoto a little longer and my return to Koya will be delayed. I trust that you will continue to pray devoutly on behalf of the regent so that when I meet him for our next long discussion I shall find him fully satisfied." In addition to the prayers, Saigyo accommodated the regent by tossing off "public poetry" of the kind a poet laureate is expected to produce; for example, a poem commemorating the opening of a new port built to facilitate trade with China. Certainly there were few others among the holy men of his time who could campaign as effectively as Saigyo.

It is a mark of the changing times that the regent Saigyo dealt with was not a Fujiwara; he was the head of a powerful warrior clan that now was dominant. Emperors and the Fujiwara were permitted ceremonial roles but they danced to a military tune.

The last decade of Saigyo's life began with a great war between two military families to determine which would rule Japan.

In the world of men it came to be a time of warfare. Throughout the country—west, east, north, and south—there was no place where war was not being fought. The count of those dying . . . climbed continually. . . .

> There's no gap or break
> In the ranks of those marching
> Under the hill:
> An endless line of dying men,
> Moving on and on and on . . .

When the conflict broke out, Saigyo, as if acknowledging that in time of war it was futile to seek funds to rebuild temples, retired from Mount Koya to the great Shinto shrines at Ise. There was a cluster of poets there and it would be a haven from the fighting. There was no rupture in his beliefs for, as he pointed out in poetry, the Sun Goddess enshrined at Ise had come to be considered a manifestation of Dainichi, the central Buddha of Shingon—so close had Shinto and Buddhism become in a process advanced by the Daishi and continued ever since.

In five years of bloody fighting the control of Japan passed from the family Saigyo had known in the capital to another whose strength was in the northeast. In 1186 he undertook his last major journey and again he went north, though it was not out of a desire to cultivate the new ruler, for his loyalties were tied to the defeated. He did not even intend to seek an audience but he was recognized as he was sightseeing in Kamakura, the new seat of power, and was summoned by the new strong man, Yoritomo. They talked all night, as the Japanese are wont to do, in what must have been a delicate fencing match. Yoritomo suspected Saigyo of being a spy and tried to find out by leading him to discuss the martial arts that had engaged him when he was young. Saigyo tried to pry a contribution out of Yoritomo for he was again campaigning, this time to rebuild the Todai-ji at Nara, that eminent head temple for the state-established temples in the provinces; the Todai-ji and its great bronze Buddha—Gyogi's supreme accomplishment—had been destroyed in a senseless act of war by Yoritomo's enemies. (Saigyo's soliciting for the Todai-ji indicates no change of heart toward Koya; holy men often shifted from one effort to another, and the Todai-ji campaign was the great effort of the day.)

Yoritomo, however, could truthfully state that he had already given generously and all Saigyo got was a personal gift, a silver cat, which he gave to a child in the street as he left—an act that must have been calculated to show disdain for the giver, since Saigyo could easily have asked that the valuable gift be kept for him until he passed through on his way back; the cat would have fetched a tidy sum to be added to the funds for the Todai-ji.

In all religions there is a constant theme in the stories of men who come to be canonized or deified, as the Daishi has been and as

Saigyo has been. Invariably such a man is said to have prophesied the time and circumstances of his own death. Saigyo had written—

> *Let it be this way:*
> *Under the cherry blossoms*
>   *A spring death,*
> *At that second month's midpoint*
> *When the moon is full.*

The moon would of course be full on the fifteenth of any month according to the lunar calendar. In his beloved Yoshino mountains the cherry blossoms would be at their peak in the middle of the Second Month. And as any educated Japanese would know, that was the traditional date for the death of the historical Buddha.

Saigyo died at a temple in Yoshino on the sixteenth day of the Second Month of 1190, just as the blossoms were beginning to fall.

10 The Daishi's birthplace—or, to avoid argument, the site of his family home, where he was reared and grew to young manhood—was naturally a magnet to the holy men of Koya. Very early a temple was founded there, drawing its support from the family lands and named Zentsu-ji to honor the Daishi's father; in time it became the seventy-fifth temple of the pilgrimage.

In the times we speak of, one of the major problems facing the priests of the temple was how to cope with the steady stream of visitors, practically all of whom were, or professed to be, priests. There were orthodox priests of Shingon from Mount Koya or the hundreds of Shingon temples scattered over the land; there were priests trained in other doctrines who came to pay their respects and seek inspiration; and there were the holy men—sometimes there seemed to be a deluge of holy men.

Early in the fourteenth century the elderly chief priest looked back on a lifetime of trying to deal with holy men. He had come to the temple as a very young acolyte (from a good family, to be sure); he had been trained and ordained here; he had slowly risen through the ranks until eminence and the blessing of longevity made him abbot.

All through his career the holy men had been a concern. When he was young and junior his most onerous assignment was to watch over them: to try to control them without rebuffing them, for most of them seemed to have a sincere faith in the Daishi; to try to prevent abrasive confrontation between them and the senior priests of the temple.

A great irritant was the noise they made. Quite often a group would descend on the temple, led by a man whose charisma and skill garnered sufficient offerings to support that many. At night they were likely to break into clamorous worship, chorusing their homage to Amida Buddha while beating bells and drums. A few of the more doctrinaire of the temple monks inveighed against this on the grounds that worship of Amida had nothing to do with Shingon, though it was true that the holy men's lusty hosannas usually mingled praise of the Daishi along with Amida. But most of the temple establishment railed only that the racket disturbed their meditations or their sleep. The abbot managed a smile: he supposed many more of the monks were sleeping than meditating. But oh my, the noise was an affliction; he knew that the monks on Koya had the same complaint.

Most of the holy men had blurred in his memory, no matter how unforgettably difficult they had seemed at the time. But one of them he would never forget, a man whose reputation had preceded him and whose later deeds were on such a scale that it was no problem at all to keep abreast of them. His name was Chogen.

The abbot closed his eyes and the vision of Chogen came flooding back: a comparatively young man then but already stamped by a passionate will. Hatchet-faced, shaved head thrust forward from his shoulders, eyes narrowed in appraisal, he was so thin there seemed to be no flesh on him. He was the revered leader of one of the largest groups of holy men ever to appear at Zentsu-ji.

Chogen performed all kinds of good works—built and repaired

The holy man Chogen *(detail of a sculpture by an unknown artist)*

roads and bridges, built irrigation ponds—but he had made a name for himself as a builder of bathhouses. Yes indeed, he told the young monk, and he rattled off the places where his bathhouses gave the people the blessings of cleanliness plus a sense of ritual purity—bathhouses with huge cast-iron tubs and boilers that provided a constant supply of hot water. Some of his tubs were eight feet in diameter, and rather boastfully he asserted that he had followers who could do anything. Back in 746, when they set about to create the Great Buddha at Todai-ji in Nara, there were no Japanese who knew how to cast such a mammoth statue and Gyogi had to import craftsmen from Korea. Not now—his craftsmen knew no limitations. He had built bathhouses in the teeming cities of the capital district, in faraway provinces, and more than one on Koya, "our holy temple" he called it. And for every bathhouse he had found patrons who provided the "hot water of virtue" by giving the cost of fuel for a hundred or a thousand days so that the baths were free to the people. (He did not have to say—the young monk knew—that out of the generous offerings he collected he supported his little army of followers and carried worthwhile sums back to Koya.)

Now he had come to build a bathhouse at Zentsu-ji—what spot more appropriate than the sacred birthplace of the Daishi? The young monk carried the word to his abbot, who frowned—it would mean an extensive stay for that "rabble"—but acquiesced, and the construction and the casting went forward. The monk watched closely. He marveled at the craftsmanship and discipline of Chogen's workers and his unquestioned authority over them.

Occasionally he would find Chogen in a talkative mood. The holy man would gaze at the mountains around them and recall his hard training deep among the peaks as a young mountain ascetic. He was no stranger to Shikoku, he said.

One day the monk asked Chogen what Mount Koya was like. Chogen gave him a close look, as though he were measuring a prospective donor, then closed his eyes and recited as he would a litany: "Mount Koya . . . is silent and far from the habitations of men; untainted are the breezes that rustle its branches, calm are the shadows of its setting sun. Eight are its peaks and eight are its valleys, truly a spot to purify the heart; beneath the forest mists the flowers blossom; the bells echo to the cloud-capped hills. On the tiles of its roofs the pine-shoots grow; mossy are its walls where the hoarfrost lingers." The young monk sensed that the passage was from the repertoire of those holy men who moved the hearts of the people by storytelling; *his* heart was moved and he vowed that he would cross the Inland Sea and climb to Koya, someday. (He never made it.)

Mostly Chogen talked about his bathhouses, sometimes about his "invention": in hilly districts he had taught the people to build fires in the caves and then pour water on the hot rock; result—a steam bath.

The people, even the ignorant common people, needed baths, he insisted. If they could keep themselves clean they would avoid many of the diseases that devastated them. But perhaps more important was the spiritual benison, for bathing expunged pollution, the pollution everyone incurred from death in the family, a wound, intercourse, menstruation, childbirth. He spoke of how the Daishi always lustrated himself in some pure swift-flowing stream before he began ritual training or a challenging mission. And Chogen confided that he had taught his campaign workers to tell the story of the eighth-century Empress Komyo of blessed memory. Pious and humble, this lady vowed to wash the bodies of a thousand beggars; she had bathed nine hundred and ninety-nine when the last appeared before her as a loathsome leper. Without a sign of repugnance the Empress bathed him. When she had finished, a glory of light radiated from his body and he ascended heavenward.

Not everything that Chogen said rang true. He boasted of having visited China three times, though vague about exactly how or when. The monk was young and naïve but when Chogen described gold and silver pagodas and silver bridges that no sinful man could cross, he was not convincing. The monk considered this and then rationalized that Chogen had the right to invent legends about himself if they furthered his good works.

Midway in the construction of Zentsu-ji's bathhouse Chogen sought out the young monk again. He had noticed, he said, that the golden canopy above the principal image in the main hall was cracked and some of the glittering pendants were missing. He uttered no word of reproach but his attitude said this was unseemly. He said he had craftsmen skilled in working with brass and gold; he could make the necessary repairs. This time the abbot had not frowned; he gratefully accepted the offer, and for the rest of the time that Chogen and his men were there he had given short shrift to complaints about their nighttime chanting, dancing, and beating of drums and bells.

When all the work was finished, when patrons had been lined up to supply wood for the boiler (they were so eager to part with their money that the monk wondered if Chogen had cast a spell over them), the abbot received the holy man in formal audience to express his gratitude. The young monk attended; it occurred to him that Chogen, though there was nothing wrong with his manners, seemed abstracted, almost bored: the completed tasks no longer interested him; his mind was fixed on his next undertaking. All the rest of his life, given the slightest provocation, the monk would reminisce about the holy man. "Ah there was no tranquillity about him. He gripped his prayer beads as a soldier does his sword; he fingered them as a merchant does his money." The junior monks heard that speech so often that they mimicked it when they were safely private, and some suggested that the priest tried, unsuccessfully, to display the same intensity.

When years later word came that the imperial court had summoned Chogen from Koya to take charge of the reconstruction of Todai-ji and its gigantic bronze Buddha, the priest professed no surprise at all. Nor was he surprised when he learned that Chogen had actively campaigned to get the job; that was like him, he did not lack self-confidence. Other priests may have been considered, but of course Chogen was the right choice, though it was a matter for regret that Mount Koya would lose his services.

Certainly Todai-ji had to be rebuilt. Situated at the old capital, Nara, it was the headquarters temple for the Kokubun-ji, the national temples, one in each of the sixty-odd provinces, established in 741 "for the protection of the nation." Its Great Buddha, a towering figure in gilded bronze, was a national symbol. Much of the nation's energy was dedicated to recreating it; a man like

Saigyo felt compelled to come out of retirement to enlist in the effort.

It had all gone up in flames in 1180, a prelude to the long, bitter war of 1181–1185. Soldiers had fired it in a senseless act of vengeance against militant monks who favored the other side. More than a thousand perished who had sought sanctuary in the temple, crowding into its upper stories: "those too old to flee, children and girls." The colossal Buddha "melted into a shapeless mass."

Todai-ji had to be rebuilt and Chogen had the job. It meant that he must mount a nationwide campaign for funds, that he must marshal men, material, and technology. It was the construction project of the century, and the priest at Zentsu-ji was avid for reports of progress.

He chortled when he heard that Chogen had devised a wheelbarrow to carry priests while they solicited contributions, a covered cab on a wheel. On the left side was pasted the emperor's decree bidding all to cooperate, while the right side bore the official appeal for funds:

THOSE WHO MAKE OFFERINGS, THOUGH BUT A SHEET OF PAPER OR A TINY COIN, SHALL IN THIS WORLD ATTAIN HAPPINESS BEYOND COMPARE, AND IN THE NEXT WORLD FIND EVERLASTING PEACE. . . .

It would take a husky man to push that contraption but Chogen had husky men. He had six of those barrows built; he himself rode around Kyoto in one and he dispatched the others on the main highways leading from the capital, each accompanied by at least fifty of his holy men.

Of course there were vast areas of the country that no wheeled vehicle could penetrate. Though war was still being waged, groups of holy men fanned out to cover the remotest districts. One such group reached Zentsu-ji, carrying a personal message for the monk: "Although a vast responsibility has been heaped on me, do not think that I have forgotten our holy temple. On Mount Koya I have established a hermitage where twenty-four holy men of deep faith insure that the invocation to Amida rises continually. Two

The holy man Chogen in his wheelbarrow, soliciting donations to rebuild
Todai-ji (*detail of a painting by Tessai*)

men at a time chant for two hours—that is their only duty, that
their devoutness may serve as a model to others. Now at Todai-ji
when I find one among the workers whose profound faith and
great accomplishment are exemplary I reward him by sending him
to that hermitage on Koya for a period of retreat and devotions."
The letter was signed "Chogen, who crossed over to China three
times."

The monk could see that the holy men who visited him were
sustained by hero worship. One of them told how Chogen chose a
chief carpenter. Summoning all the master carpenters he asked
them to do something that was quite impossible. One after another
they said so and refused, but one of them took up his tools and
said, "I have never done such a thing or seen it done, but if the
High Priest instructs me to do it I shall try." Chogen stopped him
then, saying he did not actually want the job done; he was testing

their faith in him and absolute obedience to his orders. And the carpenter who set out to try was appointed foreman.

At Zentsu-ji Chogen had boasted that his men could do anything, but faced with the technical difficulties of casting the Great Buddha he was not above impressing a Chinese caster who had come to Japan several years earlier for another project and whose attempts to go home had been frustrated by shipwreck.

Chogen was not one to wait until he had enough funds to pay the bills before starting work. He knew that contributions would flow faster if construction was underway, and shortly after his appointment he made a round of calls on high officials in the capital, beginning with Sutoku's half brother, the Retired Emperor Go-Shirakawa (who had taken the tonsure on leaving the throne and was himself in priestly robes), Go-Shirakawa's favorite consort, and the prime minister. He was seeking large contributions and he was able to report that the molds for the Buddha's spiral tresses were already completed.

In the first flush of the campaign, contributions poured in and work on the Buddha went smoothly. It was completed in four years and the monk at Zentsu-ji heard glowing accounts of the magnificent ceremony staged to invest the statue with its sacred spirit. Go-Shirakawa was master of ceremonies.

But construction of the mammoth hall to house the Buddha did not progress with that same speed. Stories were still heard of Chogen's technical innovations: the huge logs that would become the pillars had to be moved more than two hundred and fifty miles from mountain forest to Nara; he devised a new system of trundles and pulleys so that sixty or seventy men could do what before had taken as many as two or three thousand. But it was not easy to keep the contributions rolling in year after year. The court and the shogun made him governor of three provinces so that he could use their revenues; he promptly got into boundary disputes with the governors of neighboring provinces. Hearing of such things, the monk at Zentsu-ji worried: he was afraid that to Chogen the ends justified the means.

He was not prepared, however, for the great blow. In the hills southeast of Nara is the temple called Muro-ji; in a pagoda at this temple Kobo Daishi was said to have interred a sacred ball containing thirty-two grains of the holy remains of the historical Buddha that he had carried from China: belief in these relics was fervent. In 1191 the sacred ball disappeared. Chogen was accused of stealing it.

To defend himself he appeared before the prime minister, who had always been one of his staunchest supporters. He maintained that he had nothing to do with the disappearance, that it was the deed of a Korean priest who was quite mad. But the investigation continued and grew more heated and a few days later Chogen abandoned work on Todai-ji and vanished. The distraught prime minister rushed to report this to Go-Shirakawa. His majesty the retired emperor seemed not in the least surprised; he merely grinned. Now the prime minister was even more upset; he suspected the worst. Nevertheless he quashed the charges against Chogen, who then reappeared at the construction site.

A week later it all came out. Go-Shirakawa summoned Chogen and the Korean priest Chogen had accused and to them handed over the sacred ball—minus two grains, one of which he had given to that favorite consort, the other to a sycophantic courtier. It was obvious that Chogen had conspired to pander to that "dark ruler." And indeed large contributions followed.

As bits and pieces of this story drifted down to Zentsu-ji the monk was forced to the same conclusion the prime minister had reached: there was no trick Chogen would not stoop to; he would complete his mission by fair means or foul. The monk retired to pray alone. He recalled the face, the posture, and the blazing intensity in the eyes of the holy man he had come to idolize, and he told himself it was all in character. "He has to live in the world," he murmured; "he cannot help becoming worldly." And for the rest of his life he offered prayers for the salvation of Chogen's soul.

Chogen and Saigyo were not the only holy men of Koya who had access to the nobility. There was, for example, Butsugen, who for twenty-five years enjoyed a familiar relationship with the prime minister. Chogen was indebted to Butsugen, for the latter had used his considerable influence in high places to smooth over the mess concerning the theft of the Buddha's relics.

Butsugen knew all the important people of Kyoto—those who could make substantial contributions or cause them to be made—including the wealthy merchants, one of whom figures in a letter he wrote to Koya during a visit to the capital.

I discussed certain problems with the prime minister and then visited the home of the merchant M——, a devout believer who has been most generous. I was distressed to find him very ill.

"Please forgive me for being unable to greet you properly," he said. "My allotted span is up and I shall soon be leaving this vale of dreams." I chanted a service for which he expressed deep appreciation. As I left he was preparing to compose his farewell poem.

Late that evening a messenger appeared with word that he was about to breathe his last. I summoned the followers who had accompanied me from Mount Koya and bade them bring the painting of Amida Buddha that hangs in our hermitage here. We hurried to his house. As the messenger had stated, he was barely able to turn his head.

From among his relatives and my disciples we gathered the prescribed fifteen believers. Since there was no possibility that he would survive being moved to a chapel, we converted his room to a "hermitage of transience." I placed the painting of Amida on the wall he faced, and attaching the five colored ribbons to the image I placed the other ends in his hands. Bending low to be certain he understood me, I gave him my word that I would carry his ashes to rest near the Daishi on Mount Koya, thus assuring him of entry into Paradise. His eyes signaled understanding and gratitude.

His head was raised so that he could see the holy image and I instructed him to summon whatever strength he could to join the fifteen in chanting faith in Amida. Meanwhile I recited the Mantra of Light which, as the Daishi taught, destroys all evil karma. It was a great joy to see him meet death in this manner, strong in his faith, the ribbons joining him to Amida entwined in his fingers, the mystical syllables of Shingon rising around him. Beyond doubt he will attain Paradise.

His son delivered his ashes to me today. They will accompany me to Mount Koya, where I shall superintend burial and conduct the anniversary services. The family's offering was generous indeed.

The service for the dying man illustrates how Butsugen yoked the Daishi's Shingon to faith in Amida. He was a learned man and he felt it necessary to reconcile the two. He started from the Shingon concept of the Buddha Dainichi as constituting the entire universe, the Buddha from whom all other Buddhas were born. Therefore Amida emanated from Dainichi, and therefore to worship Amida was to worship Dainichi, to become one with Amida was to become one with Dainichi, to attain Amida's paradise was to attain the paradise of Dainichi and all the Buddhas. Which made it perfectly all right for the holy men to preach faith in Amida even if they never mentioned Dainichi, especially as they also proclaimed the Daishi as a savior and Koya as the gate to Amida's paradise.

This is a crude statement of the thesis that Butsugen expounded in a weighty treatise that he carried to the prime minister for perusal. The prime minister—current head of the Fujiwara family—was certainly the one to take it to, for besides occupying the highest position at the court he was a man of wide learning and an excellent writer, as his diary demonstrates.

In that diary he noted the visit when Butsugen brought his six-volume work. "Dipping into it I found a number of mistakes in style and I pointed these out." (This should occasion no surprise, because it took the highest education Japan had to offer, plus earnest application, to master the highly Sinicized language that a serious writer of that time had to use.) "The holy priest accepted my corrections with great gratification."

Sometime later Butsugen delivered a revised manuscript and the prime minister wrote that he had spent the entire day reading it. He declared that "Without reservation, it is a work of genius." What was more, he added, he had heard that it was the tonsured retired emperor who had urged Butsugen to write it. A holy man like Butsugen had links even to the imperial family.

But it is doubtful that studies of doctrine, however brilliant, would have brought Butsugen close to such important people. On a more practical level, he was renowned as a rainmaker, but he was even more famous for his incantations to cure illness, as the prime minister noted: "The holy priest Butsugen came today and we discussed various religious texts and scriptures. I also asked him about the treatment of colds. He is highly skilled in medical matters."

Butsugen may have relied on more than incantation. In their sojourns in the mountains some holy men acquired a knowledge of herbs that they put to use on the sick. And considering the state of medicine at the time, their patients probably did as well as any.

Still, from prime minister to peasant, people placed more faith in incantation than in medication, and they shopped around for the best available practitioner. From the prime minister's diary: "During the hour of the monkey"—sometime between three and five P.M.—"the Koya Holy Man Gyosho came. I spent several hours in discussion with him. He has undergone many strange and wonderful experiences. In the spring of last year he demonstrated his powers as a healer; I and my wife, together with our son—the Commander of the Imperial Guards—and our daughters, all received the benefit of his incantation to protect our bodies from illness caused by evil spirits. The Commander came especially to meet him. This saint has practiced abstinence from cereals on Mount Koya and is said to have done so with great efficacy."

To a Westerner the idea of going without bread or pasta poses nowhere near the shock of deprivation facing a Japanese told to exist without rice. Twenty-five years later another diarist wrote: "The Holy Man Gyosho is now eighty-one years old and practices abstinence from the six kinds of cereal. His spiritual energy seems to be at a very high level. Has he attained Buddhahood in his own body?"

This was a crucial question. It went back to Kobo Daishi, who was believed to have abstained from eating grains the last three years of his life, a practice that was thought to purify the body and so to aid in attaining enlightenment.

The heart of Kobo Daishi's doctrine is that man is capable of attaining enlightenment in this existence—"in this very body," without having to wait for rebirth in the next world. This optimistic doctrine holds that all things in the universe reveal the presence of the eternal, timeless Buddha, and that man has within him the possibility of experiencing union with that eternal and timeless essence: the possibility of achieving enlightenment, of attaining Buddhahood.

Had Gyosho attained Buddhahood? If he had, his incantations would be powerful indeed. He had abstained from cereals—was that corroboration?

There had been charlatans. There was the case of the ascetic who came to Kyoto in 854 proclaiming that he ate no grains. He was so impressive that by imperial edict he was provided with lodging in one of the imperial gardens. There the citizens of Kyoto, women especially, came to worship him and to shower him with gifts, asking that he offer prayers in their behalf. But after about a month of this, someone grew suspicious, did a little spying, and then announced that he was eating rice at midnight and going to the toilet early every morning. Piles of rice excrement were discovered, he was labeled the Saint of Rice Dung, and his vogue ended even more swiftly than it had begun.

At any rate, Gyosho reestablished on Koya the custom of refusing to eat cereals, and for several centuries it was part of the training for some groups of holy men.

11 The steep, rocky path up the mountain—the holy man grew irritable. Why couldn't the villagers keep it in better condition? They had to come up here, to the forest, for firewood and for the fallen leaves and decaying vegetation they used to fertilize their fields; couldn't they see that their punishing toil would be easier if they improved the path? But no, they were dirty and ignorant. Until some holy man who specialized in that sort of thing came along and rallied them to build a road or a bridge and so make their lives easier they remained apathetic, resigned to the misery they had always known because they couldn't imagine anything better. "It can't be helped," they would say. Roads and bridges were not his line of work, he didn't know the first thing about them, but he could see the opportunities. He stumbled and muttered to himself.

He was the more vexed because he couldn't find what he was looking for. They were plentiful enough when you didn't want one, staring at you from the roadside accusingly, or pitifully, but when you needed one they disappeared. Perhaps at the summit: sometimes they managed to make it to the top and then collapsed.

The trail crested and he looked about him—nothing. This was maddening. He had planned on holding a big mass at the village below. It was a bit more prosperous than most, and said to be a bit more devout. He felt certain that an impressive service would not be wasted there.

He began thrashing through the underbrush. How could there not be one here, after that grueling climb? He struck at the weeds with his staff; burrs and thistles scratched his legs. He tore at one bramble almost without looking, but there—there inside! He beat down the prickly branches. There it was, almost buried by rank grass, bare and weathered. He dived for it, caught himself, raised one palm in quick prayer, and gripped it. He brushed off a bit of humus with a pinecone, put it on a rock so that the sun would dry the dampening of the earth, and sat on another rock for a little rest. He had found the skull he needed.

He could see the crossroads now. A good thing too, for the sun was low in the west. He had heard that in the old days the headman and elders used to come to meet a holy man, but nobody had ever come to meet *him*.

As he entered the village a couple of small children ran to hide; an emaciated dog snarled but retreated quickly enough when he brandished his staff—almost toothless, he saw, too old to forage for itself.

He sought out the house of the headman, the biggest in the village. At the gate he jangled the rings on his staff and began to chant. The headman took a little too long to emerge, but when he did he was civil enough and without prompting invited him to lodge there.

When he said that he wanted to hold a three-day service for the dead his host demurred; the villagers were just too busy. But when he displayed the skull and explained his mission the head-man sucked in his breath and agreed. He sent his son to summon the elders; they concurred that in view of the honor to befall their village a three-day mass was entirely proper. Early in the morning they would dispatch the young men's association to collect rocks for the burial mound.

The headman's wife tried to keep her in the shadows but the holy man could not help noticing a nubile daughter; he thought there was concupiscence in her eyes. Surreptitiously he tried to fan the flame.

The villagers were gathering when he strode to the meeting place. He assessed them: a scruffy crowd but they were what he had to work with. He mounted the flat rock from which village officials held forth and holy men had always preached. He thrust the skull high over his head.

"Come on, come on, all of you," he cried. "This is the skull of Priest Shunkan! Gather round, look close, for this is indeed the skull of that ill-fated priest! I have carried it here—with the great-est reverence I have brought it a long distance to your village—so that at last, after all these years, it may receive proper burial. Come close and gaze upon it, for this is Priest Shunkan's skull, nobody else's and no doubt about it!

"Now listen: this skull must be interred properly. This is the skull of a priest who was abbot of a great temple at the capital! This is the skull of a priest who moved in the circle of those around His Imperial Majesty! Think of that! No matter how wretched his end, this is the skull of a priest who once dwelled among the clouds.

"Ceremony—reverent ceremony—is required to bury the skull of Priest Shunkan! It cannot be performed in haste. It cannot be performed without due honor. We can do no less than hold a three-day mass! We can do no less than erect an everlasting monu-ment to his memory!

"Not only Shunkan, once exalted, finally undone. We will at

the same time, with the same reverence, also honor the spirits of *your* dead—the restless, anxious spirits of those who have died since I last came to your village, who wait for me to conduct them to Mount Koya, to bury their earthly remains in that sacred earth, as Priest Shunkan's remains were buried there—except, of course, for this wretched, unhappy skull. The ashes of your dead I will receive during this service, the spirits of your dead I will assuage, and when I return to Koya I will usher them to eternal peace in Amida Buddha's paradise of the next world.

"And not only those recent dead. We will pray here for the spirits of all your ancestors. Together our prayers will rise to them and they will know that they are remembered and esteemed. Do not be unfilial! Do not make them feel forgotten, for great resentment can arise from neglect!"

He thundered and cajoled, and when he thought they were ready he changed his tone. "Let us pray as the Daishi taught us to pray," he began. "Homage to Amida Buddha, glory to Amida Buddha!" He got them chanting, rhythmically, hypnotically, and when he judged they were keyed up he again slowly elevated the skull. His eyes glazed, he seemed rapt, no longer aware of the villagers before him but transported to another time and place. When there was absolute quiet save for the distant cry of a crow, the anguished words came out: "I am Shunkan!"

Shunkan's story harked back to the turbulent years that marked the passing of power from the aristocracy of the court to the ascendant military class, a time when conspiracies sprouted like weeds. That of 1177 was relatively minor. It was led by an obtuse Fujiwara nobleman, who, not grasping the import of events, cherished an overweening ambition to be appointed Minister of the Left, a position rather like that of a modern prime minister. He pulled every string available to him and even hired a holy man to set up an altar in a hollow tree behind a major Shinto shrine and there recite a Buddhist mystic formula for one hundred days; forebodingly, on the seventy-fifth day lightning struck the tree, setting it afire and endangering the shrine, so that its priests, who recognized an evil omen when one flared in their backyard, drove the holy man from their precincts. But the myopic Fujiwara missed the point and was infuriated when he was passed over in favor of a son of the real ruler of the realm, the head of the warrior family then ensconced in the capital—Saigyo's friend. The Fujiwara man swore vengeance and hatched his plot.

His fellow conspirators were mostly Fujiwara nobles of no great importance with a scattering of men from the rival military clan. Priest Shunkan entered the picture because ancestral loyalties tied him to that rival clan. His own ancestors had not been warriors, but his grandfather had been a redoubtable bully who terrorized all who passed his house by standing at the gate and grinding his teeth in a most ferocious manner; Shunkan inherited his pugnacious nature. He was a priest of quite high rank, abbot of a rich Zen temple. The plot was shaped at his mountain hideaway.

As is usual with botched schemes of this sort, one of those in on it decided it was bound to miscarry and he had best save his own skin by betraying the others. All were rounded up. A satisfying number were beheaded and the rest banished (the Fujiwara ringleader was first banished, then executed).

Priest Shunkan was exiled with two others to a truly remote place, a little island almost two hundred miles from the southernmost tip of Japan's main islands, about halfway to Okinawa: "a place that even sailors cannot find unless quite certain of the way, an island where few men live. There are some people there, it is true, but they wear no clothing and neither can they understand our language. Their bodies are covered with hair and are black like oxen. There is a high mountain that burns with eternal fire and the land is full of sulphur. Thunder rolls continuously up and down the mountain. It is not possible for anyone to live there for a moment"—"anyone" meaning of course any cultivated resident of the capital.

Two of the exiles were earnest believers, and despite the chilling description of the island they found a place that was surpassingly beautiful and there set up an altar where every day they offered prayers for their safe return to the capital. Sometimes they spent the whole night in prayer. One of them carved a thousand pieces of wood in the holy form of a Buddhist stupa, cutting into each his name and a prayer for pity; these he cast into the sea one by one as he invoked the Buddhas and gods of heaven and earth.

But Shunkan, though he was a priest, was a skeptic and he would take no part in their devotions.

Back in the capital there was great excitement. The military ruler of the realm, whose name was Kiyomori, had married one of his daughters to the reigning emperor, just as the Fujiwara had made a practice of doing. The young woman fell ill, which greatly worried Kiyomori until it was discovered that she was pregnant, and then he rejoiced, for the emperor was as yet childless and should she be safely delivered of a boy it was certainly within Kiyomori's power to have the emperor abdicate in favor of his infant son. Kiyomori already had almost every honor available but he wanted his grandson to be emperor. He summoned "all the priests of high rank and saintly reputation and bade them use all their knowledge both open and secret that a son might be born."

As the months of her confinement passed the lady suffered more and more, and divination revealed that it was owing to evil spirits. It was then that the banished Sutoku, seventeen years after his death, was given back his title of emperor in an attempt at pacification. At the same time the Fujiwara ringleader of the plotting at Shunkan's lodge was posthumously forgiven to placate *his* spirit, and Kiyomori's son urged that the exiles on the island be pardoned as another act of expedient mercy. Just recently one of the stupas cast into the ocean had by some miracle floated into the Inland Sea and washed ashore at a shrine to which Kiyomori was devoted, so he was feeling soft-hearted. He agreed to recall the two, "But as for Shunkan," he declared, "this is the man who held meetings at his villa to plot audacious designs against me. Him I will certainly not pardon."

An envoy was hastily dispatched. Coming ashore, he called in a loud voice for the two who were pardoned, but they as usual were on the other side of the island at their prayers; only Shunkan heard him. The envoy produced the letter of pardon and Shunkan opened it. "He read it from the beginning to the end and from the end to the beginning, but two persons only were mentioned, there was nothing said of three. 'Ah,' he cried, 'the three of us were exiled for the same offense and to the same place, how then is it that two only are granted a pardon and I only am left out?' He looked up to heaven and cast himself down to the earth, weeping and lamenting, but all in vain."

When the ship carrying the other two put off he seized hold of it. He was "dragged out up to his loins and then to his armpits, following after them as long as he could and entreating them: 'Comrades, how can you thus abandon me?' Giving himself up to despair, he flung himself down on the beach. 'Take me with you! Let me go with you!' he cried, but it was all of no avail. The ship rowed away till it was seen no more. Shunkan did not return to his poor hut but spent the night lying where he was, wetted by the spray and dew." When the two reached the capital they did everything they could to obtain a pardon for Shunkan but they were not successful.

When Shunkan had been abbot of his temple he had a faithful servant named Ario. Hearing that the exiles had been pardoned, Ario set out to meet them where they would disembark. It was there he learned that Shunkan had been left behind. Grief stricken he determined that he must go and join his master. Officials tried to block him and he suffered a hard sea passage but he reached the island. He could scarcely communicate with the primitive inhabitants but he managed to learn that the one who had been left behind had wandered hither and thither as though beside himself; lately he had not been seen. "On learning this Ario plunged deep into the uncertain mountain paths, climbing the peaks and descending into the valleys, but never once did he see his master. Then he searched along the shore—none answered his cries but the sea gulls. At last one morning he saw a figure creeping along by the rocks, emaciated as a dragonfly. Over his skinny, wrinkled frame a few rags were hanging. He was trying to walk but staggered like one drunken. Ario had seen many beggars in Kyoto, but never yet had he seen one like this." But he thought even such a creature might know something of his master, and going up to him he asked, "Can you tell me where I can find Shunkan the high priest?" The servant did not recognize the master but how could Shunkan forget Ario? The exile cried out, "Here! here he is," and sank down senseless on the sand.

Ario took him on his back and carried him to his hut of bamboo and reeds. Shunkan begged for news of home and Ario had to tell him that his property had been confiscated, his retainers had been put to death, and his wife and all his children but one daughter had died. From this time Shunkan refused all food and earnestly gave himself to invoking the Buddha Amida and saying the death prayers. On the twenty-third day after the coming of Ario he expired at the age of thirty-seven. Clasping the lifeless body, Ario wept unrestrainedly. "Ah, how gladly I would follow my master to the other world, but because there is no other to pray for his happiness in the afterlife, I must continue to live and to pray that he may attain enlightenment." He broke down the hut and heaping dry pine branches and reeds upon it, he lighted the pyre. Afterward he gathered up the ashes and hung them in a pouch around his neck, and when a merchant ship appeared he returned to the home islands. He climbed up to Mount Koya and there he buried the earthly remains of Shunkan near the innermost place, where Kobo Daishi sleeps. Then he joined the foremost temple of the holy men and set out to perform pilgrimage through all the provinces while praying for Shunkan's salvation in the next world.

Other holy men heard from his lips the story of Shunkan, and after Ario's death they continued his prayers. Wherever they went they would gather people about them and recount the plot and its discovery, the grief of exile and death. People wept to hear it, and made offerings that prayers might be said on Koya in Shunkan's and Ario's behalf.

A whole new method of campaigning developed—storytelling. Holy men learned to heighten the effect by relating the tale in the first person with a suitable prop. In telling the story of Shunkan a holy man would produce a skull, would seem to be possessed, would cry, "I am Shunkan!"

The villagers were weeping; it never failed. He ended with a bit of poetry:

> "Oh endless days of banishment!
> How long shall I languish in this place . . .
> How terrible the loneliness of these wild rocks!"

Transforming himself at a deliberate pace, he let his trance-like state flow from him. He stood before them as himself.

"This is the skull of Shunkan," he sobbed. "I beseech you to offer all you can so that prayers for him may rise on Koya. And let us at last reverently inter his skull and here in your village erect a proper monument."

They would give till it hurt.

Graves of Shunkan dot the countryside but there were other stories in the repertoire of this breed of holy man, stories of awakening and repentance.

One told of a young courtier who fell deeply in love with a serving girl, a match his father forbade, for he intended that his son should make an advantageous marriage and rise in the world. Trapped between love and disobedience, reflecting that the prime of life is but "a flash of fire," the young man renounced the world and entered a temple. The girl followed him and sent word into the rough cell where he was chanting the sutras that she had come to see him one last time; he only sent someone out to say: "The person whom you seek is not here." So there was nothing left for her "but to swallow her tears and wend her way back to the capital, sad and bitter of heart."

But since she had discovered where he was and he did not trust himself to steel his heart against her should she come again, he climbed to Mount Koya, where no woman could follow. She too left the world, but even in a nunnery "she was unable to forget the past and brooded over it until she fell sick and died." When he was told of this he redoubled his religious austerities, so that he came to be known to all as the Saint of Koya.

There is also the story of the warrior Kumagai. In a climactic battle of the great war between military clans, Kumagai found himself forced to kill an enemy captain who was a mere youth, of delicate features and about the age of his own son. " 'Alas,' he cried, 'what life is so hard as that of a soldier? Only because I was born of a military family must I suffer this affliction! How lamentable it is to do such cruel deeds!' From this time the mind of Kumagai was turned toward the religious life." He too climbed Koya and became a holy man.

Stories like these, in which Mount Koya always figured, moved men's hearts and opened their purses, helped to rebuild Koya and keep it prosperous. Today these tales are embedded in the epic literature of Japan. They are one of the legacies of the holy men.

The third day was over. The holy man lay on his mat in the darkness and congratulated himself that the offerings had been quite satisfactory. He calculated how far he would have to walk before he could safely repeat his performance. He always enjoyed doing Shunkan; he thought he did it well.

The people had to *believe;* that was the crux of the matter. They had to believe in the holy man who came among them. Whether by withdrawing to commune with the gods in secret places in the mountains, or by living on a diet of nuts and berries and a few green leaves (he had himself noticed that those who eschewed rice and the lesser grains acquired a gaunt and saintly look), or by climbing Koya for training presumed arduous, the people had to be convinced that a holy man possessed a power.

He had a gift for storytelling. When he recited tales of the old days he could catch and hold an audience. He could make them believe that the tortured spirit of Shunkan entered and possessed him. He could make them weep, and give. Some storytellers accompanied themselves on a lute and music was a help, but he couldn't play an instrument and handle Shunkan's skull effectively. Even without music he knew he was good at his work.

And it was infinitely preferable to some of the things other holy men did. Standing under an icy waterfall while chanting a sutra was bearable: he had done it a few times himself and it really seemed to cleanse the spirit. But some of the other mortifications!—pouring oil in the palm of the hand, lighting a wick, and holding steady with no show of pain while the oil burned; burning incense on one's arm. He had heard that even Kuya had done that: burned incense on his forearm for seventeen days and nights without sleeping. The holy man shuddered. Setting oneself afire was prohibited in these modern times, of course, but he had heard of one crazed ascetic who did it. That was reverting to the primitive.

All in all he was pleased with himself tonight. He was disappointed only that the headman's daughter had not made her way to his bed. He was sure she wanted to. The headman and his wife had put her pallet between them and one or the other apparently stayed awake all night; they were overprotective. He listened for the sound of their breathing; both seemed to be snoring. He heard a rustle and she was beside him.

His hands were all over her. No need to arouse her; she was hot and eager. Twice he had to stifle her cries to keep from waking her parents. At last she crept back to her own bed.

He was half-asleep when he heard rustling again. Had she come back? That was dangerous. But the body that embraced him was firmer. "I heard you," the son whispered. "I can't sleep." There was nothing like variety, the holy man thought, and took him in his arms. The boy was an unabashed lover, as satisfying as his sister.

He did not think the headman and his wife had been wakened but he was not surprised when he was treated coldly in the morning. He did not linger in the village.

Temple Forty-five; the ladder at left rises to a pinnacle where Kobo Daishi
is said to have meditated *(detail from a print by an unknown artist)*

12 There are places along the pilgrimage route where
we can almost feel the presence of those holy men of
long ago.

Such a place is Temple Forty-five. We ap-
proach it through a gorge carved through cliffs mottled gray and
yellow. Towers and minarets sprout amidst humped forms that
loom over us like prehistoric monsters. Every rocky face is pocked
with holes. Geologists say that about fifty million years ago this
conglomerate was deposited near the sea, then thrust up into
mountains that were slashed and scoured by torrents. The sense of
ancient forces is overpowering. We walk in silence.

It is a sharp climb up to the ledge where the temple clings. Attaining it we stop in wonder. A wall of scarred rock rises six hundred feet above us. The main hall and the Daishi Hall back against it as if bearing its weight. Of the priest's residence we see little more than the facade; it is built into a huge cave. A ladder rises to a deep, twisting tunnel that widens into a chapel. The temple song says that the Daishi carved all this:

> *The power of prayer of the Great Saint—*
> *Witness caves in a mountain of rock!*
> *Witness here also Paradise!*

One cannot stand dwarfed before this towering natural altar without knowing that it has been a sacred place since man first found it. A god resides here. And holy men have come to sojourn with him.

Such another place is the waterfall at Temple Thirty-Six, where briefly we emulate ascetics by standing under the chill cataract as we chant our prayers.

Still another is the rocky cape called Ashizuri. The crescent-curve of Tosa's Pacific coastline is anchored in the east by Cape Muroto, where the Daishi broke through to enlightenment, in the west by the cape called Ashizuri, thrust even farther south into the open sea. As Temple Twenty-four stands at the tip of Muroto, Temple Thirty-eight stands at the tip of Ashizuri.

At Ashizuri as at Muroto it is a three-day walk from the preceding temple; again alike, the old henro-path has been overlaid by a modern highway, painful to walk along. There is a strong temptation to take the bus and sometimes I have done so. So did a friend of ours, the novelist Tosa Fumio, and he felt as guilty as I did. He wrote of looking out the window to see, in the swirling dust, a family of henro waiting for his bus to pass: on a rough cart sat the father, a cripple, bedding and cooking utensils piled about him; the mother was pulling the cart, a daughter of twenty or so pushing from behind. "Their robes were as brown from dust as if they had been dipped in soya sauce, their skin was dark, their hair tangled and matted. The daughter was staring vacantly at the bus, envying those on it, when she caught sight of us in henro robes. For a moment she glared, then relapsed into dull resignation. I felt as if I had eaten lead."

But unlike Muroto, there is an alternate approach to Ashizuri, a quiet road along the coast linking fishing villages. Morikawa and I walk that road and are rewarded with unspoiled headlands, coves, and white sand beaches. Still it is a long walk and a relief to reach the temple. We drop our packs and go to cliff's edge, stand there gazing out at the limitless ocean and down a dizzying drop to rocks scoured to fantastic shapes and colors; the sea pounds at them, white water explodes over them and falls back into blue pools.

This place is infamous for suicides. We understand why. The contorted rocks seem to beckon; the endless breakers offer surcease. Maudlin stories abound: our guidebook tells of a young geisha who danced off this ledge. There is a well-known novel about a young man who came bent on killing himself but who here found strength to live: the writer intended her story to end the suicides; it multiplied them.

The name Ashizuri means "foot stamping"; there are legends and chronicles to explain it. I quote from *The Confessions of Lady Nijo,* the memoirs of a remarkable lady of the imperial court. Concubine of a retired emperor, she managed several other love affairs simultaneously and with great style, until her luck ran out. Then she became a wandering Buddhist nun. She writes that in 1302 she came here.

The main image in the temple at Cape Ashizuri was a figure of Kannon. The temple grounds were not fenced in, there was no head priest, and traveling monks and ascetics could gather there without regard to class or position. When I asked how this had come about I was told the following story: "Long ago a monk came here with a young disciple to act as his servant. The disciple put compassion above all else. One day another young monk arrived—no one knew where he had come from—and joined them for their meals. The disciple always shared his portion with the newcomer, but his master admonished him, 'Once or twice is enough. You must not continue sharing your meals so freely.' When the young monk came at

お顔そばほつみきの

お魂さ海罪もするどさき

どふう里しし

Henro on the cliff at Ashizuri *(a book illustration by Shugetsu)*

mealtime the next day, his friend said to him, 'I would like to share with you, but my master has scolded me, so this must be the last time. Please don't come again.' Then he shared his meal with the newly arrived monk, who said, 'Such kindness as you have shown me is unforgettable. Please come and see where I live.' The disciple accepted the invitation, and they went off together. The old monk grew suspicious and secretly followed them to the cape, where the two young men got into a small boat, took up the oars and headed south. The old monk cried, 'Where are you going without me?' The young monk replied, 'We're going to the realm of Kannon.' As the older monk watched they stood up in the boat and turned into Bodhisattvas. In grief and anguish the monk wept and stamped his foot, giving the place its name, Cape Ashizuri, the Cape of Foot Stamping. Leaving his footprints in the rocks, the old monk turned away empty-handed. He met this sad fate because he had considered himself superior, so ever since then, people living here have avoided making distinctions."

This is much more than the usual temple legend. The part about there being no head priest and hence no protocol of rank has a simple explanation: in Lady Nijo's day the temple had fallen on hard times. Despite its distance from the capital it had in the past attracted aristocratic supporters; now they had lost their estates and could no longer provide for a priest. But wandering holy men had come to train here long before there was a temple or a priest and they continued to come when there was no longer a priest and the temple had fallen into disrepair. More important, the part about the young monks' putting to sea on a voyage to the realm of Kannon is not fantasy: such things happened.

Kannon has always been popular among the Japanese. The embodiment of compassion—not a Buddha but a Bodhisattva, one who has postponed Buddhahood in order to work for the salvation of all beings—this gentle figure attracted a great following among both the upper classes and the common people. More temples of this pilgrimage are dedicated to Kannon than to any other deity. From the ninth to the twelfth centuries worship of Kannon came to full flower: of the treasured statues from that period, the majority are of Kannon; there came into being a pilgrimage to thirty-three Kannon temples stretched across the waist of Honshu, the main island; and it was then that men actually tried to sail over the seas to reach Kannon's blessed realm.

They sailed to the south, reflecting a belief that had its origin in India, where Kannon was said to abide at the very tip of the subcontinent, Cape Comorin, on a rocky mountain called Po-talaka, a name that in Japanese becomes Fudaraku.

As Buddhism traveled east, mountains in Tibet and China came to be called Fudaraku. In Japan many temples bear the name but none so aptly as the one built on this rocky promontory. It was a long hard distance from the capital but that only enhanced the longing to come here. There were many who yearned for rebirth in Amida's Pure Land in the West or in Yakushi's Pure World in the East, but it was Kannon's Fudaraku, the Pure Land in the South, that men tried to reach in this life.

There are stories besides the one told by Lady Nijo, stories that give names and dates. Especially we are told of a saintly holy man named Kato who came from Awa in 997 and entered into retreat here. He prayed devoutly for an opportunity to go to Kannon's Fudaraku and finally received a holy sign. On the eighteenth day of the Eighth Month of 1002 he boarded a boat hollowed from the trunk of a tree, and with his disciple Einen cast off at the Hour of the Ox, "and breasting the waves which stretched for thousands of miles, he departed as if he were flying."

Holy men sailed from other places too, most often from Kumano. Kumano stands at the tip of the mountainous Kii Peninsula, jutting into the Pacific east of Shikoku. Many of Kii's peaks were sacred: En the Ascetic came out of Kii; Mount Koya rises there. A rocky cape directly south of the capital, an ancient goal of pilgrimage—it was natural that Kannon should be worshiped at Kumano.

In 1142 a priest of Kumano wrote of how, when he was a boy, a monk desiring to sail to Fudaraku carved a statue of Kannon and put it in his boat and placed the tiller in the hands of the statue; then for three years he prayed for a wind out of the north; finally it came, strong and steady, and the priest, overjoyed, boarded his boat and, praying all the while, sailed into the south. The narrator told of climbing to the top of a mountain to watch the little craft disappear in the distance, "and the wind continued to blow for seven days."

There is the case of a warrior, renowned as an expert shot with the bow and arrow, who was a direct retainer of the shogun. On a hunt one day, ordered by the shogun to bring down a stag, he missed, and so great was his humiliation that he disappeared. For years the shogun's records listed him as missing. Then on the twenty-seventh day of the Fifth Month of 1233 the shogunate received the man's own record of his subsequent life, and it was duly entered in the chronicles. He had become a holy man, his wanderings had brought him to Kumano, and there he had decided to seek Fudaraku. His letter ended with a description of how he would set out: entering the cabin of his boat he would seal the door so that the light of neither sun nor moon could penetrate; he would lock himself inside with a single lantern and provisions for thirty days; and he would let the wind and the currents carry him where they would.

Surely most of those who set out, either from Ashizuri or Kumano, drowned at sea. But some ended on the shores of Okinawa, as the chronicles of those islands make clear. How many sailed from Kumano, or from here at Ashizuri, we have no idea. Wandering holy men are not the kind who leave records. Perhaps, as some scholars suggest, the frail craft most often carried the dead or dying as a way of burial (they could not be buried here at Ashizuri—this temple has never had a cemetery—for this is a training place, imbued with ancient ideas of death as pollution). But that living men also set out from these rocks, borne by small boats and great faith, there is no doubt. They sailed into the void seeking Kannon's Fudaraku.

Later the priest talks with us about this. "Fudaraku is a mental state, but in those times long ago men tried to reach it physically. It took faith to sail and whether they drowned or reached some island I believe that they achieved that blessed world. Yet it is close at hand, as Kobo Daishi tells us. It is in our minds and it is there we must search for it."

* * *

Nothing remains at either Temple Forty-five or Cape Ashizuri to show that holy men came there but at other places they left tangible evidence. A small mound by the side of the pilgrimage path; one might pass it without noticing. . . .

The pain was sapping his strength. He tried to walk softly but every step was a jolt and with every jolt pain shot through his skull, shrieked in his ears, glazed his eyes. He had endured toothaches before but nothing like this. He felt nausea creeping over him. His legs were giving out.

He saw a tree ahead, casting a haven of shade. He made it his goal, slumped against its trunk. His eyes closed. The pain was unrelenting. It throbbed . . . like the drum he had sometimes beat on Koya. . . . Hail Amida Buddha. Homage to the Daishi.

He struggled free of his pack, leaned back. He forced himself to open his eyes. The valley was softly green in the haze of spring. At least the path was level here. He shuddered, remembering the rocky descent from the mountain pass. Then ice gripped his heart: he knew he could not climb out of the valley. The spasms were beating a knell. He would never see Koya again.

Ahead was a village he had sometimes ministered to . . . ahead but too far to go. An ordinary village, but they had welcomed him as best they could; they had given what they could . . . he remembered a cool drink of water carried to him on a blazing day . . . good people.

He sat there until he felt the chill of the ground beneath him seeping into his legs. This would not do. He pulled himself erect, clenched against the stabbing pain. Over there . . . he half crawled, half stumbled. With a flat stone he began to scrape away the earth.

He was almost elbow deep when they began returning from their plots of land. They stopped and stood silent, watching him. He knew they were there but he did not greet them. He could not let himself stop.

An old man squatted beside him. "Holiness, what are you doing?" He felt the man's hand on his shoulder. "What is this that you are doing?"

He stopped then, looked at the old man, saw the concern in his eyes. He looked up at the people ringing him. In a voice he scarcely recognized as his own, strangled by his swollen jaw, he told them he had a toothache that was unbearable. "When this grave is deep enough I shall enter it. I shall meditate. I shall meditate on Amida Buddha and Kobo Daishi. I shall pray to Amida Buddha and the Daishi that I may attain Buddhahood in this life at this place. As I meditate I shall pull the earth over me. And through all the days and years to come, forever, I promise that anyone with a toothache who comes to pray at my grave, that person will I grant relief. For no one should suffer as I suffer now." And he turned again to his digging.

Again they watched silently. The old man studied his face, then stood. Hands under his arms pulled him gently away. The old man stepped forward with a spade.

Young men in turn took the old man's place. When the hole was deeper than their hips the old man looked at him questioningly. He nodded, bowed deeply, pulled himself forward. A strong arm on either side lowered him. He entered into meditation. He chanted. "Hail Amida Buddha. Homage to the Daishi." With each invocation he reached up and pulled down some of the cool damp earth. He covered his legs. "Homage to the Daishi."

The old man kneeled and, taking a handful of earth, dropped it about him. He felt it as a benediction and he bowed in gratitude. Others of the elderly knelt above him. The earth reached his chest. He took a breath and again began to invoke Amida Buddha.

As the earth rose over his shoulders a young man brought a slender length of bamboo that he had hollowed out. When the earth reached to his face he leaned back his head, chanted his last "Hail Amida Buddha" and accepted the tube into his mouth. He closed his eyes. The earth covered his aching jaw and seemed to soothe it. The earth covered him over. He felt at peace.

They kept vigil all through the night, long after breath ceased to come from the tube. In the morning they brought flowers from the fields. They still do.

A small mound by the side of the pilgrimage path. One might pass it without noticing, but they still come, nobody knows how many centuries after, to pray for relief from toothache. They go away feeling better.

Carvings on the rock face of the mountain at Temple Seventy-one:
Amida (center) attended by Kannon and Seishi

His is not the only such mound. Not much farther along is
another. Farmers come to it to pray for rain. They say that long
ago in a time of searing drought a holy man came this way. Seeing
the distress of the people he said: "I shall enter into a state of
meditation in order to bring rain to you." Silent, immobile, the
holy man sat in meditation for twenty-one days, still as a statue.
On the twenty-first day bounteous rain began to fall, but the holy
man now was still as death. The people buried him reverently and
come to his grave even now to pray for relief from drought.

There are many such burial mounds. They are among the
traces left by the holy men.

One of the most spectacular of their memorials is behind Temple
Seventy-one, the rock face of the mountain on which the temple
stands. The whole wall, from one's feet as high as the eye can scan,
is deeply carved: with images of Amida Buddha and his attendants; with, repeatedly, the six characters that read, *Namu Amida-*

Carvings on the rock face of the mountain at Temple Seventy-one:
the five forms of the stupa

butsu—"Hail Amida Buddha"; and with the five forms constituting
the stupa that stands over so many Buddhist graves, on Mount
Koya and elsewhere—the five forms representing the elements that
make up our world: earth, water, fire, air, and the quintessence.

We cannot count the carvings; the priest tells us there are
more than fifteen hundred. Of course they are attributed to the
Daishi but the priest says most date from the thirteenth to the
fifteenth centuries, when the holy men flourished. Standing there
in wonder, we can almost hear their chisels ring in time with their
rhythmic chanting. Perhaps they sang something like this ancient
song:

> *Oh let the reverberations from this rock . . .*
> *Reach to the heavens*
> *And cause the very earth to shake—*
> *For the sake of our fathers and mothers,*
> *For the sake of all men.*

This wall of rock testifies to the holy men's faith in Amida and the Daishi, but it echoes too an earlier belief: in the bottom form of the five forms of each stupa, the square base (earth), and sometimes in the round form above (water), are deep niches, receptacles for bones and hair and ashes. Like the mountain on which Temple Ten stands, Seventy-one's mountain drew the souls of the dead.

Spirits ascended the mountain to become purified, as ascetic holy did in life, and for a year after death their relatives held them in awe. They accompanied the spirit to the mountain, carrying the ashes to sanctuary in a niche, and during that uneasy year they returned as often as they could—certainly on the haunted days of spring and autumn equinox—for reunion and prayer that the soul find repose. On their way they visited seven temples, beginning at Number Seventy-seven and ending here at Seventy-one. Like the ten-temple pilgrimage to Temple Ten, this ancient seven-temple pilgrimage became a link in the pilgrimage to the Eighty-eight.

They still come, even from across the Inland Sea. They come every spring, in groups of three hundred and fifty or more, so crammed into their boats that they must sail and land clandestinely, for harbor authorities would not permit such overcrowding. They worship at the seven temples and spend the night here at Seventy-one and the next day they offer *settai*—gifts to henro who come by, gifts of money and food, of help and encouragement to pilgrims walking with the Daishi.

I have special feelings toward this temple, for it was here I first learned about the pilgrimage. Morikawa has heard the story often. I had come to Shikoku on the advice of an old friend to investigate the prototypes of Japanese inns: temples that took guests, and farmhouses that in the spring pilgrimage season were opened to henro to earn some extra income. I came only just aware of the pilgrimage and not interested in it; it was the origin of inns I wanted to study.

I had an introduction to a local scholar who volunteered to guide me. He took me to some temples, showing me their big rooms where henro slept, the tubs they bathed in, the cavernous kitchens with huge vats to cook the rice they ate. He introduced me at two farmhouses where henro could lodge. And he said, "There is another place I want you to experience, a teahouse and pilgrims' inn on the path up to Seventy-one. You should spend the night there." Late afternoon saw us toiling up that path. Rounding a curve I was swept by a sense of déjà vu. There was the teahouse with its shady veranda to rest on, its banners announcing the specialties. I knew I had seen it before. Then I realized: of course I had seen it and others like it countless times in the woodblock prints of Hiroshige. This was a teahouse out of history.

The owner told us that he was the third generation to operate it. Not long after the war he had come by as a young henro and when the old woman who ran the place invited him to stay, he did. Her husband had been clerk at the temple until he and she moved down the mountain to take over the teahouse. The old man was fond of saké and one day when his wife was away he asked a passing henro to join him for a drink. The "henro" did, and then bashed his host on the head with a hammer and, leaving him to die, fled with the little cash on hand. So the old woman was quite alone and needed help. She adopted the young man and when she died he inherited the place. He hung the walls with haiku composed by guests. The Haiku Teahouse, people call it.

He was open and friendly but when I asked to stay the night he turned me down. "I have two businesses," he said. "I run this place and I raise chickens. I've been working with the chickens all day and I'm tired. I don't want a guest. Why don't you ask up at the temple?" So we climbed the rest of the way.

The priest took me in and I found myself in a rambling structure built against the mountain on more levels than I could count. After supper, the priest and his son, who is now the priest, came to my room and for two or three hours told me about Kobo Daishi and the pilgrimage and henro. (I learned only later that in another part of the temple there was a gathering of haiku poets that they missed to talk with me.) The thought of performing the pilgrimage was planted in me then, though I didn't realize it. The next morning they showed me the carved rock face of the mountain.

One sees images carved in wood too. Numbers of holy men expressed their dedication in this way; their works are found all over Japan. Some are statues of great artistry, worthy of any temple or museum, but most are primitive sculpture, crudely carved, perhaps disappointing until you visualize a wandering holy man of long ago, hewing a log, cutting and chiseling it with only ardor to guide his hand, struggling to realize the being that illumined his devotions.

Almost invariably people say that the Daishi carved these statues; this is a matter of faith. Most of them are kept secret but through a gift of kindness Morikawa and I have seen one of these revered sculptures, in the late-night service at Temple Twenty-six, when the image of the Daishi was revealed as it is only once a year.

At Temple Twenty-eight the priest told us that behind the main hall there used to stand a huge camphor tree with an image of Yakushi carved in the trunk. "It was said that the young monk Daishi carved it in the living tree—carved it with his fingernails, an act of extreme asceticism. My teacher used to say that the Daishi carved a Kannon in the trunk of a living tree in Awa (but it has been lost), this Yakushi in Tosa, and a Jizo in Iyo (it still exists); he didn't feel it necessary to carve an image in the fourth province, Sanuki, because Sanuki is small and the henro-path through it is short and easy.

"A little more than a century ago the old tree here fell in a typhoon and the carving was destroyed. A small statue of Yakushi was moved from the temple and a little chapel built for it. But most people choose to believe that the image Kobo Daishi carved with his fingernails still exists and is enshrined there."

We have seen the statue of Jizo in Iyo. Its tree, too, fell in a storm but the carving was not hurt and is kept in a chapel. At another temple they say the Daishi found a sick farmer; taking up the farmer's sickle he carved his own image with it, praying as he did, and so cured the man. A temple not far away enshrines a statue believed to have been carved by the Daishi when he was forty-two, a man's unluckiest age: to rid himself of that year's bane and to make a covenant with the future, he carved his own image.

Carving an image in a living tree *(a book illustration by Mikuma Katen, Collection of the Art Institute of Chicago)*

There are many others. They are rarely shown, some never—they are too sacred.

Some of the holy men's bequests are less tangible than carvings, but no less real. Each temple has a song, a short hymn reflecting the temple's tradition and faith. Henro sometimes sing these songs as they walk. The words of almost all of them are deeply dyed not with Kobo Daishi's assurance that man can attain Buddhahood in this existence, but with the holy men's faith in Amida's paradise of the next world.

At the sanctuary on the mountain where the Boy Daishi leapt into the arms of angels, the priest prepares a bath for worshipers on the fifteenth of every lunar month—at the time of the full moon—and on certain other holy days. He draws the water from a spring the Daishi is said to have brought forth, heats it in a big tub, and blesses it with prayer and incantation. Can anyone doubt who began this custom?

As the mountain behind Seventy-one demonstrates, the holy men carved both images and their invocation, "Namu Amida-butsu." At Temple Forty is a worn old woodblock, black with ink, about two feet tall. They say the Daishi carved the temple's central images, and when he finished he had this piece of wood left over so he put it to good use. Within the graceful stylized silhouette of a roadside statue—a standing deity with a halo, a suggestion of grasses at its feet—are carved the six characters that read, "Namu Amida-butsu." The temple sells all sorts of articles imprinted from this block. We are told that its miraculous powers have cured blindness and heart disease, enabled a mute to talk; a person whose body bears this stamp will not fall ill; a woman who wears a bellyband with its design will have an easy pregnancy.

One of the best-known bangai of the pilgrimage bears the name Crippled Pine Life-Prolonging Temple. The pine is a huge circular tangle of twisted low-spreading limbs suggesting a snarl of octopi. There is not a needle on its branches: traffic fumes have killed it.

"With the blessing of Kobo Daishi it lived more than a thousand years," the priest says. "He planted it on one of his pil-

A cloth printed from the sacred woodblock at Temple Forty

grimages. When he came here a second time he found a cripple lying by the tree. The man crawled toward the Daishi, begging to be cured, so the Daishi carved "Namu Amida-butsu" on a little piece of wood, made a print from that seal, and gave the cripple the paper to eat. As soon as he had swallowed it he stood up, cured.

Thereafter he became a priest and a follower of the Daishi, and the tree grew low with gnarled limbs like a cripple.

"And ever since, to gain the blessing of the Daishi's seal, people float in a cup of clear water a paper printed from it, they recite the Mantra of Light because when it is chanted all evil karma is destroyed by the light of the Buddha, they chant "Namu Daishi Henjo Kongo" and "Namu Amida-butsu," and then they drink the water and the paper.

"The temple still has the seal the Daishi carved," the priest says, but he indicates that since it is very precious and naturally much worn, a reproduction is used today.

"Oh yes, people still follow the same ritual and gain great blessing by doing so. They buy the papers from this temple: they are called Talismans of the Thousandfold Blessing. One is used for good fortune in general or for recovery from illness; two are used for easy birth, one being for the baby's health. Here is a letter that came just this morning."

I made a pilgrimage by bus, coming to the temple on March 13, when I bought some Talismans of the Thousandfold Blessing. I cured a cold with just one, and my mother and my aunt, who have been suffering from rheumatism, are able to get out of bed and walk after taking them. I have given them to so many people that I am running out, so I ask you to kindly send me ten more. I am enclosing three thousand yen. I treasure the talisman with the strange blessing.

"We get many letters but most people do not write: they revisit the temple and express their gratitude in person. Here's a letter addressed to Kobo Daishi from a Nagoya man who tells about his recovery from a gastric ulcer after using the talisman. And here's a letter I think will interest you."

He hands Morikawa a letter from a province in the far north; it is brushed in cultured calligraphy on fine paper. It tells about the birth of a baby to a neighboring family. The mother-to-be had taken two talismans; when the baby was born, the nurse at the hospital found one in the baby's right hand. In the writer's words,

"This has been a big topic of conversation, a story of great blessing."

I ask to buy a Talisman of the Thousandfold Blessing. The priest takes my money, raises it to his forehead, and returns it. The talisman is a gift—it is settai.

13 The most compelling legacy of the holy men, the one that through the centuries has worked upon more lives than any other, is not sculpture or woodblock seals or literature or songs or bathhouses. Their transcendent creation is Kobo Daishi.

The Daishi's life was one of the greatest that any Japanese has ever lived but as it receded into the mists of time the great master that he had been was forgotten. In his place the holy men evoked a miracle worker, a deity, a savior.

A deity and a savior does not die. Nor did their Daishi. They told how, long after his disciples placed him in his tomb, he sent a request in a dream to the reigning emperor. In answer the emperor hastily dispatched to Koya an imperial minister accompanied by a high priest; they carried a new robe.

When they "opened the doors of the holy tomb to put the new robe on the Daishi, a thick mist arose and hid his figure from their eyes." The high priest burst into tears and cast himself on the ground: "Why are we not permitted to see him? Never have I received such a rebuke." Then "the mist melted away and the Daishi appeared like the moon from the clouds, and the priest, weeping now for joy, clothed him in his new garment and also shaved his hair which had grown very long.

"Though the imperial messenger and the high priest were able to see and adore the Daishi, the high priest's acolyte was unable to do so on account of his youth, so the priest took his hand and placed it upon the knee of the Daishi and ever after, this hand had a fragrant odor all his life."

The Daishi's tomb, Mount Koya's innermost sanctuary *(a painting by Kawabata)*

Now the Daishi sent a message to the emperor: "In everlasting pity for the people of the world I took upon myself an unparalleled vow. In these far-off confines I wait the coming of Miroku." Miroku

Miroku, the future
Buddha *(a print by Saito)*

is the future Buddha, and the holy men calculated that, three hundred years having passed since the Daishi entered nirvana, he had yet "five billion six hundred and seventy million years to wait for the rebirth of Miroku and the salvation of the world."

In the meantime, they preached, he walked the countryside as a pilgrim, helping those who were worthy, rebuking those who did evil, seeing into the hearts of all, performing his miracles. His robes had to be replaced periodically because they became tattered in his travels.

The Daishi that the holy men created is so powerful a figure, he so seized the hearts and minds of the people, that he has displaced other figures who once lodged there. He has taken over legends once devoted to other heroes. The process still continues. A contemporary Shikoku folklorist writes of a tower of stones in the countryside; it dates from the sixteenth century, an age of almost incessant civil war, and clearly was erected as a memorial to the war dead. When he visited it thirty years ago he was told by the local elders that it was the work of a wandering Buddhist nun. Returning recently he found the people now saying that Kobo Daishi built it—built it in one night.

Morikawa and I have ourselves found examples of the same mutation. Moving on from Temple Twenty-two we wanted to seek out a bangai Morikawa had learned of from an old guidebook. Entering a village we found three women chatting at the roadside: a girl, a young wife holding a baby, and a granny—an *obaasan.* We asked directions and Obaasan said she would take us there. "I have a feeling that Kobo Daishi has asked me to guide you," she said, "and while I'm there I'll say a prayer myself. I was on my way to vote but that can wait." It was election day.

She quickly established her credentials. "I am eighty years old," she told us, a fact I would not have guessed from her straight back, smooth face, and firm step. "I was born in a house just below the chapel, though when I married I moved to a village half a mile or more away. As a young wife I opened our house as a henro-inn each spring. There used to be three such inns around here but they've all gone out of business."

I asked if there were stories of the Daishi in these parts. "Oh yes," she said. "A village you passed through a little way back, there used to be a clear brook running through it and stepping-stones to cross on. An old woman was washing clothes when the Daishi came by and asked her for a cup of water. She was a surly one and she refused him, saying the water was dirty. Ever since then that brook has been dirty and the village has had to dig wells to get good water, though every other village hereabouts gets plenty of clear water from streams.

"At another village a little more than a mile from here, the Daishi was crossing a riverbed filled with shells when the sharp point of one pierced his straw sandal and hurt his foot. He touched the point of that shell with his staff and since then the shells in that river have had no points."

She led us off the road up a hill to two small weathered buildings and a cluster of stone statues snug against a slope, in the shadows of tall trees. But for her we would have passed by unknowing. No priest lived there. The people of the village took turns in caring for it, she told us.

We shed our packs, sat on the veranda to rest, and asked her to tell us more about herself. "Once I was possessed by a badger," she began, badgers being notorious for their mischievous nature and magical powers. "It was when I was much younger, forty-six or forty-seven. I could foretell things, like the direction a tangerine tree would grow, and I could make dumplings faster than anybody else. People took me to the shrine near Number One Temple and the Shinto priest there said I was a person with miraculous powers, like a medium, and that the people of the village should consult me about everything. When I was counseling someone I felt as though I was simply repeating what a voice was telling me. But I grew tired of this role—it was hard on me—and I prayed to the Daishi to relieve me of those powers so I could go back to being an ordinary farm woman, and he did. Yet some people still call me *sensei.*" Sensei means "master."

We prayed and left our name-slips and offerings, and she too prayed and made an offering. Then she gave each of us ten yen, "as settai." We have been given settai often; in return we present our name-slips, as henro should, the same offering slips left at altars. As we were writing ours to give her, she considered, reopened her purse, and over our protests gave us each ten yen more. I put her name and address in my notebook and asked if I might take her photograph; she posed in prayer and I promised to send her some prints. We moved to the Daishi Hall to offer our prayers there. Once more opening her purse she gave Morikawa the last money in it, a hundred-yen coin. We begged her to keep it but she was adamant. It was settai.

Then she told us the chapel legend. "Kobo Daishi came here—

he followed a strange fragrance—on the third day of the Eighth Month, when the moon was new. He could find no clean water to drink, so he struck his staff into the hillside and prayed. Pure water came forth and at the bottom of the pool he saw a glittering stone. The Daishi wanted to carve an image of Yakushi from this stone but it was too dark: there was only the slender crescent of a moon, but he called on it to be bright and then there was moonlight all about him. So he was able to make the Yakushi and a Jizo as well. Then from the trunk of a cedar he carved his own image."

Morikawa and I had reviewed the old guidebook before we set out. Its version of the legend is much like hers but for one important difference: it says that the image Kobo Daishi carved from cedar was of Fudo, one of the few frightful-looking deities of Buddhism, smiter of the wicked. A legend has been altered: an image once called Fudo has come to be called the Daishi.

It was clear that Obaasan's affection focused on the image she said the Daishi had carved in his own likeness, "a beautiful statue, about a foot high." She wanted us to see it but the buildings were shuttered tight. She showed us to our path where it continued; "Now I will go to vote." We said good-bye and we called her sensei.

The last pilgrimage temple in Awa is unnumbered, a bangai, a big bustling institution called Saba Daishi. *Saba* means "mackerel." The priest, seated in the office where he writes inscriptions, told us the story.

"Kobo Daishi passed this way one evening, looking for a place to stay the night. There was no habitation, but he found a great pine tree and he slept under that. As a matter of fact, the pine had been planted by the priest Gyogi and during the night Kobo Daishi dreamt that Gyogi came down from heaven to bless and protect him. Waking in the morning, the Daishi realized that this place was sacred to Buddhism.

"As he was leaving he met a man leading a packhorse with a load of dried and salted mackerel. Kobo Daishi asked for the gift of one fish but the man refused and walked on. Suddenly his horse stumbled and fell, stricken with colic. Then the man remembered having heard that a very great priest was peregrinating Shikoku, and he realized that the one who had asked for the fish must be that priest. So he ran back, gave the Daishi a fish, and begged him to cure his horse.

"Kobo Daishi handed the man his iron begging bowl and told him to bring water from the sea. When the man did, the Daishi performed a service over the water and told the man to make the horse drink it. At once the animal recovered.

"The man was so awed by this that he knelt before the Daishi and vowed to enter the Buddhist way of life—to become a priest. Kobo Daishi was touched: he said to the man, 'Let me show you one more thing,' and carrying to the shore the dried and salted fish he had been given he placed it in the water and said a prayer. In the man's eyes the fish came to life and swam away."

The priest looked at us to make certain we grasped the nice point he was making: "The spellbound packhorse man thought that the fish swam away—it so appeared to his bedazzled eyes. . . . Then the man asked where he should build a hermitage to live out his life as a priest, and the Daishi answered, 'Under that pine tree, because that is a place sacred to Buddhism.' And since the man's experience had so much to do with mackerel, people called his chapel Saba Daishi."

The priest paused. "The story as I tell it is different than it is in the guidebooks." Indeed it was. It was even different from the printed account he handed us, which stated explicitly that the dead fish really came to life and swam away—not that "it so appeared" to the bedazzled packhorse man. I wondered if the priest had modified his story for a foreigner, but I decided it would be rude to press him on that. Instead I asked when it is considered that the temple was founded, expecting him to say 815, the year the Daishi is said to have founded the pilgrimage. His answer surprised me. "As a chapel, when the packhorse man entered the religious life here; as a temple, in 1945, when I came. Before that it was just a hermitage; it had no supporters; no priest ever stayed for long. It was I who founded a proper temple here."

It struck us that 1945 is probably when the legend was transformed. We know from reading that the central figure originally was Gyogi, not Kobo Daishi, and that the legend used to be much simpler and involved the kind of punning poem the Japanese love. Gyogi met the packhorse man, asked for a mackerel, and was refused, even reviled as a beggar; whereupon Gyogi made a poem: "On Yasaka hill he refuses to give even one mackerel to Gyogi, so his horse is felled by colic"—and the horse was. The astonished man begged Gyogi's forgiveness and gave him a mackerel, whereupon Gyogi recited another poem, which in sound differed from the first in only one syllable but meant: "On Yasaka hill Gyogi was given a share of the mackerel and the horse recovered from his colic"—and the horse did.

That was the whole legend. The hall of worship that is now called the Daishi Hall used to be called the Gyogi Hall, and the age-darkened statue enclosed at the altar (the priest said he regretted he could not show it to us), a carving of a priestly figure holding a mackerel by the tail, used to be called Gyogi and is now called Kobo Daishi—another example of how legends all over Japan have altered, the Daishi superseding some other figure, imposing but with less appeal. There is no counting the times this has happened. At Saba Daishi, Gyogi still appears in the legend as the priest tells it, though relegated to a decidedly secondary position—perhaps a transitional phase before he disappears entirely; the latest guidebooks do not mention him at all.

The Saba Daishi story has been modified still further by grafting on an old legend of Mount Koya: Kobo Daishi found a woman roasting a fish on a skewer; compassion moved him to beg for the cooked fish, which he returned to the nearby stream, where it came to life and swam away. The small trout that are found in the brook just below the Daishi's tomb have three dark spots, at the gills, in the middle, and near the tail—the marks of the skewer, they are called.

Legends have a way of procreating, but I cannot help feeling that here at Saba Daishi is a modern and self-conscious case of borrowing. At any rate the priest has made it clear that Saba Daishi as a flourishing bangai is his own creation and not at all the ancient institution most of today's henro suppose it to be. So not only legends but the pilgrimage can still be altered, as it has been in the past, by one gifted priest and special circumstance, the circumstance in this case being that the temple is just off the national highway at a convenient place for henro buses to break a three- or four-hour trip. One of them pulled in as we sat there and the temple was suddenly crowded. The priest had to busy himself inscribing albums and our interview was ended.

Having created the charismatic figure of the Daishi, a savior who descends from Koya to walk as a pilgrim, it was natural that the holy men should urge the people to follow in his footsteps. First they promoted pilgrimage to Koya, where he rested. Then they advocated pilgrimage to Shikoku, where he was born, where he came many times as a young monk searching for the right way, where he achieved enlightenment. Eventually they shaped a pilgrimage that went all around the island.

They had a model, an older pilgrimage on the main island; it began in the tenth century when the aristocracy of the court journeyed from the capital down the length of the Kii Peninsula to Kumano, where holy men sometimes set sail for Kannon's Pure Land in the South. This pilgrimage to Kumano became such a fad that one retired emperor performed it twenty-one times, another thirty-one times, and a third made thirty-three visits (the last was Go-Shirakawa, that "dark ruler" who banished his brother, Sutoku; pilgrimage does not seem to have bettered his character). Worship was always cited as the reason but there were other lures: escape from the constraints of court life and the adventure of travel in what the nobility considered remote and quite uncivilized territory. Soon adventure beckoned in the opposite direction and what evolved was a pilgrimage that twisted its way from the Pacific Ocean at Kumano through the capital across the country to the Sea of Japan; thirty-three temples, all dedicated to Kannon, were the stations along the way.

Thirty-three is an important number in worship of Kannon: in trying to save sentient beings Kannon appears in thirty-three manifestations. Eighty-eight is also a significant number—Buddhism counts eighty-eight passions or defilements that man is heir to—and is therefore a suitable number of temples for pilgrimage.

Exactly how the route on Shikoku was set and the eighty-eight temples chosen out of all the other temples on the island no one knows. Few of the holy men were literate and they left almost no records. Moreover, the Shikoku pilgrimage has always been a common man's pilgrimage and historians rarely chronicle the journeys of the common people as they do those of retired emperors and prime ministers.

Some points along the route seem inevitable choices: the Daishi's birthplace and the three places he named as sites for his ascetic practice; some other places—like Ashizuri—that were famous as settings for asceticism; a few temples too important to be left out, such as the four Kokubun-ji, one in each province, the national temples established in 741 by imperial decree. It is clear that older, local pilgrimages, like the ones from Temples One to Ten and from Seventy-seven to Seventy-one, were incorporated. Plot these on a map and the shape of the pilgrimage emerges. The earliest records of the pilgrimage appear in the early 1600's, when for the first time peace and general economic well-being made it possible for the common people to do much traveling; by that time the temples had been designated and the route set, just as they are now.

It was a demanding route, long and with many mountains and almost no pleasure resorts along the way—unlike the most popular pilgrimage of all, the journey to the sacred shrines of Ise; that could be one long bash. With all of its difficulties, the Shikoku pilgrimage drew only the truly dedicated, yet well into modern times it and the pilgrimage to Koya were among the most popular pilgrimages in Japan. It is still popular today. It is really the only one of Japan's ancient pilgrimages that is still performed by masses of people in much the same spirit as in former times.

Though we know little about how the holy men shaped the pilgrimage, the way they promoted it is clearer. They were the first guides: they urged pilgrimage, recruited henro, then led them, guiding them along the henro-path and instructing their worship. Their story of the first henro, Emon Saburo, was their favorite tale;

it was not only an incentive to pilgrimage, it emphasized the virtue of generous giving. Telling it, the spellbinders among them could mesmerize an audience. Mounting a stump or a stone they would fix their audience with a piercing gaze. . . .

"A long time ago—in the time of Kobo Daishi—there lived in the province of Iyo on the island of Shikoku a rich man, a very rich man." They would spit out the words "rich man," for they knew their audience harbored no love for the rich.

"He owned much land, and many peasants worked it, but he had only one desire—to be richer still. He was greedy and cruel. He squeezed his peasants to the limit. He forced them to pay rents so high that they could barely live on what was left." They stirred; there was scarcely a peasant in the land who didn't feel he was being gouged. "Sometimes they could not survive. A man would go out of his mind watching his children and his wife starve; he would kill them and take his own life. It mattered not to Emon Saburo.

"One winter day a wandering monk came to his gate, prayed there, and held out his begging bowl to appeal for food. Emon Saburo believed in neither the Buddha nor the gods of Shinto—on this bitter cold day he refused the monk. The next day the same priest came again. This time Saburo gave him something. He put excrement in his begging bowl." The people would gasp.

"But the priest kept returning. On the eighth day Saburo went at him with a stick, struck him, dashed his begging bowl to the ground. It broke in eight pieces, like the petals of the sacred flower, the lotus." An accomplished storyteller would take a breath and give the people a knowing look. *You and I know,* that look would say, *that the priest was Kobo Daishi, but Emon Saburo, blinded by avarice, was not then wise.*

"The priest came no more, but on the next day the eldest of Emon Saburo's sons suddenly sickened and died. The following day another son died, and the next day another. Eight days passed and the last of his eight children was dead.

"Emon Saburo was struck down by grief. Now he realized that he had been punished for his sins. He went to the wayside chapel where the priest had stayed, but he was gone. Saburo was possessed by a desire to find that holy man, confess the evil he had done, beg absolution. He gave his lands to his peasants and his goods to the poor and then he set out with little more than a sedge hat and a cedar staff. Now he was the one who was asking alms, begging for food to stay alive. He followed that priest's trail all around Shikoku, never catching up, but at each place where the priest had stopped Emon Saburo wrote his name and left it as a record that he had been there and was searching. He circled the island and came back to where he lived. Without even pausing he began the second round of his pursuit.

"He made the long circuit of the island again and again; he wore himself out in his search. After four years and twenty rounds, his health failing, it occurred to him that he might have a better chance of meeting the priest if, instead of endlessly following after, he went in the reverse direction. On his twenty-first time around that is what he did. On a day in early winter he struggled against a biting wind on a mountain trail climbing to a temple high above the clouds. He was sick, exhausted, near death. He could go no farther. He collapsed on the rocky path.

"At that moment Kobo Daishi appeared before him. He heard the Daishi tell him that his sincere repentance and hard training had washed away his sins; he was forgiven. He was asked if he had a last wish, and he prayed that he might be reborn as the lord of his home province of Iyo, for then he would have great power to do good: in the next life he could atone for the evil he had done in this one. Kobo Daishi picked up a small stone, wrote on it, and pressed the stone into the man's left hand. Emon Saburo slipped into death as though going to sleep. Kobo Daishi buried his body and marked the grave by planting Saburo's staff there. The staff grew into a great cedar.

"Late next summer—nine months later—the wife of the lord of Iyo gave birth to a baby boy. This baby was a handsome child, well formed in every way except that his left hand was convulsively closed. They tried everything but they could not open that hand. At last they called the head priest of the family temple. He came and chanted powerful prayer and secret words over the baby. The little fist slowly relaxed and opened. Inside was a stone and on it was written 'Emon Saburo reborn.'

"From that time on, the name of the temple was changed. It is now called Ishite-ji, 'Stone-Hand Temple.' It is a temple that all pilgrims visit. And they also worship at Emon Saburo's grave beside the mountain trail leading to Temple Twelve on the opposite side of the island."

They would be weeping now, and the holy man would drive home the lesson. "A man may sin greatly and yet be forgiven. All of you!—you have sinned greatly in this life and in previous lives. But the Daishi will wash away those sins if you put your faith in him. He will save you if you seek him and beg his help, if you repent sincerely, if you demonstrate that you have repented. How do you show that you have repented? By giving generously! Heed well the lesson of Emon Saburo, who refused to give to the Daishi. Give, and then give more! Prove that you repent your sins. For otherwise beyond doubt you will twist in the fiery tortures of hell!"

The legend of Emon Saburo is not without flaws. First, it pictures Kobo Daishi as vindictive; but the holy men knew, like all evangelists of all creeds, that the threat of damnation is a more powerful stimulus to giving than the promise of paradise. Their Kobo Daishi punished evil as well as rewarding good, and not only Emon Saburo: when a churlish woman refused him a potato, saying they were inedible, the potatoes of that place became inedible and remain so today—a story told with variations from one end of Japan to the other.

Second, it is impossible to believe that Emon Saburo had truly achieved enlightenment if he was gripped by such a worldly desire as to be reborn a ruler. But this is a point of doctrine that did not much concern the holy men or their audiences.

Despite these defects the legend is significant. It points to the basic concept of the pilgrimage: that the henro travels always with Kobo Daishi, for as the holy men would point out, it is clear that the Daishi was always at Emon Saburo's side, guiding him, though Saburo, because of his sins, could not see him. The tale validates the practice of leaving one's name-slips at each sacred place. It suggests that there is a special merit, or a special advantage, in walking the route in reverse, counterclockwise. It attests that the first henro was a layman, that this pilgrimage is ascetic practice for the common man. It emphasizes that at any point along the way the pilgrim may meet and see the Daishi. "He did not die. He descends the sacred mountain to walk among the people."

Emon Saburo was not concerned with doctrine, nor is the henro. The henro puts his faith in the Daishi. Beyond that, doctrine is for priests.

14

Sadly, the history of the holy men is one of slow deterioration. From the beginning few of them were saints. Most came from the common people and they worked among the common people. The temptations of worldly life were strong and all about them.

Because they made Koya famous they became conspicuous themselves. It was evident that one could make a living as a holy man of Koya, and inevitably men joined their fraternity who were interested only in making a living. In 1464 and 1521 fires again swept Koya and again it was necessary to campaign for great sums. Many of the new volunteers were drifters, outcasts, even ruffians. Some boasted that they had never climbed the sacred mountain, that they knew not a word of Sanskrit—not one syllable of Shingon's mystic formulas. Their lack of devotion was evident to the people: the campaigning went badly.

Even the pious and gifted among them faced painful difficulties, for the country had slipped into another long period of civil war. Once more the central government had deteriorated and all over the land local barons fought each other for supremacy. Previously those lords had welcomed the holy men because they traveled widely and had useful information about other districts. Now they were distrusted as spies and often were turned away at borders.

But it is true that many of the holy men were coarse and

commercial. Some began by giving "gifts" in return for contributions—noodles, medical plasters, remedies for diarrhea—and ended by becoming common peddlers. Others, less scrupulous, sold ordinary ashes as holy ashes from the fire ceremony at the altars of Mount Koya, "efficacious against any disease"; or, to hold charms and amulets, they sold little cloth cases, vowing that they were made from robes that had clothed the Daishi. Holy men were found to have sold images they had stolen from temples. Their lascivious behavior and homosexual affairs were exploited in popular fiction. A punning slur became current: "Never offer a night's lodging to a holy man if you don't want your daughter raped." At festivals in the capital, celebrants masqueraded as degenerate holy men, burlesquing their entreaties.

He could see the crossroads now but he felt only bitterness. He had never been treated well in that village and it was no pleasure to be coming toward it late in the day, after the wearying climb over the mountain, after depressing days when he had garnered few offerings.

He had heard there was a time when the headman himself had come out along the road to welcome a holy man and escort him to his own house. That must have been a long time ago. He spat.

True, the first time he had come here he had been given lodging. Eagerly too. The young wife had given him the glad sign and had whispered that once asleep nothing could wake her husband. Well, something had, or maybe the deceitful rube had only pretended to fall asleep. She had scarcely reached his bed, was just stretching out to enter his arms, when a sword had plunged into the pallet between them, cold steel barring two bellies about to fuse. He had been terrified, he admitted. He had pleaded innocence, blamed the wife (of course she had started it), but that young ruffian had run him out of the village in the middle of the night, rousing everyone by shouting that he was a seducer and flashing that sword so that it almost nicked his backside. It was a nasty experience, but he hadn't even got his arms around the woman—why should the whole village bear a grudge for so many years? He wondered what she looked like now. She was tempting then—probably would have been a good piece. Why was it he remembered so vividly the ones he'd never had, while his conquests were a blur? He forgot his miseries for a bit, imagining the pleasure he had been denied in this village.

He was brought back to reality by a couple of mangy curs who raced out to growl and snap at him. This was his welcoming committee. He gave one of them a good whack with his staff but the brute only bored in closer.

He slowed as he approached the first house. It was so shabby that he could tell the family had virtually been cast out of the village. Because of that they might be more friendly; perhaps he should ask for lodging there. But as he neared it a woman who looked as mean as a witch peered out the door and then slammed it shut.

He began his cry, "A lodging, a lodging!" He spun out the syllables to make them more plaintive. That took no acting but he was afraid his voice sounded as if he knew no one would take him in. He tried to alter the tone—defeatism would only lessen his chances—but now he was aware that his bitterness put a hard edge on his voice. A band of small boys circled around him, hooting.

He stopped before each house—"A lodging, a lodging, give this holy man lodging!"—until it was quite obvious the door would not open. At the center of the village, where he knew everyone could hear him, he stopped. He beat his breast and bellowed. "This holy man comes from Mount Koya, from the sacred precincts of Kobo Daishi! This holy man brings the blessing of the Daishi! A lodging, a lodging, give this holy man lodging for the night; the Daishi's blessing will flow upon the house that gives this holy man lodging!" The only response was from the jeering boys.

Anger welled up. When these people rejected him they rejected the Daishi—for did he not come in the Daishi's name? He burned to scourge them. Oh, to hurl retribution! "Curses upon you who refuse this holy man! The Daishi walks this land—you refuse him lodging! You will be punished! You will suffer the torments of hell!"

An old woman came out of a house and hope leaped up. "A lodging, a lodging . . ." She threw back her head and laughed. She laughed without mercy. She extended her arm and gave him an obscene sign. The boys around him shrilled and mimicked her.

She finished him. If people were merely cold there was still hope. When they laughed at him it was no use.

He turned to leave this village. He would sleep another night on the hard ground. He would search the fields for a turnip they had overlooked. The boys gave up but the vicious dogs snapped at him far past the last house.

Many of the holy men were vulgar and some descended to evil, but I want to remember that most of them were devout and strong-willed. They tramped thousands of miles through the countryside, bringing the people the kind of religion they thirsted for, giving hope and solace to those who otherwise would have had little of either, dutifully carrying the ashes of the dead to Koya for burial in its sacred soil, conferring its promise of paradise.

The holy men glorified the Daishi and made Mount Koya preeminent. The contributions they brought rebuilt its temples and kept it prosperous. They made it the burial place for all Japan and a goal of pilgrimage for nobility and commoners alike.

Yet there was always friction on the mountain, friction between the holy men and the proper priests of Shingon. There was conflict over doctrine, for the mysteries, the complexities of Shingon scarcely brushed the holy men. The priests were irritated by the holy men's loud chanting, their gongs and bells and drums; annoyed that the holy men outnumbered them, seemed to have taken over the mountain.

For centuries the priests and the holy men needed each other, and so a strained and often rancorous alliance was maintained. But when the holy men became ineffective, when the contributions they brought dwindled to a trickle, when scandal and ridicule changed them from an asset to a liability, the priests went on the offensive. They accused the holy men of living worldly lives of pleasure, of harboring evildoers and criminals, of destroying the original intent of the monastery. There were armed clashes. In 1606 the priests' warriors battered the leading hermitage of the holy men. The holy men instigated a lawsuit against the priests, took their case directly to the shogun. They lost. The ruling noted that Koya was, after all, the monastic headquarters of Shingon; the holy men must renounce their Amida doctrines and "return" to Shingon.

Some did and were absorbed. Their own temples disappeared. Today little remains to suggest how they once dominated the monastery. But the system of hermitages they established to lodge pilgrims still exists; the vegetarian dishes they created are still served; visitors still throng the mountain to bring the ashes of their dead or to request memorial services for them. The vast cemetery is a monument to the holy men's evangelism.

Though some stayed on Koya, numbers of the holy men held to their faith and left the mountain. Some settled down as priests in the villages they had ministered to. Putting an end to their wandering they founded many of the temples that stand today in the countryside.

Many continued to wander as they always had. Temple Seventy-eight of the pilgrimage became a base for such men, a place to return to as before they had returned to Koya. "The temple had been leveled in warfare," its priest says. "They rebuilt it and made it a center for their beliefs, their blend of faith in Amida and faith in the Daishi. Holy men of every stripe came here. It was a kind of headquarters for the ascetics who did not eat grain, who lived on roots, nuts, and greens that grew wild. Some sought Buddhahood in this life by burying themselves alive: we find their graves in the temple precincts. But most never gave up wandering. They died as they wanted to, along the road."

The holy men faded from the scene but the pilgrimage they had founded drew more and more worshipers; the Kobo Daishi they had created became more and more compelling: a deity, a miracle worker with the power to bring forth springs of pure water, to grant easy birth to women suffering a difficult pregnancy, to make the blind see and the crippled walk, to punish evil and reward good.

From one end of these islands to the other he crept into hearts and lodged there. He inspired faith and hope. There arose a deep longing—to be with the Daishi, to be at his side, to walk the path he trod to enlightenment. They came in ever greater numbers: the young making a rite of passage to adulthood, the elderly seeking a bridge to whatever comes next; they crowded the doors of the temples with the supplications and the testimonies they affixed.

They still come, to pour out their hearts to him, to beg his help, perhaps to meet him face to face on the long road around Shikoku.

III
Pilgrims

15 At Temple Number One the present priest's grandfather and father gave all henro starting there a leaflet, *Exhortation for Pilgrims to the Sacred Places of Shikoku.*

The pilgrim is not to veil his body in impurity or harbor evil thoughts in his soul; he should enter upon the penitential journey with a cleansed body and a pure heart. In whatever difficulties and disagreeable situations he may find himself, he should let no thought of anger rise in him. He should take care, that he may attain the fulfillment of his vow.

Arriving at a temple, one should first perform one's devotions with a quiet heart, then complete the written offering without haste, not getting too far from one's baggage if there is a crowd, but being careful, since mistakes are easily made even without evil intent. Pocketbook, money, and the like should under no circumstances be put down or shown to others.

Those who set out together should assist one another lovingly and obligingly. If they meet a weak pilgrim or one troubled by illness, they should spend themselves in caring for him; that is charity after the Buddha's heart. In the choice of companions met along the way one must be cautious; one must consider that there are times when it is pleasant to have a comrade to talk with, but there are also occasions when one's faith in a companion is betrayed. For there are bad people who have the most honest appearance; they approach and pretend that they want to point out a shorter way, to deliver efficacious prayers, or to teach a secret magic; they end by forcibly taking money or even violating women. Such people are to be found here and there upon the roads of Shikoku: those who wear pilgrim garb to hunt for their livelihood. It is not necessary that other people pray for one; he who merely follows the Daishi with his whole heart can have his prayer granted. . . . Also one should not write name and address too clearly on one's pilgrim staff, name-slips, and the like, since every year numerous people fall victim to swindling through the mails.

The rule of setting out early and putting up early is as good for today as it was for earlier times. Where one is invited to spend the night one will surely not be dealt with badly: one should therefore turn in, even if the sun is still high. If one tries to go on a little farther, the way often stretches out; before one realizes it, it is late and one does not know where to stay.

Ascetic training in the form of standing before the gates of strangers and asking for alms is to be performed every day at about twenty-one houses, following the example set by the Daishi. To do so is very good practice toward forming a pious nature. One should not think that one does it in order to receive money or other things; he who makes that his goal is only a beggar and his piety is degraded. . . .

In the spring there are everywhere settai, gifts from the hands of pious people or free sojourn in their houses. If such favors are bestowed on one, they should be accepted in the most thankful spirit and one's name-slip given in return.

A hasty journey with a heart full of business does not lead to piety. One is only brought to shame by it. Without other intention or thought, calmly and without haste, with "Namu Daishi Henjo Kongo" upon one's lips—that is how to make the true pilgrimage.

Namu Daishi Henjo Kongo.

Postscript: Whoever upon the pilgrimage experiences spiritual disturbances or has other cares should turn with confidence to the priests of the pilgrimage temples.

Morikawa and I consider this nice mix of spiritual and practical counsel. Much of it is still valid and the rest summons up times past.

The warning against those who preyed on gullible henro is out of date. The shark who masqueraded as a pilgrim has disappeared. In a more sophisticated world he has moved on to more sophisticated endeavor.

Begging alms as ascetic training has all but disappeared, though it is still prescribed. (Imagine a busload of pilgrims swooping down on a village.) I have not practiced it. I tell myself that a foreigner has no business begging from the Japanese; I suspect the real reason is that I lack the very humility the training is supposed to foster.

But settai—giving to the henro—persists. People still come forward to press a gift into the henro's hand. Settai cannot be refused. Following those old instructions, we accept in a thankful spirit and give our name-slips in return.

In giving to the henro a person gives also to Kobo Daishi, who travels at his side. In some districts a housewife used to bring two little dishes of rice, one for the pilgrim and one for his invisible companion (uncooked rice, for the henro would cook his own if he stopped at a simple shelter, or he would hand over to his innkeeper as much as he wanted cooked and so substantially reduce his lodging fee). Then there is the old belief that the Daishi still walks the henro-path: one might press a gift into *his* hand. But essentially settai is a way of participating in the pilgrimage, of joining in what the giver considers a pious and meritorious endeavor.

Settai may be spontaneous or planned, offered by an individual or a group. When we began our pilgrimage at Number One we were greeted with an outpouring of settai. Within minutes we were clutching tissues and handkerchiefs and caramels. As soon as we entered the gate we were saluted by a beaming group of white-haired men and women; they were giving each henro an orange, a coin, and wishes for a "good pilgrimage." I recognized some of those smiling faces. Three years earlier they arrived at the temple the same evening I did, having crossed the same strait I had from the Kii Peninsula, where Mount Koya and so many other sacred mountains rise. The priest's wife told me that they come every year on the same date, as the traditional season for pilgrimage begins, and take up residence in their own building, which years ago they constructed just inside the temple gate.

Early the next morning I went out to talk with them. In the kitchen the women were singing hymns of the pilgrimage as they cooked breakfast. I was welcomed by three old men who were keeping themselves warm around a hibachi; it was late March and there was a chill in the air. Their village had been offering settai at

Number One for more than a hundred years, they said, meaning longer than anyone could remember. There had been only one interruption, a couple of years during World War II.

Each spring they collect money and the oranges for which their district is famous. They make the four- or five-hour voyage in fishing boats belonging to some of their members—no problem to get boats because any boat making that trip is bound to haul in lucky catches all through the ensuing year. Others of their group are farmers and shopkeepers. The name-slips they receive from henro are carried home and distributed to the households who gave. Families treasure them as powerful talismans against misfortune. (Later in our pilgrimage we hear of a family who have traditionally offered settai at a ferry crossing. About fifty years ago a terrible fire swept the town. That family's house was in the middle of it but on a straw rope they tied the hundreds of name-slips they had received that year from henro and strung them around their house; it was saved.)

In the old days people often gave straw sandals and breech-cloths for the long journey. There were those who offered to carry a henro's pack for a while (Morikawa and I appreciate the blessing that would be). Villagers sometimes set up a stall along the road where they offered to dress the women's hair and give shaves to the men.

A well-known story about settai originated near Temple Six. I was reminded of it before that temple came into view, when I caught a whiff of the heavy, sweet aroma of a small old-fashioned sugar mill. . . .

Toward the end of the eighteenth century a diligent young farmer named Tokuya lived in a nearby village. It was a desperately poor village, cursed with soil that would not grow rice, wheat, barley, or the money crop of the province—indigo, the source of an enormously popular dye, a soft, glowing blue. Tokuya was an enterprising and intelligent young man and he tried hard, but with no success, to find some crop that would do well in that soil.

One day a henro passed by to whom Tokuya wanted to offer settai. Since there was nothing in the house to give he massaged the man's back and shoulders. While his hands worked, Tokuya

The sugar mill near Temple Six in the old days *(a book illustration by an unknown artist)*

talked of his village's plight, and the pilgrim mused that perhaps sugarcane would grow there; his own home on the island of Kyushu was near a fief famous for its production of sugar and the soil there appeared to be quite like that here. Beyond that the henro knew little: the plants and the secrets of cultivation and manufacture were jealously guarded.

Excited by this tip, Tokuya slipped away from home, smuggled himself into that sugar-producing fief, and worked as a farmhand for a year. At the end of that year he succeeded in stealing three stalks of cane such as are used for planting. He secreted them in a bamboo walking stick, escaped, and returned home.

Plants sprouted from his cuttings; three years later he had propagated them and knew that they thrived. Unfortunately he had not learned how to make sugar so again he stole away to Kyushu. It took him two years to land a job in a sugar mill and three years more to learn the whole process. At last he was able to come back to his village and make sugar, sugar even better than that from Kyushu. His village prospered; sugar production spread up and down the valley; the province's sugar became famous and brought a high price on the commodity exchange in Osaka. The lord of the province made Tokuya a samurai, a member of the military aristocracy with the right to carry two swords, and he was installed as chief of sugar production for all the province. And no one has ever forgotten the anonymous henro who set Tokuya upon his quest.

There are other stories of the benefits that henro brought. They are credited with teaching the use of herbs in Chinese-style medicine, with teaching the art of the potter, and with teaching an especially efficacious version of that popular remedy and restorative, moxa cautery, in which little cones of vegetable fiber are burned on the skin to draw poisons out of the system (it is called, naturally, Kobo moxa). Shikoku was an out-of-the-way place and travelers from the other islands brought new and better ways of doing things.

Over the centuries the most valued act of settai has been an offer of lodging. Food and lodging are the major expenses of the pilgrimage and as the *Exhortation* said, "Where one is invited to spend the night one will surely not be dealt with badly." Morikawa and I heard a story about that from a companion who walked with us the first few days of our pilgrimage, a man who had made the pilgrimage before.

"It was just about *here,*" he told us between Temples Nine and Ten, "that some years ago I was invited to spend the night at a farmhouse. I accepted, of course. Later I learned that a daughter in the family was soon to be married and at bedtime I was told that the women of the house had finished making the new bedding she would take with her as part of her dowry. That night they asked me to sleep in it and so give it a henro's blessing. I did; I stretched out in it but only briefly. Then I moved to my own bed, which had also been laid out."

Hearing his story, we pondered another dimension of this self-imposed mission of being a henro. For the henro is associated, he has associated himself, with Kobo Daishi, and he has taken on a trace of the Daishi's aura. When one puts on a henro's robe he puts on something more, something he should cherish and protect. I told myself I must remember this.

From time to time Morikawa and I travel with companions. Some, like Kobo Daishi, are not visible. Two of those whose company we most enjoy are from the province of Tosa. One is a man who made the pilgrimage in 1819 with a friend from the same village. He kept a diary and as we walk we sometimes dip into it to see what it was like along the same stretch of path more than a hundred and fifty years ago. The two of us have vowed to walk the entire pilgrimage but in 1819 henro had no choice, and it was easy for no one. Leaving Temple Seven we remembered an entry from his diary: "Just outside the gate of Number Seven we found the body of a dead henro. A companion told us that a child henro died last night at the inn where we stayed, and soon we came across another body. So many dead in close succession depressed us."

At Number Eight we could not help thinking of our other companion from Tosa, our friend Tosa Fumio, the novelist and journalist who has taken his pen name from his province. He finished his pilgrimage about a month before we started ours. He undertook it because the newspaper he writes for asked him to do a series of articles, a long literary diary, about the pilgrimage and his experiences as he performed it. His articles are now appearing daily and we read them eagerly whenever we find that newspaper.

Temple Eight is deep in a valley. Even the great gate, which is all we can see of the temple as we approach it, is set far back from the road. The gate, built in 1688, is the biggest among the eighty-eight temples. They say a band of robbers once lived in its second story but that tale seems overly romantic for this peaceful countryside.

The temple halls stand under old trees in the narrowing ravine: a pagoda in a sad state of decay, the middle gate, and then a long flight of stone steps up to the bell tower and main hall. More steps rise higher to the Daishi Hall. We strike the bell and as the tones echo and die we look about us. This is a temple that once

Temple Eight *(a painting by Kawabata)*

had splendor. It has suffered years of neglect, moldering in the shadows, but we can see that restoration is being undertaken; we hope the priest can find the money to continue it.

It was on the doors of the main hall that Tosa found an almost illegible letter, a letter directed to the Daishi:

> My husband, Nakagawa Ineki, disappeared at the end of last year, leaving me and our children. He had immoral sexual relations with Kimura Sachi, a twenty-eight-year-old divorced woman of the neighborhood, and he ran away hand in hand with her. My husband is a good man but everyone knows that Kimura Sachi is wicked and they say she had sex with every man in the village. Obviously my husband was deceived by this sinful woman. I have five children, the oldest only fourteen, and I am at a loss without my husband to provide for us. I think I would rather die than live this way. So please, O-Daishi-sama, please punish Kimura Sachi, a wicked woman, and bring my husband back to me.
>
> Please!
>
> Nakagawa Toyoko, age thirty-three
> Minami Uwa-gun
> Ehime Prefecture

The letter is not there now, but the setting—quiet, lonely, redolent of decay—brings it to mind. We picture the distraught woman, come from the far side of the island. How long did she pray here in the shadows? "O-Daishi-sama, please!"

Tosa found other letters from her at succeeding temples. The tone altered. Although her rancor against the other woman remained feverish, some of her bitterness shifted toward her husband. At Temple Twelve, high in the mountains, she had begun to examine herself. "If I have given cause for complaint, I will change. If I have bad points, let me reform. . . ." That was the last of her letters Tosa found.

Henro who begin at Number One commonly experience a change at Twelve. Tosa felt this and we do too. The air is sweet; the mountains lift the spirits. The first difficult climb has been accomplished. The populated valley with its reminders of everyday problems has been left behind; the cares brought from home have dropped away. (And so has some of the too much gear we started with—mailed back to make our packs ride easier on sore but toughening shoulders.) As we set out in the morning after spending the night at the temple, Morikawa pauses to drink in the vistas. He smiles. "We're really into our pilgrimage now," he says, "no longer starting."

16 I failed and the failure still weighs on me. . . .

It happens shortly after we leave the temple, the bangai, where Kobo Daishi is said to have been schooled as a boy—on that bright spring day made gay by the temple festival, after hospitality had been lavished on us in the setting of the temple garden. The priest comes to the entry to see us off and points out a path leading straight down to the highway, the shortest way to the next temple. We dislike walking along highways but it is growing late and we know we must hurry to reach before dark the temple where we have made a reservation for the night.

Just before we reach the highway there is a cluster of new houses. A woman emerges from one of them and invites us in for a cup of tea as settai. We have been drinking tea for the past hour and are pressed for time but this is not the kind of invitation one can refuse. In the entryway she invites us into her home but we beg off, asking if we may just sit here without shedding our shoes. She brings us coffee, which is a treat, and chats with us sociably as we enjoy it. From within I hear a hum of voices, almost a monologue, the solemn, didactic tone of a man delivering a disquisition, only occasionally broken as a young woman assents.

We start to thank our hostess and go our way when she asks if we will come in to meet her family. Please, won't we come into the living room?

I assume she wants us to admire her children, perhaps to give them the chance to say they met a foreigner, but Morikawa and I both know that once we enter we cannot break away quickly. We make excuses—it will soon be dark and we have a long way to go.

Now she bares what is on her mind. She focuses on me. Will I, she begs, examine her daughter, who is suffering from a chest condition? The urgency in her tone, the sound of the voices from within—I have the feeling that the illness is serious.

I know what this woman is asking. Just this morning we encountered a healer. Morikawa spotted a sign saying that a couple of hundred yards off our road was "a temple related to Kobo Daishi." Curiosity took us there, a small chapel adjoining a house. A woman answered the door, a priestess. Over tea and cookies she sketched the chapel's brief history: it was opened by an aged nun who settled here after making the pilgrimage; when she died an elderly priest came from the city to live out his life here; then it was taken over by two nuns "who were unsuccessful"; when they moved on about three years ago this woman came, after (like that first nun) completing the pilgrimage. What was it, I wondered, that she was evidently successful at but the two nuns were not. She told us: "People suffering from illnesses, physical and mental, come and ask me to perform rituals of prayer for them." She was a shaman, a healer.

Now I am asked to be one. As a man with hair gray enough to imply some wisdom; as a stranger—there is mystery in that word, the mystery of a person unknown unexpectedly appearing from a world unknown—and doubly a stranger, a foreigner; and above all as a henro, I am being asked to minister to a sick girl.

I panic, utterly at a loss. Nothing I have studied has prepared me for this. Suddenly I am not a henro, I am a misplaced doctor's son from Illinois (one who instinctively shied away from his father's profession). I have no religious power, I tell this woman. I am wearing a henro robe but I have no religious power. I have no ability to diagnose an illness or to cure it.

She pleads with me just to look at her daughter. Another daughter, an attractive young woman, comes to the entry, kneels, and smiling, joins her mother in urging us in.

I repeat that there is nothing I can do for the girl, that I am afraid anything I might do would only make things worse. I urge them to call a doctor.

I try to explain, to justify. It's not that I don't want to help, I say, it's that I can't. I have no power, no competence. Morikawa I know is as agonized as I am. He is caught between these pleading women and his demoralized companion. Full of apologies, we make our escape.

We plod along the highway, single file for safety's sake. There is no chance to talk. I am shaken. I feel painfully inadequate. Why didn't I ask Morikawa what to do instead of showering him with a torrent of excuses to interpret? What should I have done? I know only that I have failed.

The fates are not slow to punish me, and Morikawa because he is with me. Darkness overtakes us. We phone to find that because we are so late there is no room for us at the temple. (We have violated a cardinal precept of the *Exhortation,* "the rule of setting out early and putting up early. . . . If one tries to go on a little farther, the way often stretches out; before one realizes it, it is late and one does not know where to stay.") We end up at an unpleasant inn where we are served an unpalatable meal, which (that and weariness and failure) promptly makes me ill.

Several days later we come across another of Tosa's articles about his pilgrimage and I learn what I should have done. With his permission I quote; he speaks of himself in the third person.

The scene is of thatch-roofed farmhouses and peach trees in full bloom. A lone pilgrim, weary, his white robe soiled, walks with dragging feet, trying to keep his eyes on the blossoms. He hears someone calling him: "O-henro-san!" He turns to see an old lady running after him and he stops to wait. When she reaches him, all out of breath, she offers tea at her house. He is thirsty and he thinks it will not take much time. "It's very kind of you," he answers, and follows her back.

It turns out to be quite a distance, but remembering how she had run after him he puts down any temptation to refuse and continue on his way. Finally she points out one of the thatched houses. Like the others it has a peach tree blooming in its garden.

He sits on the veranda, she serves tea and cakes, and they chat. Suddenly the old lady straightens and becomes formal. "O-henro-san, will you do me a favor? I have a granddaughter who is eighteen years old. She has been sick in bed for a long time. Will you pray at her bedside to charm away her illness?"

The henro is astonished by this unexpected request but he realizes that it is a serious matter. He tells her, "I can pray but I am not Kobo Daishi. I too am seeking the Daishi's help. I am just one of many henro."

Earnestly she says, "That is enough. What I ask is that you pass your album over her sick body."

Now the henro remembers that when he was a child, every time he had a stomachache or a fever his grandmother would pass a thick book over him while she repeated, "You will get better soon; you will get better soon." The book was the album of her pilgrimage to the Eighty-eight Sacred Places of Shikoku. She treasured it and when she died it was buried with her. This comes back to him very clearly now and he nods in assent.

She is gratified, and leading him into the house she shows him to the room where her granddaughter lies. Her bed is by the window so that she can look at the peach blossoms. The old woman speaks lovingly to the girl, who silently turns her face to the henro. It is clear, unclouded. She smiles and greets him with her wide eyes. He looks into them, at a loss for words.

He hears the grandmother explain . . . when the girl was nine years old she was attacked by tuberculosis of the spine . . . she was taken to doctor after doctor but it was no use . . . since then she has lain in bed.

It is her pure eyes that hold the henro. Then she speaks: "I'm sorry to trouble you. I suppose my grandmother asked you in. I keep telling her that we should not interrupt henro because they are in a hurry."

Her voice is bright and it banishes the depression he has felt. He finds it easy to talk now. He introduces himself and tells her where he's from. She listens alertly and sometimes she asks questions. In a short time they are talking freely.

"I have made more than a hundred friends among henro." She pauses and then she confides, "When I become dejected I turn the pages of my diary and try to remember each of them. I'm so grateful to them. And now, will you pray with your new album?"

He hands her his album in its cover of golden brocade. Her eyes shine. "Albums get more gorgeous every year. This is wonderful." She puts it on her young breasts and closes her eyes. His heart overflows and he prays silently, afraid to trust his voice. He sees something he should not: a tear flows gently, gently down her cheek.

Along the same stretch of road where the girl's grandmother hailed Tosa, Morikawa and I catch up with a lone henro and walk with him as far as the bus stop he is heading for. "Two years ago I made half the pilgrimage," he tells us. "Now I want to complete it. . . . My reasons? Well, my grandson has heart disease—he's just a little fellow, only six years old—and I pray for his recovery. I'm not in good health myself: there's a hole in my heart. And I have a neighbor who is mongoloid. I say prayers for my grandson, my neighbor, and myself."

There are literally numberless stories of cures wrought by the Daishi, of the blind given sight, of the crippled enabled to stand and walk. One hears of such miracles at every temple and along the path between. Several temples have collections of casts and braces and crutches left by those who no longer needed them.

The doors of temples are crowded with written supplications: for a sick child, often with a photo that gives my heart a wrench; for better sight or hearing—sheets filled with a single character for "eye" or "ear." There is a chapel—unnumbered, a bangai—whose deity specializes in diseases of the breast; its walls are covered with replicas of breasts brought by women who prayed there. At several temples there are altars enshrining a god, more Shinto than Buddhist, whose province is woman's anatomy "from the waist down." "It was holy men who installed that god here," says one priest; "its altar had two or three centuries of prosperity but almost no one visits it anymore." Yet some temples report that it is popular with women of the entertainment quarters who come to seek protection from venereal disease, and others that it is visited by women who suffer ill health after giving birth. As for birth, I have not been able to count the temples with deities noted for their power to grant pregnancy and easy delivery; the sheer number of such altars speaks eloquently of the life that Japanese women have lived—the obligation to bear children, the perils of childbirth in the past. Temple Sixty-one has in two generations changed from the poorest to the richest among the eighty-eight based largely on a single premise: that prayers and guidance there will enable a childless couple to have a child. It seems evident that for many Japanese medical science needs all the help it can get, if indeed it is the remedy of choice.

I do not mean to belittle the importance of state of mind. Though it is difficult for me to believe that the pilgrimage can cure cancer—we encounter a few henro who say that is what they are praying for—I know that there are diseases it can cure. Polio or a stroke, for example: if the victim can walk at all, then the hard physical exercise (some would call it therapy) and the getting out into nature (for nature has therapeutic powers), if accompanied by faith, can work miracles—but not without faith.

A priest at one of the temples has told me: "In the old days many who were ill made the pilgrimage; lepers, for instance, were numerous along the henro-path. Nowadays the physically ill go to hospitals. But these are times of strain and mental illness, and so today the benefits of pilgrimage are greater than ever."

The young Shingon priest I traveled with on my first pilgrimage was named Mizuno. Late one day we found ourselves in the river valley between Temples Twenty and Twenty-one. It had been a hard day: down from one height and a long walk before we climbed to Twenty and then lurched and stumbled (I speak of myself; he was surer-footed) down its mountain. There we faced the forbidding form of the mountain on which Twenty-one stands. Night was coming on and we were all in. There is a village in the valley by the river and we asked if there was a house that lodged henro. There was; we found it and were taken in.

Shortly after we arrived a couple appeared, a man and wife whom I guessed to be in their sixties. They were shown to a room upstairs, we being downstairs, but when it came time for supper the housewife called them down to eat with us. And so it was I heard their story.

They introduced themselves as Mr. and Mrs. Ishii from Okayama City, across the Inland Sea. They owned a small apartment building, they said, but they were not really city folk; they had been farmers until they had to sell their land because Mrs. Ishii's health was so poor that she could no longer do her share of the work. For twenty years or more she had suffered from a nervous ailment: headaches, sleeplessness, malaise, her condition becoming progressively worse. She lost weight: "I looked like a ghost." They went to physician after physician; each ended by saying he could do nothing for her.

They explained that for years they had been worshipers of Kobo Daishi. Their farming village had had no temple and they had joined with their neighbors to form one, of the Shingon sect.

"About a year ago," Mr. Ishii continued, "my wife's health was so bad and worsening so fast that we had just about given up"—I got the impression that they had contemplated suicide together, though they certainly didn't say so. As a last resort, they decided to undertake the pilgrimage. "We realized that she might die attempting it," Mr. Ishii said, "but no other hope was left to us."

They started at Number One. For several days it was agonizing for her, and for him at her side. They were able to walk only a short distance each day but they went as far as they could, and they prayed, they prayed. Slowly she began to gain strength; the days became a little easier. They went all the way around and by the time they reached Temple Eighty-eight she was in truth cured.

A year later, as we sat there at supper, her weight was normal, her color was good, and she looked fit. I told her so and she demurred a little: "I'm not completely well. But I can live again. Each morning and evening I pray in gratitude to Kobo Daishi." Mr. Ishii finished: "We have returned to give thanks. We won't do all the pilgrimage—only Awa—but every year for the rest of our lives we intend to do at least one province." (There is a tradition of doing Shikoku's four provinces one at a time, with an interval between.) "We cannot forget that we have been blessed."

I went to bed conscious that I had heard the story of a miracle. I knew that the regimen of the pilgrimage had been vital—the physical exercise, the closeness to nature, and just getting away from home; but without faith they would not have been enough. I have thought of the Ishiis often in the years since. I hope that spring still brings them back as henro to worship in thanksgiving.

It was the next day, on that first pilgrimage, that we fell in with a young henro. I had glimpsed him first at Temple Twenty. A slight, pale young man with long hair, he stood out among the elderly. We met again at Temple Twenty-two. It was noon, and the young priest and I had improvidently neglected to provide ourselves with lunch. He offered us a box lunch, saying he had an extra one, and the two of us shared it.

I wondered why a young man would set out alone on the pilgrimage. He was a little shy and he volunteered nothing but he did not seem to mind my questions. He came originally from a town in northern Japan, in the "snow country." Of his family he said that they did "nothing much"; no, they were not farmers. He was the second of three sons. At fifteen, as soon as he had finished junior high school and the years of compulsory education, he left home for Tokyo. With little to offer in skills or experience, he found a job in a potato chip factory. I looked at his hands: they were slender and soft.

As is usual, the shop provided a dormitory for its workers: he and about thirty others lived in a loft above the factory. Each had a low-ceilinged cubicle about six by nine. I asked about recreation. Nothing, he said, but television and once in a while a movie. He worked six long days a week.

He was twenty-four. After nine years of working in a small factory for small wages, of a life that was leading nowhere, he was fed up. He said he was having "personal problems"; I took that to mean friction with his boss and co-workers, a suffocating sense of futility, and perhaps the onset of a nervous breakdown.

He had been given few holidays; now he was taking one for himself. He had quit his job and set out on the pilgrimage. "People in Tokyo said I'd find Shikoku dead, but I like it here." I asked his purpose; he said he had none. Obviously he was bent on escape from a life that was strangling him, but he was not running aimlessly: he was seriously engaged in the pilgrimage. Unlike the few other young people we saw, he wore the henro's white robe, a bell hung from his waist, and he was earnest in performing the rituals at the temples.

He was making the pilgrimage with no time schedule and no

deadline; he said he would take as long as he wished. I sensed that he was hungry for companionship but our schedules did not mesh. We drifted apart at Temple Twenty-three. When I last saw him he was praying ardently before the main hall. I hope his pilgrimage brought him what he was looking for, someone or something to give his life direction. I will never know.

Morikawa and I, deep in Tosa, are searching for a bangai, an unnumbered temple we have found listed in old guidebooks. We have been told that it was abandoned for a time but that some years ago an energetic priest restored it.

With Temple Thirty-six behind us, we began this day by riding a ferry up a mountain-rimmed inlet that thrusts miles deep into the coastline. There is a tradition, which we were happy to honor, that at this one place in the pilgrimage the Daishi granted henro permission to travel by boat. Landing we found a dirt road that took us first among flooded paddy fields, then through tangerine groves, now up the easy slopes of a forested mountain. We meet almost no cars and there is birdsong all about. The temple is said to be at the crest of the mountain, the Crest of the Souls of the Dead Who Have Attained Buddhahood. This is another of those mountains where the souls of the dead gather.

There is no mistaking the crest: the road falls away in both directions. We stand there beneath the trees. There is no sign of a temple. Then sighting a path that enters the woods, we follow it to a swift descent of steps hewn from the mountain.

It is not at all what I expected. I thought that we would find a small hermitage in the forest. We stand where a ravine ends against the mountain but from here the compound stretches wide and open toward a broad valley. The ground underfoot is raw gravel; the scarred walls of the mountain show where it came from. The utilitarian buildings have no patina of age. We move to the newest; it is the residence and we are ushered into the priest's study.

It is unusual for henro to come this way these days, he says as he welcomes us. He is a big, vigorous man, taller and huskier than I, open in his speech. Several times he is called to the entry to speak with people who have come to him, yet with us he is unhurried. I piece together his story.

"During the war in the Pacific I was in the navy medical corps. I served in Saigon and in a general hospital in Singapore. I came safely home because of my mother's prayers, because of her great faith in Kobo Daishi. Our home was beside the henro-path. She wanted to make the pilgrimage with me after the war, but she died just fifty days before I got home. The following year, at the age of thirty, I decided to become a priest. I wanted to pray for the peace of the dead, all the dead, Japanese and those we fought against.

"And I had worked beside doctors. I had learned that there are sicknesses that medicine cannot cure; only religion can help. Cancer—people suffering from cancer come here to pray for recovery.

"The university on Mount Koya offers an accelerated course for those like me who are called to the priesthood late in life. I went there to study. I learned about this place from a henro who had discovered it on his pilgrimage—a small chapel in the forest, about to be destroyed. He urged me to save it. No one knew what had become of the former priest. During the war he had prophesied Japan's defeat, said it had been revealed to him that the nation would be scourged by fire; the secret police had taken him away and he was never heard of again.

"I searched the records back five generations to find the owner and I bought the land. Where we are sitting was a ravine sixty feet deep. To fill it in I cut away the mountain, leveled the land. I built a road, following the old henro-path, more than half a mile down the mountain so that cars could get up here. I myself felled the trees, hewed the timber, built these buildings. I have labored here twenty-four years trying to follow the example of the Daishi. Without faith I could not have done what I did.

"You know the legend that Kobo Daishi founded the Eighty-eight Sacred Places. I do not believe that, but he did wander all

In a spring rain henro cross a mountain between Temples Thirty-six and Thirty-seven *(detail from a book illustration by Shugetsu)*

through Shikoku. It was a backward, primitive place: he built roads and bridges and irrigation ponds; he did social work among the people; he brought them a higher faith. He founded some temples and restored others. I have done what I've done to prove that the Daishi could do what he did."

As he has talked between goings and comings he has given us souvenirs, he has invited us to attend a goma fire ritual he will

conduct presently, and he has told us we are welcome to spend the night here.

Returning after another talk with a caller he conducts us to the goma hall, the one building surviving from the temple's earlier existence. Speaking of the prayers he will offer he uses the word *kito:* it indicates prayer powerfully reinforced by rites and mysteries, rites with an ancient flavor of exorcism, mysteries most often directed to cure sickness. It is beginning to dawn on me that this priest is a shaman.

Four women are kneeling before the altar; I wonder how long they have been waiting. We kneel a bit farther back. The priest checks the name, address, and age of each person present. The two women on our left are mother and daughter. He asks the mother how many children she has borne. He asks the daughter if she is menstruating; the way he puts the question flusters her. When she answers yes he rephrases his query; now she states that her period is finished (he must be guarding against ritual impurity). Satisfied, he asks her what year she was born: "The Year of the Snake." It is clear that she has come to be cured of some illness (from the conversation Morikawa thinks it is a throat condition).

The women on our right, though by their ages they could be mother and daughter, are not related. His questioning of them is less probing.

He announces that this will be a goma for the purpose of making our wishes come true. He turns to the altar and prays, naming each of us. For Morikawa and me he asks simply that our desires be granted and that we complete our pilgrimage safely.

A tower of sticks has been built. Intoning a litany, striking gongs and bells, he sets the fire. It flares high. He is silhouetted against flame. When the blaze begins to subside he rises and moves to the left of the altar. He summons the daughter. With his three-pronged ritual instrument—heavy with brass and symbolism—he thumps her back and shoulders, then massages them forcefully. From a foot-high stack of tissues he grabs a few, moistens them with his mouth, holds them over the fire, and with those hot and smoky papers rubs her brusquely; throwing the tissues aside he seizes more; he rubs her hair and shoulders, her back and chest, her face and head. Once, the papers catch fire; he does not notice, rubs her head, and her hair flames. I start to cry out but he sees, beats out the flame. With hot papers he massages her neck, then grasping her head he snaps it to the right, to the left, forward and backward; each time we hear the crack of her spine. He seizes her by the thigh and the neck, picks her up bodily, thrusts her at arm's length face down over the fire; reversing his grip, he flips her over, face up. He sets her on her feet, kneads her again with his hands, thumps her with the three prongs of brass, propels her back among us.

I am mesmerized. It has been a violent, almost fearful performance—it would have been fearful but for his strength and his assurance.

He calls the mother. Her treatment is briefer and he does not hold her over the fire. I look to see which of the women on my right he will summon.

"America-san!"

Me? If I could speak—but no words come. I find myself rising, advancing to the altar. I am thumped, massaged, rubbed with hot and smoky papers. My neck is snapped, my spine cracked. And then, incredibly, he picks me up, holds me outstretched over the fire; the heat flares on my face. He reverses me; my back glows. I am again massaged and thumped. I float back to my place.

Morikawa is called. He does not get held over the fire.

The flames are burning low now. The priest sits again before the altar. The other two women are called in turn to kneel before him, receive a relatively perfunctory treatment. He is now ready to answer their questions.

The older woman is concerned about her grandson. He is twenty-three and has not yet found a wife; what should they do? Nothing, he answers; he will not find the right girl until he is twenty-six; she will come from the direction of such-and-such a village. Will he have more traffic accidents?—he has been involved in several. He cannot avoid such misfortune, she is told; he will have another and serious one in December.

The young woman's husband is giving her trouble. The priest listens, comments briefly, advises her that the man's name indicates he will never be a success as a farmer: he should change his occupation.

The priest rises. The women murmur their thanks, bow gratefully, and leave; I am certain they made an offering earlier. Others are already coming in to pray and to be counseled. We are again invited to stay the night. I have a feeling that we should, that I should talk more with this man. Morikawa points out that it is early afternoon and that we are expected at a temple in the next town. The priest does not press us. We set out.

My body is light, all soreness gone, but my thoughts are whirling. Is this priest exploiting superstition or do people need what he offers? I truly believe that faith can work miracles. I know that all religion has an element of magic. But how slippery is the line between seeking enlightenment in this world and seeking favors—the priest said "happiness." I wish we had stayed to talk longer with him, to explore the role in which he casts himself.

The road down the mountain is not as pretty as the road up. The hills are bare; road construction is in progress. One sight I will remember: a plot of clover between beds of rice seedlings, lavender bracketed by tender green.

The experience continues to haunt me. Occasionally, when we are talking with another priest I ask an opinion. One reply seems defensive: that kind of prayer has always been an element of Japanese Buddhism and of Shingon in particular, and after all, the bangai in the mountains has no members to support it; the implication seems to be that somehow the priest has to make a living. It is an answer that leaves me troubled.

A highly respected priest is unequivocal. "Proper priests of Shingon are not faith healers. When they perform goma they may feel that they receive a message but they do not divulge it. They keep it inside, and pray. Faith healing, telling fortunes—this is walking the back road."

The priest of a temple on a mountain that for ages has been a center for ascetic practice touches on the issue without my asking. "The spiritual descendants of the ancient holy men still come here to perform the religious exercises that they believe give them power. Some of these men and women are good people but some of them worry me—those who tell the fortunes of the gullible or try to cure illness by prayer. Sometimes the seriously ill depend on them: everyone hopes for a miracle. Priests must admonish such faith healers since they won't accept counsel from laymen."

As we near the end of our pilgrimage, the priest of the mountain bangai is still on my mind. I realize that we must talk with him again. Morikawa phones; he says that he will welcome us. We catch an early morning train for the four-hour trip across the island over its high spine of mountains. From the station we take a cab up into the hills to the temple. The driver doesn't have to be told how to get there: he says he makes the trip often. Nor does he seem surprised to find four women sipping tea in the entry, waiting for a taxi in apparent confidence that one will be along soon. We get out; they get in.

The priest appears, as tall and sturdy as I remembered. He receives us warmly, asks about our pilgrimage, thanks us for coming so far to see him again. He talks of the holy men of Koya (as if he knows the reason we are here) and of the mystic power of the goma fire. "There are things that cannot be explained by science."

We are several times interrupted. When we were here before I thought perhaps he was busy because it was a Sunday and a day off for most people, but this is a weekday and there is a steady stream of visitors. Many of them he turns away because we are here; we ask him not to but he says they can come anytime and we cannot. He does receive a few: from his study we can hear the murmur of their worried voices and his confident one, and the sounds of shoulder thumping and spine cracking; they leave looking grateful.

He take us up the mountain, guides us into the forest along traces of the old henro-path a few yards from the road we walked forty days ago, points out gravestones along the path. On one we make out a date: the Month of the Boar, 1803. "There are twenty or thirty stones along this path but actually only a few graves are marked—those of pilgrims whose families were well-to-do, who could send money or come themselves to erect a stone. The poor and sick came to Shikoku hoping to die along the pilgrimage route and become part of its sacred soil. The bodies of most of them were just thrown down a mountainside or tossed into some ravine.

"About twenty years ago when I was digging to widen the road I heard a voice crying from the ground. Working very carefully, I unearthed a skeleton, a rice bowl, a pipe, and some old copper coins. I conducted a service and reburied the bones."

Back at the temple I ask what kinds of problems, what kinds of sicknesses, people bring to him.

"The kinds that can't be cured by medicine—stomach and intestinal disorders, neuroses, diseases that the doctors can't diagnose. The tensions of life today, the mental strains that we are subject to, combined with rich food and lack of exercise—these produce intestinal ulcers and all kinds of muscular pains. From neuroses to the athlete's foot we get when we put on shoes, modern life is hard on us."

He summons two women from the kitchen. "This woman was once a section chief in a telephone office. She had a breakdown and was put in a mental hospital. The doctors said she could never be released but I cured her four years ago.

"This other had an operation on her throat. They cut a nerve, destroyed it so that she was left with psychoneurosis. I cured her." The women second him. There is no questioning their sincerity. They work at the temple out of gratitude.

"You must not misunderstand. The Esoteric Buddhism of Shingon was not developed to cure disease but to achieve peace and a calm heart. We must know ourselves and see the interrelationships that bind us together and to the universe. Shingon is very profound, difficult to master. Most priests don't study hard. I undertook many spiritual exercises; I trained seriously. It is possible to see Buddha. I did once: I felt an ecstasy far greater than the climax of sexual intercourse.

"Now when I meet someone I can tell what kind of agony or disease possesses him. I know when someone is going to die soon or suffer a tragedy: I don't tell what I foresee but I try to implant the power to endure."

At last I ask the question I have crossed Shikoku to put to him: "You worked in a hospital during the war. You were a medical assistant. You have some knowledge of medicine. If someone comes to you with a disease that a doctor could help, do you recommend that he or she see a doctor—as well as offering your help through prayer?"

"I always ask first if they have been to a doctor. If they have not, I tell them to consult one. If it seems necessary I send them to a hospital at once." This is what I wanted to hear.

It is dark before we recross the mountains. Morikawa is dozing. I tell myself that this hard day has been worthwhile. My eyes close.

17 More than thirty of the pilgrimage temples claim the Daishi's great precursor, Gyogi, as their founder. (Scholars think Gyogi never came to Shikoku but this is not entirely relevant because some of his followers must have, and whatever they did they would have done in his name.) Of these many temples, Number Nineteen seems to me closest to Gyogi's spirit of involvement with the towns, of service to the people of the plains. Nineteen lies at the heart of its town, not at all aloof from the streets and shops around it. In its big, busy compound one feels the rhythms of town life; the temple seems attuned to the concerns of townsfolk. This morning a woman is walking back and forth the half block between the main hall and the Daishi Hall, deep in prayer. She will walk this course one hundred times for whatever number of days she has set for herself. I tell Morikawa I have never come here when there was not someone praying thus.

This temple is famed as a barrier gate for henro, a barrier gate in the religious sense just as for centuries there were political barriers at the boundaries of every province—posts where travelers faced examination, where henro had to present a passport issued by their home authorities, identifying them and authorizing them to make this pilgrimage. At a temple barrier the examination is subjective, a spiritual testing: if a henro is able to worship and move on without difficulty he has passed the barrier, but if he is confronted by trouble or ill omen he has failed and he should go back to where he began his pilgrimage and start all over again. There are those who say that having passed a temple barrier, a

Temple Nineteen *(a painting by Kawabata)*

henro is permitted one night's relaxation of his vows of abstinence, that he may drink, eat fish, and have sex. But of course this is outrageous.

There is supposed to be a temple barrier in every province but the lists vary. There is agreement only on this temple for Awa and on the one for Tosa. Nineteen's famous legend has to do with its role as a barrier. It has been told and retold but I feel I have it straight, for I heard it from the temple's distinguished high priest.

It begins in a port town on the Sea of Japan. A merchant called Gimbei had three daughters; our story concerns the second, Okyo. Okyo's parents were not models for their daughters. They wrangled constantly. Gimbei kept a mistress; his wife had taken a lover. In such an atmosphere it is not surprising that Okyo grew up wild.

Nor is it surprising, given the extramarital involvements, that Gimbei had financial problems. In this situation he and his wife were able to agree on one thing: weighing Okyo's nature and their own need for cash, it was expedient to sell her as a geisha. They accepted the offer of a house in Hiroshima, across the island on the Inland Sea. Before she had completed the term for which they had sold her, however, another monetary crisis loomed. She was sixteen when they spirited her away and resold her in Osaka. It was a comedown: in the new house she was more prostitute than geisha.

In Osaka she took a lover named Yosuke. He paid the fee to release her from her contract and set her up as his mistress. She journeyed home and asked her parents' permission to marry Yosuke. They were outraged by her unfilial conduct, because once she married they would lose control of her and would not be able to sell her again, but she threatened to kill herself if they didn't consent, so they gave in and she returned to Osaka. She knew very well she could not marry Yosuke because he already had a wife, but she had escaped her parents' grasp.

Life with only one man was dull, however, and Okyo soon acquired another lover, a gangster named Chozo. For a time she enjoyed the favors of her two men, but then Yosuke became suspicious. He announced he was going on a business trip, doubled back, and caught Okyo and Chozo in bed together. Some very unfriendly things were said.

Okyo and Chozo brooded about this and a few days later they acted. Okyo lured Yosuke to a secluded spot and there they killed him in a most cruel fashion. (The priest was not certain how, but

he speculated that they may have cut him up alive, piece by piece.)
The murder was so barbarous, in fact, that when it was done they
were seized by remorse. They discussed double suicide but decided
that Osaka, where they were both so notorious that the deed would
create a sensation, was not the proper setting, and so they crossed
the Inland Sea to Shikoku. It was the spring of 1803: the boat they
crossed on, the port, and the road were crowded with henro. They
decided to move with the pilgrims.

When they arrived here at Number Nineteen, the barrier gate,
Okyo tried to pray at the main hall. Suspended above her was the
acorn-shaped brass bell that worshipers jangle (it is called croco-
dile mouth because of the wide slit in it). She grasped the bell rope.
Suddenly her long hair rose on end and twining itself around the
rope began to twist its way up, lifting her bodily. Chozo rushed for
the priest, who was already coming in response to Okyo's screams.
He prayed, and finally she dropped, leaving most of her hair and
part of her scalp enmeshed in the rope.

She had in truth been tonsured and, accepting this, she
begged the priest for tutelage and became a nun. She lived in a
small chapel belonging to the temple and devoted the rest of her
life to prayer. Chozo lived out his days as a temple laborer. The
temple still has that bell rope, displayed in a case behind the altar
in the main hall. A young priest lights a dim electric bulb so that
Morikawa and I can peer at it.

When we emerge into daylight on the veranda that stretches
across the front of the hall, the priest points to the statue placed
out there. It is Binzuru, he says, and asks if we know his story.
I have seen such an image at every temple, always outside like
this, always seated resignedly, always red-faced—clearly a mortal. I wonder how I could have been so unmindful as never to ask
about him.

"You see how shiny his body is? Many hands polish him.
Someone sick rubs him and then presses the part of his own body
that hurts, for Binzuru was a physician from a long line of physicians. He was first among the sixteen disciples of Buddha. He had
just one weakness—he was too fond of liquor. One day a rich man
came to Buddha and begged him to overcome an evil spirit that

was afflicting his house. The Buddha could not go, for he had been summoned to expound his doctrine to the king, and so he sent Binzuru, cautioning him under no circumstances to drink while on this mission.

"Binzuru went to the rich man's house and found that indeed the evil spirit was there and all the residents were suffering from it. Binzuru confronted the evil, struggled with it, and by proclaiming Buddha's teachings overcame it. The rich man was so grateful that he insisted on setting forth a banquet. Again and again Binzuru refused drink but he was sorely tempted, and at last he convinced himself that he should take just one cup so as not to offend his host. Of course he could not stop at one cup. He became quite drunk, his mastery over the evil spirit dissolved in the alcohol, and soon the people of the house were suffering again.

"The Buddha was greatly vexed and cast out Binzuru from his disciples. But Binzuru was remorseful and he continued to go where the Buddha taught; he could not enter, but he listened from outside, and the Buddha knew this and did not prevent it. As the Buddha was about to enter nirvana, he called Binzuru to him and told him that he was forgiven but that he could never enter nirvana: he must remain forever outside, in this world, ministering to the people. That is why he sits outside at every temple, red-faced from his love for drink, but curing the people's ills and protecting them from evil."

We have lingered an hour here at Temple Nineteen. The elderly woman who was walking between the Daishi Hall and the main hall has completed her hundred rounds and gone; two others have appeared. Back and forth, back and forth, one moves a little faster than the other: they pass at a different spot each time. Their eyes do not meet; each is intent on her own prayer. Half-hypnotized by their ritual, I am tempted to sit here in the sun until one of them finishes and then try to strike up a conversation. I would ask her age, not a rude question in Japan; old folks like to be congratulated on their longevity. Has she lived all her life here by Nineteen and worshiped at this temple? How many days has she pledged to walk the hundred turns? And (diffidently) what is she praying for? I am quite certain it would not be something for herself; more likely for some member of her family. Perhaps if I wait I can talk with both women.

But that would be prying, and we should move out; we have a considerable walk ahead of us. Morikawa signals that he is ready to go. We slip into the harness of our packs, thank the priest who talked with us (he is now busy selling an amulet), take up our staffs, bow toward the main hall and the Daishi Hall, and leave.

The past few days, since we descended from Temple Twelve, we have been in the lowlands, close to the sea. Now we turn again to the mountains. The next three temples are mountain temples. Our goal today is not Number Twenty but its innermost sanctuary, another temple that is on a mountain a valley apart from Twenty. We start out along a highway busy with trucks coming down from the mountains, loaded with logs. Somewhere along this road those 1819 henro from Tosa found a stall where villagers cut and dressed their hair, as settai. Then they bought new straw sandals for the climb ahead. Actually, Morikawa reminds me, henro did not wear regular sandals; they wore half sandals that barely covered the foot. They were cheaper, which was important, but also one just slipped into them; there were no strings to be tied and untied, dirtying the hands and making one unclean when one wanted to enter a temple hall. Henro usually carried extra pairs, for they were of course fragile.

Since our first rainy days the weather has been good to us: generally sunny though blurred with the haze of spring, warm but not hot, and only occasionally with gusty winds that whip our sedge hats, trying to sail them across the fields. Then the cord under the chin strains tight and we clutch the rim with our free hand. But today the breeze is gentle.

Once in a while we see a henro-stone—a survivor along this concrete highway—one of the stone markers that point the way, many of them placed long ago by holy men. We walk beside a river, passing on our left the beginning of the path up to Twenty. Then we enter a valley. There are sawmills and tangerine-canning plants along the road. The grade becomes noticeable and the peaks begin to close in on us. We come upon a henro-stone and take a path off to the right.

A henro-stone
marking the route

It is a climb but not a hard one, on the pleasantest kind of path to walk, earth packed firm by generations of farmers. For much of the way we move through tangerine groves. Higher, where we get vistas of the terraced valley and the far-ranging mountains, the path is bordered by buttercups and violets, by dandelions, which are friendly here though spiteful in my own garden, and by clumps of wild iris. The valley narrows and becomes a canyon. Our path clings to its side, close to sheer drops. On the opposite face we spot a waterfall, a slender sparkling strand.

We reach the head of the canyon. Here it has pinched to a rocky gorge filled with a tumbling stream that we cross on a wooden bridge painted bright orange, pausing on it when we see in the shadows a stone statue of the Daishi as a pilgrim. From here a tree-shaded path lined with thirty-three stone images of Kannon brings us to a level area carved into the side of the mountain. The hall before us clearly has a roof of thatch but it is covered by sheet metal painted the same gay orange as the bridge. It's a traditional color for temples and perhaps it's one that the tangerine-growing supporters of the temple have an affection for, but one becomes accustomed to weathered unpainted wood and black tile: I blink.

This is the Daishi Hall and priest's residence. Here we will spend the night. Cliffs overhang us. High up there is a cave where legend says the Daishi meditated, and up there is the main hall. It is past four o'clock and I, at least, am tired; we decide to postpone our visit to the main hall and cave until tomorrow morning. The priest nods and shows us to our room next to the altar. It is comfortable and pleasant here; we are told they can accommodate a hundred but tonight we are the only guests.

During the night I am wakened by rain beating on the metal roof; the foot or more of thatch beneath the metal cannot muffle the sound. It is still pouring when it comes time to get up and it is chilly on this mountain. I bundle up for the trip to the cave.

We climb through a gray cloud, a diminished world: following Morikawa I can just make out the figure of the priest who leads us. Accents of yellow-green appear and disappear, the new foliage of spring. The priest pauses where the path jogs around two great pines. It's said they were planted by Kobo Daishi, he tells us, and their furrowed trunks look old enough—husband and wife, linked by a Shinto ceremonial rope hung with strips of white paper angularly cut.

We reach the main hall, a simple building, cold and damp this morning, where the priest leads us in a short service. He takes us then to a shed, a kind of changing room, and gives us each a coarse white gown. We might get wet, he says, implying that they are to protect our clothing, but I assume they are ceremonial. I am already wrapped in a sweater, a jacket, my rubberized rain jacket and trousers, and my henro robe; the new robe scarcely fits over all that.

He leads us up a path cut into the face of the mountain, unlocks a sturdy door across a rift in the rocks. Inside we climb a ten-foot steel ladder, move across a ledge, enter a fissure. I had expected to be shown a sizable cave containing some stone images. Instead, for the first time in my life, I am spelunking. Holding a candle, switching it from hand to hand as he directs, we squeeze through crevasses, left side or right side first, arms held overhead or down, as he instructs. We duck low, lie on our sides to inch along twisting tunnels. Two or three times I think I am stuck, manage to wriggle free and go on. I am ridiculously dressed for this: I should have shed my bulky clothing.

We emerge into a large chamber. I have made it, I think. The priest points out natural formations that bear a likeness to Buddhist deities. As in most caves, it takes a bit of imagination to see the resemblances. Then the priest starts squeezing through another passage. I manage to follow into a second chamber where we are shown a dragon sculpted by nature, probably accounting for a legend, occasionally heard, that Kobo Daishi sealed a dragon in this cave.

There is one more chamber, the priest says, the one where the Daishi meditated, and he slips into another fissure, calling back his instructions on how to twist and stoop and squeeze. I follow. On one maneuver, sideways in a half crouch, I become stuck. I squirm and strain, I feel the seam of my rain trousers split, but it is no use. I cannot get through. I call to Morikawa to go on and wriggle back with my guttering candle to keep company with the dragon. Morikawa tells me, when they return, that the final sanctum is slightly larger but much like the first.

The priest leads us out by a different way, a low tunnel—no tight places but we have to crawl on hands and knees, "like babies, because we have sinned." Outside he tells us that this cave and an aery pinnacle at Temple Forty-five, where Kobo Daishi is also said to have meditated, are the two most difficult spots of the pilgrimage. I agree. He adds, gratuitously it seems to me, that they are testing places, barrier gates. Alas, I have failed both, for previously I lost my nerve at Forty-five: I knew I could get up there but I wasn't sure I could get down again without losing my footing and plunging three or four hundred feet. Perhaps this time around . . .

Back at the Daishi Hall we shoulder our packs and start down toward the valley. It is past one o'clock when we begin the climb to Temple Twenty; the rain has not let up. The path is muddy and slippery and where the feet of generations of pilgrims have worn it into the mountain it is a gully filled with a torrent of brown water. Tosa muttered that it is so steep "one's chest hits the rise ahead" and told of a man who escaped from prison in 1952, aiming to seek refuge at the temple above; about halfway he gave up and meekly went back to jail. The 1819 diarist and his friend grew exasperated; their guidebook gave the distance in the old Japanese measure called *cho* and they watched for the stones that marked them off: "We felt that in this case every cho was too long and Hikobei proposed that we measure them ourselves. It took us 335 steps to go one cho and since usually 180 steps is enough, the cho here are almost double the usual." Morikawa and I recall that some of those stone markers are dated 1365; they have guided henro for more than six centuries but neither of us is inclined to stop in the rain and examine them closely.

We reach the temple rain soaked and cold, debate whether to stop for the night, foolishly decide to push on to Twenty-one.

It is harder going down the other side of the mountain than it was climbing up. The path is rougher and today the footing is precarious; I am continually bracing and braking and sometimes I fall. We finally reach the river. I peer through the rain but am unable to pick out the house where Priest Mizuno and I stayed and met Mr. and Mrs. Ishii. Cross the bridge, start up again; for a short while it is easy, a wide trail used by the villagers who work in the mountains. Then the climbing begins in earnest, alongside a stream that races down a rocky course—surely the same stream the Daishi followed when he ascended this mountain to invoke Kokuzo on its summit. This path up to Temple Twenty-one is steeper, rougher, and longer than the one up to Twenty; today it is more treacherous.

We take consolation from knowing that we are not the first to find this section of the henro-path difficult. Down one mountain and up another, it is traditionally one of the toughest stretches of the pilgrimage, one of its tests. Folklorists say that physical trials like this, trying the henro's will and stamina, were the original

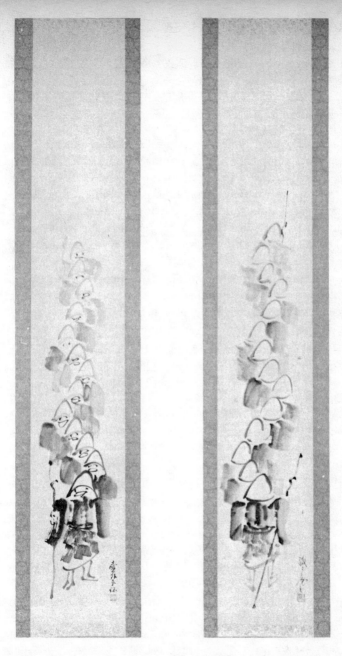

"Down one mountain and up another." *(paintings by Kogai Gyokusen)*

"barrier gates," an idea that only later was given a religious gloss and focused on temples like Nineteen.

For a long time—from the seventeenth century into the twentieth—the pilgrimage was in many districts the coming-of-age rite. Especially in Iyo and in Hiroshima across the Inland Sea, neither young men nor young women were considered ready for marriage until they had completed the pilgrimage, endured its physical trials, and been tempered by its asceticism. (Some who were poor ran all the way—a feat that seems almost incredible to me—since by shortening the time they could cut their expenses.) Bands of young folk, happy pilgrims, used to be seen often along the path. When they got home there was a congratulatory party and they were accepted as adults.

We strain upward, wet and chilled. It is almost dark when we reach the steps up to the main gate. Across the lightless compound the residence is shuttered tight against the night and the weather. We ring the bell and wait. The young priest who answers, a caretaker in the absence of the chief priest, is taken aback to see us. He remembers that Morikawa phoned to make a reservation but we were not expected so late and in such a rain. He and his wife and an elderly couple who have served the temple for years scurry to make a bath and fix some dinner for us. We are embarrassed to have discomfited them and yet, huddling over a hibachi in the dim light of one naked bulb in a room where all the cold of the night seems to have concentrated, we are grateful to be at this temple dedicated to Kokuzo, on this mountaintop where the Daishi struggled toward enlightenment.

Later, when we have been fed and made comfortable, we speculate as to exactly where the misadventures of a boy named Utakichi began. It was "in the mountains of Awa" that his foster mother died, leaving him alone on the henro-path and easy prey. But let him tell his own story as he recounted it in a deposition to officials when he finally got back to his home in Tosa. Somewhat abbreviated, it runs like this:

"I am Utakichi, aged fourteen. I was born in a village in

western Tosa, close to the border of Iyo. When I was still a baby my father died. When I was five or six my mother remarried and moved to another village. I was adopted by a distant relative in my home village; I have not seen my mother since.

"My foster father was seriously ill as a boy but recovered thanks to his pilgrimage of Shikoku. My foster mother too had recovered from illness as a result of her pilgrimage. Both wanted to make another pilgrimage of thanksgiving but he could not obtain permission from the authorities, and so my foster mother set out with me—I was eleven then—and her own son, just three years old. We passed through the border gate and began to visit the pilgrimage temples in Iyo.

"When we were near Matsuyama City my little stepbrother fell ill with a high fever. A henro who was a physician examined the boy and told us he had smallpox; that same night he died at his mother's breast. It was a tragedy but there was no help for it; after the burial my foster mother and I continued our pilgrimage. She was deep in sorrow: she could not sleep at night and every young one she saw reminded her of her lost child. She suffered a relapse of her chronic stomach disease and in the mountains of Awa she died. I had no money but the people there were kind enough to arrange a funeral and the priest of the local temple issued a mortuary tablet bearing her posthumous name and the date of her death.

"I was now so lonely and perplexed I didn't know what to do. The headman told me that the best way for me to get home was to follow the pilgrimage route and so I set out as a mendicant henro, telling passersby my situation and appealing for sympathy. Some gave me fifty copper coins and some a hundred, so that after a few days of begging I was able to change my coppers into a silver coin, which I carried wrapped up with my foster mother's mortuary tablet." Utakichi must have been an engaging tyke: he had already collected enough money to see him all the way home.

"Carrying this bundle on my back, I went on my way. It was then I met a henro monk who told me that in the mountains a temple was holding a festival where I could easily beg money. He offered to guide me there and I followed him without suspicion. At a deserted place in the mountains he told me that during my long journey I must have picked up lice and that I should undress so he could examine me. I took off my clothes, whereupon he gathered them up and made off with them, including the wrapper with the memorial tablet and my coin. When I ran after him protesting, he threatened to tie me to a tree and leave me helpless. He threw me a kind of undershirt made out of towels and disappeared.

"Fortunately at the next village people gave me some used clothing and I was able to continue. It was then I fell in with a henro about thirty-five years old. He kept me close company. He identified himself as Eizo of Matsuyama. He said his father was an evil character who, when he got drunk as he often did, beat people up and even decapitated statues of Jizo. Eizo explained that he felt obligated to atone for his father's misdeeds and consequently was making a pilgrimage through all the sixty-six provinces of Japan. Since he was going through Tosa he offered to take me right to my home and he was so sincere and friendly that I felt at ease." He was more than friendly: he made the boy his lover. Utakichi was probably neither surprised nor reluctant; he wanted to get home.

"After entering Tosa at the eastern barrier gate we visited the pilgrimage temples one by one until we came to Number Thirty-seven. There Eizo told me that the main route to the next temple was far roundabout and we had better take a shortcut. We went through the mountains for ten days. It seemed to me that we must be near my home village but Eizo said we hadn't come nearly that far. We reached the sea and took a boat. I raised doubts about this but he said we could get very close to the next temple that way. When we reached port I asked where we were and he told me we had crossed to Kyushu. To my reproaches he replied that he had to go there and he had no choice but to deceive me for he could not part with me. I prayed to the gods to bring me safely home but meantime I could do nothing but obey and follow him." In truth, Utakichi had become a complaisant, even eager, lover.

They made a complete tour of Kyushu, worshiping at all the major temples and shrines, and then returned to the same port. "I beseeched Eizo to take me home but he was silent. You see, I traveled with Eizo a long time and I got to know his character. Believing that sooner or later he would bring me back to Tosa and remembering the frightening experience of traveling alone, I put myself in his hands."

Slowly they worked their way up Honshu. Eizo outfitted his young companion in the robes of a pilgrim to the sixty-six provinces, and Utakichi wavered between pride in his new clothes and worry that he was even more deeply obligated. In Kyoto they visited the great temples. They went up to Mount Koya. They walked north along the Sea of Japan, crossed the Japan Alps, lingered three weeks in the shogun's capital, Edo, and then, though winter was coming, kept pushing north. One of Eizo's feet became infected; in the mountains at year's end he could no longer walk.

"Village officials kindly provided a place for him to rest and I stayed there with him. One night two wild monks forced their way in and stole the seals and inscriptions of all the temples and shrines we had visited. After that I was told to move to the home of a rich farmer named Magozaemon but every day I visited Eizo, bringing the food that Magozaemon gave me for him. As the weeks went by Eizo's condition grew steadily worse. In the Third Month he died.

"Officials summoned me and questioned me and I told them my whole story. They found it hard to believe but I convinced them. In the meantime Magozaemon and his wife were ever so kind to me; they let me sleep in the same room with them and they offered to adopt me as their son and even give me a share of their land. After all my bitter experiences it was like paradise.

"Then one day I was summoned again and the officials told me that a man of my own province had come to get me. He was a man of high position and I was afraid of him. More than that, it grieved me to leave Magozaemon and his wife, whom I loved so much. But I had to go. The man took me to the Edo mansion of the Tosa authorities, and in due time I was sent back to my native place.

"Since all our seals and inscriptions were stolen I have no evidence to support my story. I have tried to remember the names of the shrines and temples Eizo and I visited but I can't remember them all. I really had no choice but to go with him, I was so afraid of traveling alone. I was timid from birth: as a child I was afraid to go alone to the toilet at night.

"I want to express my gratitude to the authorities for sending me home by ship."

Descending from Twenty-one we cross a valley and wind over a hill. From the crest we look down on a huge bamboo grove rippling in graygreen waves. Then we are walking through that grove. Our path runs the middle slope: above and below us bamboos thrust their slender leaves high overhead. The mountainside, terraced with bamboo logs, is clean of brush, covered only with last season's brown fallen leaves, lovely background for the celadon tones of the segmented trunks. For me bamboo has magic. I would like to live by a grove like this, to have within sight its clean, lithe beauty and within hearing the whispers of the wind through its leaves. We find a man and wife cleaning a harvest of bamboo shoots for market; they tell us the grove is theirs and I envy them.

Most of the old henro-path from Twenty-two to Twenty-three has become a heavily traveled national highway. To avoid it—after we meet Obaasan and she guides us to her village's bangai—we cut over to the coast, a bit longer that way but a small price to pay for escaping the ambush of noise and diesel fumes. Our quiet road dips and climbs between the sea and abrupt forested hills to a craggy point where it mounts to a ledge carved in the rock. We round the bluff and across almost a mile of blue bay behold a sweep of beach, the roofs of the town of Hiwasa, and on a hill behind it the colorful tower of Temple Twenty-three.

The road slopes downward now and the old man coming toward us on a bicycle is pedaling hard to make his way up. Startled, he dismounts. "Astonishing!" he exclaims, "How rare! How extraordinary!"—doubly surprised at seeing two henro on foot and then finding one of them a foreigner. He gets out his purse to give us settai and tells us that he made the pilgrimage when he was young. After we part we look back several times to see him walking his bike and looking back at us. He is still murmuring to himself. "Astonishing!"

We climb down to the broad and gently curving beach. Far back in time a breed of giant sea turtles determined that it should be their incubator and despite the harassments of man they stubbornly persist. Each summer, beginning in late May, a few hundred females, each more than four feet long and three wide, appear from the sea and make their way up the beach. Each digs a hole in the warm sand, and with tears streaming from her eyes, deposits about a hundred and fifty eggs, covers them, and returns to the sea. The eggs are already fertilized, for the turtles have intercourse in the sea, floating on the surface, taking their time. In August and September hundreds of baby turtles emerge from the sand and crawl toward their ocean home. Until a few years ago townspeople and tourists ravaged the eggs and the newly hatched young, but now the town government tries to protect them and has reduced the mortality rate. Those that survive grow to maturity in about fifteen years and live to an age of a hundred twenty or thirty. Japanese folklore, which takes them as a symbol of longevity, claims for them a life of ten thousand years, but this is stretching the facts a bit.

We walk through the town to the temple, conscious of its enormous appeal. It is one of the most popular of the eighty-eight; more than half a million people visit it annually, many from far away. Morikawa has a mission to perform: he has been carrying forty-two coins entrusted to him by a cousin to be offered at this temple.

There are barriers at temples, there were barriers at the borders of provinces, and there is another kind of barrier that almost every Japanese is to some degree concerned about, though today they may deprecate their uneasiness. It is the matter of critical or unlucky ages. Temples and shrines all over the country offer protection against these years; one of the most famous is this that we are approaching, Twenty-three of the pilgrimage.

Morikawa mentions the prevalent legend that when Kobo Daishi was forty-two, the unluckiest of all ages for a man, he peregrinated Shikoku establishing the pilgrimage in order to combat the misfortunes threatening him that year. (One bit of lore says there are eighty-eight temples because that number is the sum of the unluckiest ages: forty-two for men, thirty-three for women, and thirteen for children.) But by Japanese count the Daishi was forty-two in the year 815 and it stretches credulity to think he walked Shikoku that year. As his biographer points out, he was then sought after both at the court and among the people; he was exchanging poems with the emperor, holding services in the capital, responding to requests for epitaphs. Moreover this was the period when he was writing his basic doctrines. Wandering Shikoku? We recall the priest who said to us with a trace of impatience, "Look, he was just too busy!" True, but it is pointless to argue against a folk belief. That is evident as we approach the long flights of steps leading up to the temple. Even knowing what to expect I am surprised by the crowds.

The temple has published a pamphlet that gives a comprehensive list of the dangerous years: "The years of Great Danger are for men 41, 42, and 61, and for women, 32, 33, and 61; for both sexes the years of Lesser Danger are 1, 6, 7, 15, 16, 19, 24, 25, 28, 34, 37, 43, 46, 51, 52, 55, 60, 64, 69, 70, 78, 79, and 82." We study the instructions. The ritual begins at the final flights of steps: "Persons at the age of Great or Lesser Danger who wish to turn aside the danger of misfortune should visit the temple on an auspicious day. On their arrival they should buy a pair of new straw sandals and when they come to the danger-hill—the men to the men's flight of forty-two steps and the women to the women's flight of thirty-three steps—they should put on these sandals and climb the steps, laying upon every step a coin." Today the steps are almost covered with coins, though the women seem to have outnumbered the men.

The pamphlet offers a note of explanation—"In order to drive out danger, there are buried in the danger-hill one thousand copies of the Yakushi sutra, each character written on a pebble"—and then continues its instructions: "One must leave one's sandals at the top of the hill and in the Hall of Votive Pictures take up the

Steps to Temple Twenty-three *(a print by Kadowaki)*

pestle and strike upon the mortar containing incense exactly as many times as there are years in one's true age. Then one must worship at all the other chapels of the temple." At the last chapel one is to strike its bell as many times as one's age and then "offer in the main hall a danger-banishing charm. Finally one should go to the office and order danger-banishing prayers."

Morikawa forgoes the new sandals and simplifies the procedure somewhat but he fulfills his responsibility. I offer a prayer for the young man I last saw praying at this temple, the young fellow who fled Tokyo and a potato chip factory for the henro-path on Shikoku. I pray that his quest was rewarded.

Then we sit for a while in front of the Daishi Hall, lazing in the late afternoon sun as pestle and bell are struck in the background. Below is the town, embraced by green hills: patterns of gray and red tile roofs, white accents of fishing boats moored in the river. Legend after legend explains the existence of this temple and its power to shepherd believers through the ominous years, but idly I wonder if the temple's power and its presence here may be somehow related to the reality of those awesome turtles, their fabled longevity, and their inborn drive to continue their kind, which spring after spring brings them back to the warm white sand of that special beach.

We have worshiped at the last temple in Awa and we have plodded another twenty miles or so along a national highway. Almost without realizing it, for there are only small markers at the border, we leave Awa and enter Tosa Province.

It did not use to be so easy. At this point in the old days henro faced the Tosa barrier gate. All those wishing to enter the fief were strictly examined. Henro were given a hard time.

They had, of course, to present a valid travel permit, issued with the approval of their own fief, signed and sealed by local functionaries and the priest of their home temple, specifically authorizing them to tour the sacred places of Shikoku. Tosa officials at the guardhouse would receive this with distaste and scrutinize it carefully. They would demand to see money, evidence that the henro would not have to beg his or her way across Tosa, "thus draining away the wealth of the province." They would ask questions, trying to screen out undesirables: the sick and diseased; beggars and ruffians in henro guise; and most of all, spies. Each fief kept vigil against secret agents from other fiefs. Then, after the early seventeenth century, they were all apprehensive about the agents of the central government, the shogunate. It maintained a vast spy apparatus to check on the semi-autonomous lords of the provinces, the daimyo. Were they engaged in unauthorized military buildup? Was there any hint of rebellious thought? Were they mindful of their subjects' well-being? Spies were at the top of any fief's list of unwanted visitors.

At last, if the officials at the barrier gate could find no reason to reject the pilgrim, they would issue a permit to travel through their land. It would specify that only thirty days were allowed and warn that overstaying would bring punishment when leaving the province; it would restrict travel to the prescribed henro-path and forbid wandering into byways (where alms might be more generously given to pilgrims, or gulls more readily found by sharpsters, or information more easily gathered by spies). Finally, reluctantly, the henro would be allowed into Tosa, assured that he was not welcome.

Not surprisingly, many henro tried to sneak across the border. Tosa guards were on the watch for them. Illegal entrants caught inside the province were whipped—forty, fifty, a hundred lashes— and deported. Repeaters, or those guilty of thieving or swindling— selling "magic" medicines or talismans—were branded on the arms or cheeks so that they might never again pass unrecognized.

In a formal scheme of things devised by priests to reinforce the idea that henro should begin their pilgrimage at Temple Number One, Awa was labeled "the province for spiritual awakening"; in Iyo and Sanuki, the third and fourth provinces, the consecrated pilgrim would approach enlightenment and Buddhahood, but only after hard labor in Tosa—Tosa was "the province for ascetic discipline." Morikawa and I speculate as to which came first: was it the concept that the second province should be the arena for hard training, or was it the fact that Tosa was least hospitable of the provinces?

Even today, Tosa is different. The other three provinces of Shikoku face the Inland Sea, a land-gentled sea studded with a thousand islands. Tosa is the other side of Shikoku. Cut off by a barrier of mountains, until recent times remote and difficult to reach except by hazardous sea routes, it faces the open Pacific. When its seamen left their harbors they knew that "Henceforth there is no island to run to." Here developed the Tosa character: independent, individualistic, proud, intrepid, stubborn—strong-minded men given to vigorous speech. Awa nurtured the ballad-drama; Tosa raised fighting dogs. Logical, practical, not religious, producing relatively few henro themselves, the people of Tosa generally shared their rulers' distaste for the grubby pilgrims in their midst. The henro faced indifference if not disapproval; he felt as though he were making a pilgrimage into enemy territory; in his special vocabulary he coined a phrase for Tosa: it was "the land of demons."

> Tosa is the devil's land—
> No lodging there, we understand.

Of course this is too harsh an epithet, though it gained currency. Not all the people of Tosa rebuffed the henro, but a welcome and settai were generally found only around the pilgrimage temples and they were few. The long road through Tosa is more than a third of the pilgrimage, yet along it are only sixteen numbered temples, less than a fifth of the eighty-eight.

Even those oases of warmth were a source of disappointment to fief officials. In a memorandum of 1810 that is typical of the directives they issued in a steady stream, they sighed that in spite of strict ordinances and their repeated remonstrations, "there is no end to henro who stray from the prescribed route and who, in some cases, feign illness to stay longer than scheduled, or practice exorcism, or sell fake medicines, or conduct gambling, or commit thievery. This is because the villagers in the neighborhood of the pilgrimage temples are such stout worshipers of Kobo Daishi that they show extraordinary kindness to henro, even to the extent of overlooking suspicious behavior." But when it came to reporting rascally henro, other villages too were lax: "Being loath to use the complicated procedure for making reports to the authorities, they neglect their duty." In short, they disliked red tape.

On the other hand, the officials also issued directives that henro who fell ill must be properly cared for until they recovered, and that children orphaned on the way by the death of parents who had brought them must be kindly treated while arrangements were made to send them home. "Negligence of these duties is inexcusable"—the people of Tosa were not inhuman. And though settai was deplored, it was permissible "to spare small coins or a handful of rice to henro who travel on the authorized route begging for alms." The henro's problem was to find someone who was willing to stretch permissible into advisable. In Tosa it was axiomatic that one must rise early in the morning to seek alms. The first at the door might get something; later supplicants would not be so lucky.

This attitude was still evident half a century ago according to Alfred Bohner. Bohner, a German, was teaching in Matsuyama; in 1927 he made the pilgrimage and wrote a book about it. Yet as I read his account I wonder whether his antipathy to Tosa hadn't been inculcated by his Matsuyama friends. I have told Morikawa my first impression of Tosa.

Priest Mizuno and I had come by train and bus from Hiwasa and Temple Twenty-three to Muroto and Temple Twenty-four (I did not then realize that the essence of the pilgrimage lies in walking it). We had a good talk with the priest and then walked on. It was late afternoon when we reached Temple Twenty-five. It looked like rain and I was ready to stop. Also I was hungry for vegetables, our recent diet having consisted of not much but rice, and so at a shop in the town I had bought large bunches of spinach and carrots. The priest who appeared several moments after we rang the bell was brusque, it seemed to me. He summoned a much younger priest and departed. After the usual discussion necessary to establish that I did not require Western food, the young man said that we could stay and accepted my purchases. The food at the temple was vegetarian, he remarked; there was no objection to preparing vegetables. He showed us to an upstairs room.

I was concerned that the head priest was going to be uncooperative about talking with us, so I asked Mizuno to press for an interview soon. The request was shunted aside with word that we were about to be served tea. A second appeal was smothered in the announcement that our bath was ready. After bathing I changed to fresh underclothes and felt better.

We were shown then to a downstairs room overlooking a little garden with a pool containing orange and white carp. The head priest appeared, now the soul of cordiality. He made tea for us himself and he talked freely and knowledgeably about his temple. I could not have asked for more.

Then, in the same handsome room, came dinner. There were my spinach and carrots, beautifully prepared, but all kinds of other vegetables too: bamboo sprouts, tender fernlike shoots, and other things I cannot name. There was a huge bowl of red-ripe tomatoes and chopped cabbage—a salad never looked so good. There was *sashimi* of tuna, uncooked, fresh from the sea a few hundred yards away. And as a final blow to vegetarianism there was *tataki,* my first taste of one of the great dishes of Japan, a special food of Tosa. The young priest—we knew by then that he was the head priest's adopted son and son-in-law—sat and chatted with us as we ate. He explained how tataki is prepared. A filet from a choice bonito is lightly toasted over a fire; there are differing opinions about what should fuel the fire, he said, but he held with those purists who insist that it must be pine needles. While being delicately browned but by no means cooked, it is beaten with straws to imbue the flavor of the fragrant smoke (beaten with straws—rather like being tickled to death). It is served in a special soy sauce laced with garlic. I am afraid I ate immoderately. Dessert was sliced apples and summer oranges which the young man peeled and sectioned for us.

In a period of three or four hours I had been made a partisan of Tosa and I have remained one. I have insisted to Morikawa that we spend a night at that temple. The problem is that a faulty memory and a too hasty reading of my notes has made me think that the temple was Twenty-six, not Twenty-five. Anyway, Morikawa and I have decided that we are not meeting and talking with enough other henro—walking henro, like us—so we have given our-

Tosa fishermen catching bonito *(a print by Hiroshige)*

selves a very easy schedule around Muroto: a night at East Temple, Twenty-four, right at the cape; a night at Port Temple, Twenty-five, only four miles away; and another night at West Temple, Twenty-six, little more than three miles farther. That should give us plenty of time to accost fellow henro.

We do meet one couple at Twenty-four. The man, retired from business in Tokyo, says he previously walked the entire pilgrimage but because his wife is with him this time they sometimes take a bus. They are making the pilgrimage simply to give thanks that life has been good to them.

Arriving very early at Port Temple we climb a sharp slope to the main hall, small and plain. Incense offered by fishermen's wives with their morning prayers is still burning in the urns. How many wives have climbed this hill to pray for the safety of their men? And how many have come here for solace?

Down by the priest's residence we loll in the compound, catching up on our diaries, waiting for henro. One finally appears: the same one we chatted with in Awa, the man with a hole in his heart; somewhere along the line we passed him without knowing. We begin to understand: the reason we encounter so few walking henro is that there are so few.

A round-faced priest appears and, seating himself in the open window where he inscribes albums, joins us in waiting. We move over to talk with him. He tells us the temple legends and its more recent history. And then he smiles the quizzical smile of someone who feels he ought to be recognized. At that moment a young priest comes out the door to welcome us. Suddenly I realize where I am. It was at this temple, not at Twenty-six, that Mizuno and I were so warmly entertained. I feel foolish.

But our stretched-out schedule has only happy consequences. It results in our staying the next night at West Temple, privileged guests at its annual festival and revealing of the statue of Kobo Daishi. And here we are received like old friends. Our packs and gear are at once moved from the henro quarters upstairs to the family's garden room where Mizuno and I feasted. I am given snapshots of the two of us standing with the family in front of the Daishi Hall, starting out from here the following morning in rain;

they have held the photos against the day I should reappear. The young priest takes us to tour the port. He shows us the market shed where the day's catch is being packed in ice for shipment; he points out the small boats that fish the warm currents offshore for bonito and mackerel, the big craft that make six- or seven-month voyages after tuna into the Indian Ocean, the Tasman Sea, even the Atlantic. Once, but no longer, whales could be hunted just outside the harbor. A henro who made the pilgrimage in 1884 kept a diary that is seldom quotable because he usually confined himself to a laconic listing of temples and lodgings, but here he got carried away. "Walking from East Temple to Port Temple we saw a whale being caught. We canceled our afternoon schedule, took lodgings, and watched the fishermen carve up the whale in the sea. As they did, scores of local housewives jumped into the sea and tried to cut meat from the dismembered carcass. Angry fishermen brandished bamboo poles to drive away the women, who did not flinch. They were like flies on the back of an ox. Some were beaten and injured about the head. It was an interesting sight."

After coffee we walk back to the temple. I did not think it possible but we are wrapped in even greater hospitality than before. Two heavy easy chairs are lugged into the garden room for us. The day has been overcast but now the sun breaks through, slanting across the hillside, picking out bursts of bloom, azaleas in pink, lavender, rose, white. Buses have arrived and white-robed henro climb to the main hall, the bells at their waists tinkling. They will be staying here tonight.

The young priest joins us for dinner, bearing a tray laden with beer, a fine whiskey, and Hennessy brandy. We feast; Morikawa and I both indulge in double portions of tataki. The bus henro are eating in a big room nearby, but not nearly so we

The head priest joins us after dinner. He has been drinking and is jovial. "I used to drink a bottle of saké every evening," he says, "but the doctor told me I was threatened with diabetes so I switched to whiskey and lemon."

His son-in-law asks us to go into town again "for just one drink." I beg off—the day has been full enough for me—but Morikawa joins him and I am left alone. There is no point in trying to sleep: the head priest is now boisterously entertaining the group of henro.

In indicting Tosa as "the devil's land," Mr. Bohner cited a 1901 brawl at this temple between two hundred henro and three or four priests. Those were the days before a fixed fee had been established for album inscriptions. The henro thought they were being overcharged and the priests "had answered a request for reconsideration in a very unholy way by insulting the pilgrims." There is another roar of laughter from the henro quarters, I think of all the kindness that has been heaped on me here, and I say to myself that there have been changes.

18 Does it seem contradictory that the province which was the most inhospitable to henro has produced Shikoku's most complete records of the pilgrimage as it used to be? Perhaps it is merely that modern Tosa—now named Kochi—has been graced with a superior group of social historians. They painstakingly assembled the diaries of Tosa henro from which I have been quoting, the directives concerning henro that fief officials issued in a steady stream over a period of two hundred years, and the records of henro who in one way or another got into trouble in Tosa.

The afternoon that we left Temple Twenty-six—its fete was still in full swing but we felt we had to push on—we walked between the shore and a ridge of hills. Sometimes the ocean was visible, stretching empty to the horizon—"no island to run to"; sometimes it was cut off by a seawall or by scrub bamboo planted as a windbreak.

We walked through a village of inviting old-fashioned houses, a place that takes pride in tradition. We came upon a goldfish peddler negotiating with a knot of intent young customers. He was attired in a sedge hat and a dark blue *happi* coat with a bold design dyed on the back, a figure out of the past.

Henro-stones marking the route

A figure out of the present was a woman driving a small pickup truck, vending produce from house to house. She pulled to the side of the road when she saw us and, smiling, announced that she wanted to give us some tangerines as settai. We would welcome a handful, we told her, but she insisted on filling a big bag and then, jauntily waving, drove off. As we walked we ate as many as we could but Morikawa, as junior partner, was left with a heavy sack to carry. (Eight days later, in one of those happy coincidences that seemed to mark our pilgrimage, we encountered the same woman and enjoyed a lively conversation with her as she walked her dog along a riverbank on a Sunday morning.)

The town where we stayed that night was where the 1819 diarist and his friend Hikobei wound up their pilgrimage. Their home was near (though we don't know precisely where because the first page of the diary is lost) and for them Twenty-six had been the last of the eighty-eight. They had spent the night at the village we found so pleasantly old-fashioned, and Hikobei fell off the wagon, "but he had kept his pledge of abstinence throughout the pilgrimage."

Their pilgrimage had taken them fifty-seven days. "I had sent a letter home, informing my family of my return. So in expectation of a party to welcome us we passed the time taking saké offered by Matsubashiya Eibei. Then we visited Kinshichi of Osada and were treated to more saké. While we were there our welcome party arrived—Gonjuro and his wife, who were leading a horse, and Tsunehachi, Tadasuke, Yoshihei, and Ofuji. We all took saké together. Then I mounted the horse, Kinschichi sending one of his men with us to carry our baggage, and we merrily started home. Many along the way welcomed us back. In the evening we had a spree at my house with saké and dishes prepared by Gonjuro. I had long missed tataki."

They had another party the next day and then the diary lists page after page of welcome-home gifts: rice and fish and enough saké to have drowned the horse. Two and a half weeks before they started out, fief officials had circulated a ban on welcome-home parties: they were "a showy folly" and they "violated every principle of austere living." Tosa people did not let their government intimidate them.

The next morning Morikawa and I have a chance to reflect on the somber side of the pilgrimage. We pass the place where, on an autumn day in 1869, a henro from Tokyo was found lying ill at the roadside. He was carried to a farmhouse where it was discovered that he had no pass, having entered Tosa illegally. He was treated by a doctor but died two days later, "thus absolved," as the record put it, "from the punishment he otherwise could not have escaped."

Another item concerns the resident of a village not far off. "Last year he met a henro priest in the mountains and was given some charms. Since then he has been advertising himself as 'a man of miracles.' He has swindled his fellow villagers and even cut off women's hair," thus presumably conferring nunhood upon them. He was meted forty lashes and an indeterminate period of confinement to the local area.

Now we begin to see what I have been watching for: bold inscriptions, mounted and hanging on the wall the way the Japanese display a prized example of calligraphy, but these are brushed in English. The first one I spot is at Temple Thirty-two:

PEACE AND INTERNATIONAL FRIENDSHIP
FREDERICK STARR
TAISHO 10. 3. 4.

I know the name. Starr was a professor of anthropology at my university, Chicago. He had retired before I got there but he was a legend. He was, I am certain, the first foreigner to perform the pilgrimage. "Taisho 10. 3. 4." is March 4, 1921.

"I was about fifteen years old when he came," the priest remembers. "As my father and he talked, I served tea. He said that the Shikoku pilgrimage was the only religious pilgrimage left in Japan; the others had become tourist jaunts. He spoke of his admiration for Kobo Daishi."

As we walk I tell Morikawa something about Frederick Starr—I try but I am not sure that the man is translatable. Japanese professors are expected to be long on dignity and short on ebullience. Starr was an irrepressible little bantam of a man who said that dignity was something no one with any force need bother about. He didn't lecture; he talked to his classes, sitting on his desk swinging his feet. Generations of students adored him, including those who registered for his classes in order to cover his pronouncements for the Chicago newspapers, to whom he was a reliable source of good copy. He fumed about spies in his classroom, professed indignation that his lectures were pilfered, but his scrapbooks appear to contain every word ever printed about him.

And how could the newspapers, from New York to San Francisco, resist a savant who, for example, called the female sex barbarians? "Women are not civilized," he declaimed. "Furthermore they should not be civilized. What is more, they can't be." In a women's magazine he carried the war to the foe: "Can anyone," he wrote in *Redbook*, "can anyone anywhere actually point to a single first-class achievement in literature, in science, in art by woman?"

No wonder the *New York World* devoted columns to him under the headline THE QUEEREST PROFESSOR IN THE COUNTRY (this being in 1902, when the word "queer" was still straight). Some of the QUEER THINGS HE HAS SAID were that "ten times too many persons go to college nowadays, wasting not only their own time but that of their teachers as well" and that "a thousand years from now all food will be in concentrated, pre-digested form and teeth will be superfluous." The *World* went on to call him a prodigious scholar and an admirable teacher. Which he was.

The newspapers really had fun with him after his 1904 trip to Japan. The occasion was a commission from St. Louis's world's fair, the Louisiana Purchase Exposition, to bring from Japan's northern island of Hokkaido some "hairy Ainus" for its exhibits of primitive people. Starr obliged with a party of four men, three women, and two children, a timber Ainu house, and a collection of Ainu objects; they were one of the fair's big hits. But he made bigger headlines with the opinions he brought back. He was in Tokyo the day that war was declared between Japan and Russia; he returned proclaiming that Japan would win. Editorial writers and military experts all over the country hooted at this preposterous notion.

They were convulsed when he amplified his remarks. The war was not between nations, he said, but between races: Japan's victory would signal the ultimate supremacy of the yellow race. "Every race has its day, just as every dog has his, and the day of the white race is about done. The yellow race is slowly and surely moving toward that great part it is to play in the world's history. Japan is opening the way for this progress, but she will not ultimately be the supreme nation. China is without doubt destined to hold this position. It has the latent power. In time it will rule the world."

On this visit, he said, he was struck by the innate power of the Japanese as a people; their life was more "real." And in words he must later have regretted, he contributed his bit to the Hearstian campaign against "the yellow peril"; we had taught them too well: "We should beware, then, lest this knowledge be used against us."

For he became a dedicated Japanophile. His prime areas of study had been the Congo and Mexico but it was Japan he fell in love with.

A generous university seems to have given him all the time he wanted for work in the field; he came back to Japan every year or two to spend six months, eight months, a whole year. Each time he arrived he hurried off his ship to a traditional Japanese inn and changed into Japanese clothes from the skin out; he didn't get into Western clothes again until he left Japan, no matter what the occasion (he designed his own crest for his kimono, a star in a circle). He never learned the language—the same devoted interpreter served him faithfully and skillfully through most of his visits—but his efforts to live as the Japanese lived while he scanned their culture broke new ground.

His approach was through folklore and religion. He made a close study of the mystic rites of the Shinto cult that centers on Mount Fuji—he quickly recognized the importance of mountains to the Japanese and of mountain worship in their religion—and very early he became interested in the Shikoku pilgrimage. He kept promising himself that he would perform the pilgrimage and do it properly, by walking the whole way, and he repeatedly stated that of all the figures in Japanese history, he admired Kobo Daishi most.

But so many things interested him. He was fascinated by the old highroads and their role in molding the country. In 1915 he was one of the few Americans invited to the coronation of the new emperor. The ceremonies were to be held in the old capital, Kyoto, and characteristically he announced that he would walk the three-hundred-thirty-mile Tokaido Road from Tokyo to Kyoto, saying that he was born in 1858, the year that Hiroshige died, and that he wanted to see for himself the road that Hiroshige's prints had immortalized. As Consul General Saburo Kurusu (whose distinguished diplomatic career went on the rocks in Washington, D.C., on December 7, 1941) remarked in Chicago, "It was a poetic inspiration," and though Starr actually did most of the trip by jinrikisha he was followed by a swarm of reporters, he was cheered in every hamlet, and if there were any Japanese who didn't know his name when he started they surely did by the time he reached Kyoto.

The coronation over, one of Japan's great national newspapers, the *Asahi*, suggested that he continue his trip to the western extremity of the island under their sponsorship. The idea delighted him and the *Asahi* published his diary of the journey in ninety-three installments. The enterprising editors then suggested that if he went north from Tokyo to Aomori he would complete a twelve-hundred-mile traversal of the main island, so he took them up on that. He loved to travel, and he loved to get into the "old" Japan, where tradition was still strong and folklore vital.

He was always a political man. He was concerned about progress toward constitutional government and the direction in which Japan was heading, and so he was dogged by plainclothesmen on all his trips, the police being not at all sure what he was up to. He climbed Fuji three times, using every route, and he did the rather dangerous midway path that circles the mountain halfway up and is seldom attempted except by cultists; the police trudged after him. He complained but he must have known it would do no good.

He went up to Mount Koya in 1917 and again in 1920, and he made a preliminary visit to Shikoku in 1917, but it was 1921 before he undertook the Shikoku pilgrimage. He had wanted to walk it all like a true pilgrim, he said, but that year his schedule was too tight, so most of the way he would have to ride. And by now he was too much a celebrity to travel anonymously in Japan; as he modestly admitted, he was the best-known foreigner in the country. Reporters chronicled his visit to every temple, climbed every mountain in his wake (the snow was more than a foot deep on the alpine path from Number Eleven to Number Twelve). Newspapers vied to provide him with a car and be his host, and every town of any size begged him to make a speech.

He started at Temple One and he went all the way around to Eighty-eight and back to where he had begun, but it is Tosa where he is best remembered, a fact that reflects a kinship of original and independent spirits.

Take for example his reception at Temple Twenty-eight. He

must have felt that he was falling behind schedule, because instead of staying overnight in Aki town, as the people there begged him to do, he gave them a matinee talk and then took the interurban train to a station half a mile from the temple. It was dark by then but as he walked he collected a crowd of local people eager to have a look at the foreign henro.

He arrived at eight-thirty, so unexpected that the priest was absent. He was received by nonplussed monks and some members of the temple. He was invited to spend the night, he accepted, and then, settling back, he asked to be shown something distinctive of Tosa. The priest's chief disciple was perplexed about how to entertain him—confronted with a guest, the Tosa instinct is to break out the bottle, but it was well known that Dr. Starr shunned liquor, as well as tobacco, women, and telephones. Even without alcohol they decided to demonstrate one of those drinking games played with chopsticks. The professor was intrigued and joined in; there was a match between the American and a Tosa man. (That was the way a local reporter would naturally put it: not between an American and a Japanese but between an American and a Tosa man.)

After the game they tried to teach Starr and his interpreter a Tosa folk song. Folk songs almost demand the lubrication they were denied that night and the effort was doubly doomed since, as a reporter noted, neither of the guests had much of a voice, but Starr ordered his companion to master the song before they left Tosa.

The next morning the professor was up early, lighted candles and incense before the altar, and then in his white robes sat at a desk to write in his diary. When he left after warm good-byes, he was delighted to find kite flying in progress below the temple and some of the villagers obligingly staged a cockfight for him. A newspaperman recorded the speculation circulating among the people: "He may have a great knowledge of Kobo Daishi, but can the Daishi understand his prayers in English?"

He went on into Kochi City, where for two days he received celebrity treatment. The two newspapers jointly sponsored a lecture at the city auditorium before an overflow crowd. His subject

Temple Twenty-eight *(a painting by Kawabata)*

was "Japan and America" and judging from the newspaper reports he touched on his favorite themes. He praised Japan for its astonishing progress since emerging from seclusion; for having amazed the world by defeating those two giants, China in 1894–1895, and Russia ten years later; for being the only nation in the Orient to maintain its independence against rapacious colonial powers: with China so carved up it had almost lost its identity, only Japan could stand by itself.

East Asia had half the world's population. Its peoples should maintain their own character, they should face the world as Asians, they should demand the right to self-determination; and in all these efforts Japan had a heavy responsibility: it must take its stand as an Asian nation, it must protect Asia, it must lead Asia.

And he chided his audience as he invariably did. Why were they losing the national character that had made them great? Why were they aping the West in the mistaken notion that that spelled progress? He had a gift for prophecy: "If you want only to play a white man's role in a white man's world, you will end as Germany has. If you rally Asia behind you, no nations can combine against you."

Some people on both sides of the Pacific talked of the possibility of war between the United States and Japan, he admitted. He didn't deny that there was tension in California, talk of expelling Japanese immigrants. But "real Americans" would never tolerate that, "real Americans" had never borne ill will against Japan, from Commodore Perry's time to the present. Japan and America must seek to understand each other; they must together strive for peace. They must work hand in hand in China.

He closed by talking of the meaning of the Shikoku pilgrimage and why he had undertaken it.

He was, the papers reported, interrupted many times by applause.

One of the newspapers provided a car in which he visited the temples clustered around the city—Twenty-nine, Thirty-one, and Thirty-two, which we have just left. At every temple he poked around looking for unusual name-slips, the placards of dedication that pilgrims leave to evidence their visit. Today most henro do as Morikawa and I do, fill in name and date on printed slips that we place in a basket or on a hook before the altar. But there have always been individuals and groups who create their own design and plaster the buildings with them, even (using a brush attached to a long jointed stick) the high ceilings, where they are least likely to be damaged or removed. In the old days henro carried plaques of wood or metal and nailed them to the buildings; it was that practice which gave rise to an expression still used by henro, who do not "visit" a temple but "hit" it. Morikawa and I have seen one henro honoring tradition with wooden plaques.

Starr's interest in pilgrimage had fanned an interest in these papers and placards; he was elected member of a society that collected them; they bestowed on him a nickname proclaiming him master of the subject. Later in his pilgrimage, at Temple Fifty-three, on the back of the cabinet housing the principal image, he found a prize: the oldest plaque for this pilgrimage yet discovered, a brass plate about 9½ by 3¾ inches, dated 1650 and testifying to a pilgrimage undertaken in the company of Kobo Daishi by a commoner from Kyoto named Iyetsugi. The temple priest will cheerfully bring it out for inspection.

Of course Starr visited the one pilgrimage temple right in Kochi City, Number Thirty; the evidence is there for all to see:

WELCOME THE COMING, SPEED THE PARTING, GUEST
FREDERICK STARR
TAISHO 10. 3. 4.

I wonder if he was intrigued to find a pilgrimage temple in the heart of a castle town, almost in the shadow of the castle—the only instance of this on Shikoku, and that in the capital of the fief that had been most unfriendly to henro. I wonder if they told him that the temple he visited had not always been Number Thirty. And I wonder if, when they took him into the countryside to visit Tosa Shrine, the province's foremost Shinto shrine, they pointed out the site of the former Number Thirty, in the shrine precincts. Probably not. It was a complicated and bitterly disputed matter and I'm certain his guides wished to avoid it.

It goes back to one of the major turning points in Japanese history, the events of 1868 called the Restoration, in which the shogunate that had ruled Japan since 1600 was toppled by a coalition of old enemies, one of whose rallying cries was that they would restore the emperor to his rightful supremacy. Those who had nur-

Welcome the Coming, Speed the Parting, Guest
Frederick Starr
Taisho 10.3.4.

Frederick Starr's calligraphy at Temple Thirty

tured the campaign and the coalition were skillful propagandists; in claiming that the emperor had a divine right to rule they necessarily used the Shinto myths that traced the divine ancestry of the imperial line and pictured halcyon days when early emperors were absolute rulers. In some areas the revival of Shinto engendered antagonism toward Buddhism. This was true in Tosa, which had never been a stronghold of Buddhism anyway, and when the new central government decreed that the native Shinto should be cleansed of "foreign" Buddhist contamination, Tosa authorities went at it with unsurpassed vehemence.

Temple lands were confiscated. Bells were seized and melted down. Buddhist priests were stripped of the government ranks they had held for more than twelve centuries. About a fourth of Tosa's temples permanently disappeared. Of Tosa's sixteen numbered pilgrimage temples, nine were closed for periods varying from three to twenty-three years; at some the buildings were destroyed and the images profaned.

Temple Thirty was a special case because it stood within the precincts of Tosa Shrine. It was closed and demolished in 1870, among the first to go. There is an indication of what was to come in a petition submitted to the authorities by the shrine priests in the spring of 1870. "This is to request that you approve our idea of prohibiting henro from entering the compound of Tosa Shrine. These days henro from other provinces enter the compound to sleep at night; they spoil the sanctity of the shrine by cooking and doing other dirty things. None has ever been found carrying a travel pass. Some even escape while officials are studying how to deal with them. Most worrisome is that they may start a fire because of their carelessness."

That fear was not unfounded. The Tosa record of crimes and punishments shows that it was about then that a novice from a temple in Awa and the two young women who were performing the pilgrimage with him—a trio that in itself might raise eyebrows—were sentenced to be flogged forty times and deported because the fire on which they were cooking rice at another shrine got out of control and burned down the shrine.

At the same time it may be noted that what the priests were complaining about was no new thing. On some of the buildings of Tosa Shrine are old graffiti like this one dated the Sixth Month of 1571: "Ah! ah! there is no place to lodge—I stayed at this shrine." Perhaps the priests of that earlier time were more tolerant.

The Tosa Shrine priests' petition continued: "Their dirty presence is desecrating. They converge in such numbers, one group on the heels of another, that they are quite beyond control. We beg you to find a way of keeping them out of the shrine." Tosa authorities found a way. They demolished the temple. Its images of Amida and Kobo Daishi were transferred to Twenty-nine, which for the next twenty-three years functioned as both temples.

In 1893 a temple named Anraku-ji in Kochi City acquired the statue of Amida from Twenty-nine (which was no doubt relieved to part with it) and declared itself Temple Thirty—it had the principal image, which is in essence the temple. And for the first time the henro route led straight through the city: in feudal days henro, always suspect as possible spies, had to skirt the castle town or court dire punishment. It is clear that with modern times the officials of Tosa—Kochi—were losing their capacity for indignation over pilgrims.

But the Tosa spirit of stubborn battle persisted in the adherents of the old temple, which had been named Zenraku-ji. In 1929 they succeeded in reestablishing it (since the national government refused to authorize any new temples, they transferred a defunct but legally existent temple from the Tokyo area)—at least in name, for they had the money to erect only a marker on the old site in the shrine grounds. Now their fight began to heat up. In 1938 they were able to erect a temporary building. They brought back the statue of the Daishi from Twenty-nine and they demanded that Anraku-ji relinquish the Amida. Anraku-ji, whose name means "peaceful enlightenment," refused and war was declared.

A battle between temples is embarrassing to the hierarchy. In this case the situation was complicated by the fact that the two temples belonged to different schools of Shingon, so that two hierarchies were involved. There has been more than one attempt at resolution. In 1942 an agreement was signed that Anraku-ji would, within three years, return the Amida and would thereafter be designated the innermost sanctuary of Zenraku-ji; three years passed and the Amida did not move. In 1952, after more negotiations of staggering complexity, Anraku-ji was declared to be Temple Thirty, Zenraku-ji was designated "a place of historic importance," and to insure that this agreement held, Zenraku-ji was transferred to the same school as Anraku-ji and the same chief priest was appointed to both temples. I have no confidence that the fighting is over. The author of our most up-to-date guidebook is wrathful on the subject. To him Zenraku-ji is indisputably Number Thirty: Kobo Daishi founded the pilgrimage and chose the temples and assigned to each its number, and nothing has changed since then. It may be mere coincidence that the author is a priest of the school to which Zenraku-ji formerly belonged.

His indignation notwithstanding, it is clear that the pilgrimage can be altered. There have been battles between other temples over which was the properly authorized place for henro prayers. Most of these occurred some centuries ago and cosmetic history has both veiled the fight and assured us that the rightful temple was the victor—for that is where we worship today.

Here in Tosa, in the case of Temple Thirty, the change was wrought by revolutionary fervor that engendered religious fanaticism. And it seems irrevocable, despite Zenraku-ji's impassioned advocates; the old temple is now well off the pilgrimage route, it takes extra time to get to it, fewer and fewer henro will make the effort (though Morikawa and I do; we visit both).

Talking to reporters in Kochi, Starr seems to have had the notion that he was making his last visit to Japan. In two years he would reach the university's mandatory retirement age of sixty-five, he said, and after that he had so many projects in mind that he doubted he could ever return to Japan. He was wrong, of course; he was too deeply committed. Those other projects went by the board; it was Japan he came back to. But in the meantime, back at Chicago, he taught as he had for twenty-five years his pioneering course called simply "Japan." "Our university is one of the few in the world where such a course exists. . . . It deals not only with folklore and customs, but with politics, social conditions, and the institutions that go to make up the life of modern Japan as based on the growth of centuries." Students called his classes "eye-openers for the mind."

And as always, he found time to make news. There was a series of debates with Clarence Darrow on the question "Is civilization a failure?" in which he optimistically upheld the negative. He had execrated the expedition under General Pershing that Woodrow Wilson sent into Mexico in 1916; now he attacked the Treaty of Versailles and the League of Nations as a carving-up of the world by callous victors, a blow to self-determination, and a slap in the face to the half of the world that was excluded: "a foolish, fatal blueprint for more war." He continued, as he had for years, to advocate independence for the Philippines: "We took them to exploit them. We are not wanted. We are not needed. We ought to go." He warned that the immigration act of 1924, directed against the Japanese, was a dangerous blunder that would hurt the U.S. He insisted that war between Japan and the United States need never happen, but he warned that if the Western world continued its present policies in Asia "there will come a war of unspeakable terror." And he continued to assert that Asia would be the future center of the world.

He retired from the university in June, 1923. It was estimated that he had taught four thousand students; one thousand of them gathered for one of the several testimonial dinners; they cheered him until they were hoarse and gave him a fund to buy a home in Seattle, where he had decided to retire. He told them he had laid out a program to keep him busy until he was 120; then he would decide what to make of himself.

Morikawa smiles.

Starr was off to Japan as soon as he had moved himself and his library to Seattle. He arrived in Yokohama on August 12, 1923, and told reporters his plans. He would climb Mount Fuji again and then two other sacred mountains; he would complete his study of the four old main highroads by traveling the Kisokaido, which linked Tokyo and Kyoto by traversing the central mountains (as the Tokaido followed the coast); those excursions would give him the last material he needed to write two of his projected nineteen books. Then he would go to Korea to study political conditions and "the effect of the Japanese experiment there" (on previous visits he had found a good bit to praise); to China for an assessment of the political and financial state of the country; to Cambodia, where he wanted to check on the French colonial administration and to visit Angkor, recently uncovered to the world; and finally to Siam for a study of southern Buddhism.

On the morning of September 1 he had checked Fuji off that list and was relaxing in his cotton lounging robe on the third floor of his usual inn at the center of Tokyo—Morikawa gives me a startled look: September 1, 1923, is a date burned into the consciousness of the Japanese. The next day would be his sixty-fifth birthday and the governor of Tokyo was to give him a party. At two minutes before noon the walls around him crumbled; he was in the midst of the most devastating earthquake in recorded history. He survived; his inn moved him to the nearest large park, where he watched through all that night as the fire that was devouring the city roared closer. At daybreak the wind shifted; he and the others gathered there were spared. With other foreigners he was evacuated from the country as soon as could be. It was his shortest visit.

He was lucky, Morikawa says. Nobody knew that better than he, I answer, for he had walked through the havoc, the thousands of bodies, the stench of death.

Morikawa and I spend three full days in the city of Kochi, resting, getting our clothes clean, and enjoying long helpful conversations with friends like Hirao Michio, a Tosa historian with a national reputation, and Tosa Fumio, who is pressing to finish his long series of articles about his own pilgrimage.

Then we set out again, stopping at Temple Thirty-three, which we visited before we entered the city, to offer prayer—to say good morning, as Morikawa puts it—by way of getting started.

Next door to the temple is a Shinto shrine that vividly illustrates what has come of the Restoration government's use of Shinto and abuse of Buddhism.

No sooner had Buddhism come to Japan in the sixth century than it and Shinto began a long process of accommodation. In many respects the two complemented each other and the priests of each soon saw advantages in coexistence and even alliance. At first, Shinto deities were invoked to protect the new religion: Shinto shrines were built alongside Buddhist temples. But before long, the situation was reversed: then Shinto deities, like ordinary mortals, were considered to be in need of salvation through the power of Buddha, and so Buddhist scriptures were recited before Shinto altars and Buddhist chapels were built beside Shinto shrines. In time the two faiths grew so close that in the people's minds they mingled and merged and it became difficult to know where one began and the other left off.

All along the pilgrimage route Morikawa and I have seen Buddhist temple and Shinto shrine side by side. Through most of their history the two were in reality one institution, most often administered by the Buddhist priests—one institution offering the option of prayer at two kinds of altars to meet any worshiper's need and inclination. The Restoration leaders tried to "cleanse" Shinto of Buddhism in order to create a new kind of national Shinto dedicated to deifying the imperial line as the focus of a new nationalism. What they were attempting was like trying to un-scramble an egg.

For a time Shinto shrines flourished because they were subsi-dized by the government. Then after the war in the Pacific they were orphaned as the American officials of the Occupation insisted on the American doctrine of separation of church and state (a radical if not incomprehensible doctrine in Japan, where religion had always been called upon to serve the nation and its people). The subsidies to Shinto shrines ended. Few of them had ever had their own full-time priests and no longer were they linked to the Buddhist temples whose priests for centuries had administered many of them. Again and again Morikawa and I have seen the answer: the Buddhist temple is alive and active; the Shinto shrine beside it rots.

The story here at Temple Thirty-three is somewhat different. There was originally only a temple. It had fallen on hard times, deserted and without a priest, until in the late sixteenth century it was rebuilt by Tosa's greatest hero, a warlord named Chosokabe Motochika. Motochika made it his family temple, and when his eldest son died in battle he divided the young man's ashes, carry-ing part to Mount Koya to rest near the Daishi's tomb and de-positing the rest at this temple, which still keeps them, the son's armor, and the roll of the seven hundred men who died with him. When Motochika died the name of the temple was changed to his posthumous name and a statue of the old warrior was installed in the main hall.

It is a measure of the mindless fury against Buddhism that swept Tosa in the 1870's that even this temple was razed. On its land they built a Shinto shrine and they dedicated that to Motochika, as if they knew better than he what he believed in.

The temple was rebuilt earlier than most, on land adjacent to the shrine. Its statues, including a magnificent group of sixteen national treasures, were brought back from storage at Temple Thirty-one.

Chosokabe Motochika *(a painting by an unknown artist)*

Morikawa and I have already taken a look at the shrine. The story is familiar: it seems deserted. No one is in attendance; the roof leaks; there is a gaping hole in the floor.

The five miles of country road we walk between Thirty-three and Thirty-four is the same that Starr traveled but today much of the land is tented in plastic: truck gardening has taken over. Each village has its co-op to market produce; we see baskets of eggplant, green peppers, ginger, tomatoes. We are told that the villages around here take turns in offering settai—often that auspicious dish, rice cooked with red beans—but we are a few weeks too late.

Coming toward us we spot a lone henro, walking the route in reverse order. When we meet he tells us that he is from Hiroshima, that he started from an Inland Sea port in Iyo. He is moving against most pilgrimage traffic yet he says he has met walking henro only about once a week, most recently a young monk.

Temple Thirty-four is built on a fill thrust like a wharf into the paddy fields. The narrow precincts are bounded by a low wall; lined up along it are dozens of weathered stone figures, small and large, mostly of that patron saint of travelers, guardian of children, and rescuer of wicked souls, Jizo. They gaze on us benignly; we are in good company.

The temple's unpretentious buildings stand in a row facing the images. The exception is a small, wall-less building in front of the main hall; it is literally filled with wooden ladles, a common item in a Japanese kitchen, but from each of these the bottom has been knocked out. Each represents fulfillment of a prayer for easy birth.

Traditionally a woman on becoming pregnant brought a new ladle to the priest; nowadays he often finds himself giving the suppliant one from a stock he keeps on hand. In either case he punches out the bottom and, placing it on the altar, offers prayers over it during the course of two nights and a day. The woman takes it home and keeps it in the alcove that is the place of honor in her home. When she gives safe birth to a sound baby she writes her name and age on the handle and returns the ladle to the temple. The young woman issuing inscriptions in the priest's absence says that women come not just for their first child but for subsequent pregnancies also, and that many come from other prefectures.

We have been told that this temple has some writing by Frederick Starr and I ask about it. The young woman opens the entrance to the residence. Above the inner door it hangs mounted and framed: PEACE AND INTERNATIONAL FRIENDSHIP, FREDERICK STARR, TAISHO 10. 3. 5.—the same hopeful message as at Thirty-two, written a day later. In the corner of the mounting is a yellowed newspaper clipping. Morikawa stands on the steps and strains up to read it, getting a crick in his neck.

It announced that Starr had died in Tokyo on August 14, 1933, on his fifteenth visit to Japan. While traveling in Korea for research he was stricken with an intestinal disease. He was rushed

Temple Thirty-four *(a print by Kadowaki)*

back to Tokyo and to St. Luke's Hospital but he died two days later at the age of seventy-five. The funeral was to be held in Tokyo. "In accordance with the express wish of Dr. Starr, who deeply loved Japan, his body will be dressed in formal kimono."

The program he had laid out to busy himself till he was 120 would not be completed; most of the books would remain unwritten. Japan had lost a staunch and vocal friend: he had been able to say good things about her rule in Korea; he had defended her actions in the Manchukuo dispute.

I do not mean to overpraise him. Scholarship has advanced since his day. But he created wide interest in anthropology, he was a brilliant teacher, and he gave his students an appreciation of Japanese culture they could get at almost no other university in the West (the course that he taught for twenty-five years was dropped when he retired).

The temple is soliciting contributions to repair the severe damage done by a typhoon last summer. Morikawa and I buy a copper sheet for the roof. We sign and date it, and add: "In memory of Frederick Starr." Then we shoulder our packs and set out again.

19 Partway down the long hard road to Cape Ashizuri there is a hermitage that summons thoughts of a holy man named Shinnen who performed surpassing services for henro. He had walked the circuit around Shikoku many times and he knew the problems pilgrims faced as they tried to trace the henro-path. To help them he wrote the first guidebook. It was published in 1685, which may seem rather late, but guidebooks are not written until there is a demand for them, and until after 1600 it was not possible for ordinary people to travel much (the first guidebooks for other pilgrimages appeared about the same time). Shinnen's guidebook shows that the pilgrimage was already popular.

This pioneering effort was a great boon to henro but Shinnen was not satisfied with it. He wanted to produce a guide that would give pilgrims all the counsel they needed to perform the pilgrimage properly—not only keep them from getting lost but tell them the story of each sacred place, explaining why it was holy and how to worship there. He knew that his book was inadequate and so he climbed Koya to seek help from a priest named Jakuhon.

"I did my best," wrote Jakuhon, "selecting and arranging his material, but many details were not clear. To remedy this, Shinnen revisited the temples with two or three companions and obtained the missing information while also making a sketch of each temple, and I was able to finish compiling this work."

The expanded and polished guide, seven slim volumes printed from woodblocks, was published in 1689. It begins at the Daishi's birthplace and it lists ninety-four temples without assigning them numbers—today's eighty-eight plus six bangai; the route is the same as it is today. Jakuhon is credited as author but the preface acknowledges that the impetus and the information came from Shinnen. It was expensive but it was quickly plagiarized by cheaper books. Henro had what they needed to guide their steps and their worship.

Shinnen turned to another need. On the three-day trek to Ashizuri, from Temple Thirty-seven to Temple Thirty-eight, pilgrims often found themselves without a roof to sleep under even in the foulest weather. At a junction, a spot passed by henro going to the cape and by the many who chose to backtrack along the same road in going on to Thirty-nine, he built a chapel and a shelter, enshrining a life-size statue of the Daishi he had carried on his back from Koya. Here he lived out his life, helping henro. Helping often meant nursing them in sickness, sometimes burying them. There are many graves in back.

Although Shinnen established the hermitage at that junction, the Jakuhon-Shinnen guidebook suggested an alternate route to Temple Thirty-nine: not the backtrack and then a path west over the mountains, but a road that went west along the coast and then veered north, where there was a temple to be visited. The temple never acquired a number—it became a bangai—but certainly some henro went there, for at Ashizuri the authorities of Tosa fief grew unaccountably liberal: they authorized both routes. Morikawa and I have no difficulty choosing. The coastal road is clearly less busy, we do not want to backtrack, and we want to visit that bangai if it still exists.

The evening that we spent at Ashizuri and Temple Thirty-eight brought to a close an especially fine day: sunny, warm, and very clear. After supper we walked again to the cliff to face the sea that holy men sailed into, seeking Kannon's Fudaraku. The only clouds were the vapor trails of training jets, marking the darkening sky with long calligraphic strokes. The moon was a slender crescent that would hold water. We remarked on the long spell of beautiful weather we had enjoyed.

Perhaps we should learn not to do that. During the night I became aware of a growling wind. When we rise the weather has changed around: it is gray, chilly, and blowing a gale.

But the road is pleasant, narrow and little used, bordered on our right by woods and our left by the rocky coast, pounded today by a somber sea.

The rain holds off until late morning, a few splatters and then a downpour. If we were bright we would stop for the day. Instead we walk on along something more river than road until two compassionate foresters stop and give us a lift to the next town, where some concerned and friendly folk find a place for us at an inn that has gone out of business but is willing to take us in. When we go to bed the storm is still at it. Sheets of rain and blasts of wind slam the old house: it trembles and groans.

But in the morning the sun is out. We skirt a coast guarded by bastions of black rock. The ocean heaves and smashes at them, still seething from yesterday's storm. A few fishermen in rowboats looking small and vulnerable ride the swells, rising and falling, appearing and disappearing. On a beach a woman digging for clams is eyed by a hawk that soars above her. Landward are black crows and black butterflies and mountains of black rock touched with spring's green.

But the wind—it fights us every step of the way. Gripping my sedge hat I watch a bird fly into it and lose headway. At my feet a woolly caterpillar is picked up and blown from the macadam.

Conversation is impossible; words are torn from our lips and scattered.

At the head of each narrow bay we thread the lanes of a fishing village. At the last one that shows on our maps we stop for lunch. It is too small to have a restaurant but we find a food shop tended by a smiling woman from her bright kitchen overlooking it. We buy half a dozen eggs and cheerfully she boils them for us. We buy a package of bread; she loans us her toaster and insists on giving us butter. We buy a can of peaches and eat them from her dishes.

Soon we leave the coast and climb into the hills. Deep in the forest we find the bangai we have been looking for. In Shinnen's time Moon-Mountain Temple, it is today Moon-Mountain Shrine. Here is an institution that weathered the separation of Shinto and Buddhism without catching its breath. The priest of those days simply changed from Buddhist to Shinto robes and continued to perform the same services he always had. He preserved his institution, kept it open.

Perhaps he was able to do this because he was a long distance from the castle town and fief headquarters, perhaps because this place always had a strong Shinto flavor, perhaps because he was the kind of man he was. Other Buddhist priests tried it; some went insane, some committed suicide.

But here is Moon-Mountain Shrine, maintained by his descendant, an elderly man retired from teaching. He tells us that the central altar enshrines the same object it did in Buddhist days, a sacred stone with the shape and the glow of the moon half at the wane; he implies that the people pray more often at a small chapel dedicated to the Daishi. He seems pleased to see us: one henro came last year; we are the first this year (only April 29 and traffic has already doubled).

The next day we reach Temple Thirty-nine, the last in Tosa. Quiet, rural, it possesses a national treasure, a bell cast in 911 at a temple called Miroku. The priest says there has never been a Miroku Temple on Shikoku, and he supposes it was cast in Nara or Kyoto. Legend says it was brought here from the palace of the Dragon King of the Sea by a great red turtle that rose, bell on

月山圖

Moon-Mountain Temple
*(an illustration from the
guidebook by Jakuhon
and Shinnen)*

back, from a pool formed by a spring the Daishi had brought forth.
For a moment I wonder whether this tale might signify that the
bell was recovered from the wreck of a boat that sank offshore.
But I put this thought out of my mind: here in the compound
for all to see is the pool, and the turtle is memorialized in red
concrete.

The priest escorts us a few hundred yards to the innermost
altar. We pass a lone farmer scything a field of wheat and come to
a flooded field with a crop we have seen in both Awa and Tosa but
could not identify: clumps of slender green grasses like long pine
needles. The priest tells us that they are the reeds that are woven to
make the covers of tatami mats. Now they are about as high as the

wheat the farmer is harvesting but they will grow almost as tall as a man. The seedlings are transplanted in the coldest season and the reeds are harvested in the hottest. They used to be grown almost exclusively in Okayama Prefecture but they do not tolerate contamination: pollution on the other side of the Inland Sea has brought this crop to Shikoku.

Hanging inside the little chapel are large red banners, many of them, each bearing the name, age, and address of someone whose prayers to the Yakushi of this temple have been attended by recovery from illness. Outside are dozens—no, hundreds—of little flags, red and white, planted in the ground, signifying the same blessing. "There are innumerable stories of cures," the priest murmurs, "from tuberculosis, blindness, paralysis—but the stories are no different, I suppose, from those of any other temple."

He reflects. "To intellectuals, religion seems strange. But the point of the religious life is mental and spiritual training, and that cannot be achieved by oneself. We need help from some source like Buddha or Kobo Daishi or Yakushi." He considers us. "The point of the pilgrimage is to improve oneself by enduring and overcoming difficulties."

Now we leave Tosa. In the old days there was just one authorized exit, a mountain pass called Pine Tree Ascent right on the border between Tosa and Iyo. There is always something significant about crossing a pass. A scholar has noted that the Japanese word for "mountain pass" originates from a verb meaning "to offer," "because travelers always had to offer something to the god of the pass as a prayer for safe journey (a custom also seen in Korea, Mongolia, and Tibet). . . . There are many instances where large mounds have accumulated from the offerings of small stones."

At Pine Tree Ascent was a barrier gate. There was a flood of Tosa edicts, one every three or four years for more than two centuries, stipulating that it was the only point where travelers might cross the long border with Iyo. Of course henro who had entered Tosa by evading the barrier gate at the other side of the province had no choice but to try to evade Pine Tree Ascent—and, if caught, suffer being flogged or branded or both before being forcibly ejected.

Tosa guards also became unpleasant if outgoing henro had overstayed their authorized thirty days, while they doggedly examined incoming henro—those performing the pilgrimage in reverse order—to screen out spies, rogues, vagabonds, jugglers, minstrels, and monkey trainers.

Many henro of those times, on leaving this province where they felt so abused, would squat with their backs to it and augment the memorial to "the Devil's Land," a quite different offering from the usual one at a pass. Writing in 1927, Alfred Bohner reported that the Dung Monument no longer existed but that vegetation grew very rank where it had.

On a contrasting note, praise was lavished on the prospect from the summit: "The entire bay of Sukumo stretched before me: its countless islands, its bizarre tongues of land, its winding arms of the sea." And, "Kyushu was within reach of my staff while the towering mountains of Iyo lay at my feet." That 1819 henro from Tosa here surrendered his exit permit and received a new pass permitting him to reenter at the other side of the province. Then, overcome by the view and sentiment at leaving his home country, he composed a haiku before continuing.

For years I did not attempt Pine Tree Ascent, having been assured by presumably knowledgeable folk on both sides of the pass that the path no longer existed, that it had disintegrated and disappeared completely when a new road was built around the mountain instead of over it. But I have learned to distrust such advice and I was haunted by the feeling that I should try to find the old path. Last year, walking with friends in the heat of summer when the dirt and roar of traffic on the highway seemed almost intolerable, I suggested that I was willing to risk losing some hours in the search if they were. We struck off into the countryside toward the hills.

Trying from our maps to figure the best approach, we began to climb along a little wooded road. Around a curve we found an old man, comfortably stripped down to some baggy cotton trousers, with a cart that had started life as a baby buggy. In it were a

Monkey trainers *(a drawing by an unknown artist)*

couple of mats to sit on and something to eat and drink. I am sure he was up there for peace and quiet away from his family. He told us we were on the wrong road; we should start from the village where he lived and he led us back.

In the village he turned us over to a farmer who said that yes indeed, the path still existed, and pointed to the ridgeline high above. "That's the border between Tosa and Iyo," he said. "On this side the path is good, but on the Iyo side it's not well maintained," and he started us out.

It *was* a good path, only a bit overgrown. The weeds had been cut back not much earlier but thistles had already sprung up and were nettlesome. As we gained altitude we began to get those belauded views, the coastline, islands, the strait between Shikoku and Kyushu. We had not gone far when a boy appeared at our heels, a smiling kid who fairly sprinted up the path wearing rubber sandals. Clearly the mountain was familar to him. When we began to find divergent paths and were unsure, we moved him up front. Someone murmured, not facetiously, that Kobo Daishi had appeared to guide us.

We had trouble only with the last hundred yards or so, where timber had recently been harvested and the path destroyed in the process, as usually happens; it takes a while for feet that know the mountain to mark the path again. We struggled up, mostly on all fours, but the ridgeline was so close there was no sense of being lost.

Once we gained the ridge all was easy again; through a break in the forest another sweeping view and then the pass. Two memorial stones, quite new, mark the site, but of the buildings that used to stand here—the barrier was a bit lower but up here were two teahouses (where everyone stopped to rest and where henro overtaken by darkness could spend the night) and a chapel enshrining a statue of the Daishi—nothing remains save a bit of stone wall.

I already knew the story of that Daishi. When the new road was built travelers over the pass became so few that the teahouses were abandoned, and about fifty years ago the people of a village on the Iyo side decided to bring the chapel down where they could care for it. A bit later a meeting hall was built nearby and the horses tethered there made the surroundings much too dirty for the Daishi. Finally the old men's club of the town at the foot of the mountain offered a suitable location and the villagers accepted gratefully. One of the members of the club has shown me to the little chapel that stands on the grounds of the chamber of commerce building, the town's social center. Inside was a crutch, offered by someone who no longer needed it; this Daishi, he told me, is renowned for its power to help cripples. And there was the image: a seated figure about two feet high, carved in sections—primitive art with simple strength.

Once we achieved the pass we sat to rest like thousands of henro before us, and pulled from our packs some of the snacks we always carried. The boy, having delivered us, vanished just when we wanted to share our food with him, but almost immediately the farmer who had set us on the path appeared. "I saw that you were having difficulty," he said, "so I hurried up to help." He sat with us in the little clearing, chatting and eating, until we started down into Iyo. He had been wrong about only one thing: on the Tosa side it was certainly a good path, except for that last short stretch, but on the Iyo side it was even better—clean, often shaded, and with lovely views of the mountains and valleys. Unfortunately it ended where a great gash had been cut in the slope to build a new highway, and we had to inch our way down to the road.

And so Morikawa and I, now that we know the path exists, cross the border from Tosa to Iyo over Pine Tree Ascent as henro should. In the town we find a comfortable inn and then we go to pray before the Daishi. Presently we are relaxing in a hot bath. As we are finishing our dinner and it is growing dark, two new guests, young men, limp past the open doors of our room. They are so evidently footsore that Morikawa grins in sympathy. "Henro," he says.

After they have bathed and dined we call on them. The older, whom I guess to be in his thirties, does the talking. He tells us that he works in an office in Osaka. Year before last he began his pilgrimage and he has continued it every time he could get a few days' holiday. Sometimes the younger chap has accompanied him,

Henro resting *(detail from a book illustration by Shugetsu)*

sometimes not. They have walked the pilgrimage not in sequence but choosing a section according to the time available. (Japanese employees are granted a week or two of annual holiday but few consider it within the work ethic to take it.)

We are now in the midst of what is called Golden Week: seven days that include three holidays—April 29, the Emperor's birthday; May 3, Constitution Day, celebrating the new constitution; and May 5, the ancient festival of Boys' Day (now given the unisex name Children's Day). By using the weekend and taking one day off from work, these two have given themselves five days. They traveled all last night to make an early start this morning. They have today walked more than forty miles, and worshiped at Temple Forty along the way. We admit that to us such a walk seems almost impossible, and the spokesman grimaces and says they don't waste time: they maintain a fast pace and they even walk while they eat.

By walking a hundred and fifty miles more and worshiping at the three temples along the way, the older will close the last gap: he will complete his pilgrimage on this holiday and he will have walked every foot of the way. We admire him for that and tell him so. He says that he enjoys walking and he needs exercise and release from the tensions of the office. They both envy our being able to do the pilgrimage all at once and in so leisurely a manner; they make us feel privileged.

As we are saying good night he asks whether we have heard that a man at the unlucky age of forty-two should make the pilgrimage. He does not look that old . . . is he thinking of his next pilgrimage?

Now we face the mountains of southern Iyo. From here to the plain where the city of Matsuyama rises is about a hundred and fifty miles, mostly mountainous and mostly beautiful. It is possible to walk nearly the entire distance on national highways as suggested by our modern guidebook with its primary concern for motorized henro. That unpleasant possibility we reject. We want to stay away from busy roads and we want to seek out the old henro-path.

It is not far, only a couple of hours, to Temple Forty but we stop there for the night, giving ourselves an easy day and time for long contemplation of the old woodblock that reads, "Namu Amida-butsu." We try to sense the magical power of that carved board, the faith that has inspired countless cures, given measureless comfort.

The next two temples are forty miles away, over a mountain four times higher than Pine Tree Ascent, with views that seem to encompass all Shikoku. We spend the night up there at a bangai that through most of its history was ambiguously Buddhist and Shinto but since the 1870's has, of course, been classified as Shinto.

Down and to another bangai in a castle town famed for bullfighting—not man against bull but bull against bull—and the next

Temple Forty *(a print by Azechi)*

morning we reach Temple Forty-one. This is another of those institutions that joined Buddhism and Shinto, here so intimately that until the severing of the two a single hall was both Buddhist temple and Shinto shrine and it enshrined as principal image a statue of a Shinto deity believed to have been carved by the Daishi. For more than a century temple and shrine have been housed in different buildings but the spleen aroused by the divorce is still mordant; each claims that it houses the image that the Daishi carved. We see that the temple priest has set up new signs identifying the buildings: main hall to the left, Daishi Hall to the right, and up the hill a "local shrine." He has chafed an old wound and while we are there a village leader comes to protest. He charges that the wording "local shrine" is derogatory in implication and tantamount to telling henro not to bother visiting the shrine. The priest says not at all; he has done no more than tem-

Temple Forty-two *(a print by Kadowaki)*

ples usually do in identifying buildings so henro know which is which. The conversation is interrupted so that we can take our leave but the man waits to continue it. We speculate about it as we walk a wooded stretch of henro-path that the priest has marked, munching cookies he has given us. It seems clear the dispute will not be resolved today.

Forty-one and Forty-two both lie in a fertile valley tucked among mountains and both reflect the concerns of husbandry: Forty-one, the growing of rice; Forty-two, the care of farm animals. I am eager to reach Forty-two. On my two previous visits it had no priest, only a kindly old woman living there as caretaker. It had an aura of age and dignity but it seemed lonely and incomplete. We have heard that now there is a priest and I look forward to a revitalized temple.

I am pleased to find that the priest is an acquaintance who was formerly at the bangai back in the castle town. "I have been searching for old records to reconstruct the temple's history," he

Talisman from Temple Forty-two promising long life to cattle *(a print)*

says, "but it's slow going. There was no priest for five years and for ten years before that the old priest was senile and it was as if no priest was here." Sad, for when Bohner made his pilgrimage he found that same man to be exceptional: "This is a temple where every henro, be it ever so early in the day, is invited, even urged, to stay overnight, and where care is taken for his edification. . . . The temple has many old documents, some dating back nearly seven hundred years."

The priest gives us a print from a centuries-old woodblock; it promises long life to cattle. "People purchased these talismans and pasted them on the ceilings of their barns to protect their livestock," he says, "but the temple was known for guarding humans as well, especially from smallpox. Letters came from all over pleading for protection against that disease."

We ask about the old henro-path to Forty-three, over another mountain, through Long Tooth Pass. It still exists, he tells us, and the temple's innermost sanctuary stands at the pass, but the path is difficult to find. He has an appointment but he phones a member of the temple and asks him if he can help us. And then he walks with us more than half a mile up the road. He must, he says; he must introduce us to Mr. Furuya because he asked him to be our guide.

Mr. Furuya meets us, a stalwart, handsome man wheeling his motorcycle; he'll ride it back, he says, but when we explain that we'd like to walk the old path, not the new road, he cheerfully takes the bike home.

He returns and we set out through fields and soughing bamboo groves. He is fifty years old and a farmer, he tells us, getting the preliminaries out of the way. I say that I think the village is lucky to have such a fine priest after a long hiatus. He agrees. "And he's a young man too. I was a member of the committee that took charge of temple affairs when we had no priest. We had difficulties. The members wanted this priest but the headquarters of the school our temple belongs to is a major temple in Kyoto, it has the authority to designate the priest, and it had a different candidate, an elderly man. Our village had had enough of aged priests after suffering through ten years when the old priest was incompetent. The situation was aggravated because our temple has high rank; headquarters argued that they must send a priest of high degree. I made four trips to Kyoto trying to resolve the issue. What it came down to was that headquarters' nominee was a greedy man; our people raised two million yen to buy him off." (I blink: two million yen at today's rate is almost ten thousand dollars and this is a rural community: they must care about their temple.) "So we got the priest we wanted, who is a good man, and the people are happy to have him."

Now we are climbing through a forest of cedars, fine tall trees. "One of these mountains belongs to the schools and the timber helps support them. It was given by the people back in the old days." The old days in this case means the late nineteenth century, when public schools were coming into their own in Japan.

We break into the open above the forest. Ridges of dark green mountains twist below us. Beyond is the strait and more islands than I can count. "On a clear day you can see Kyushu," Mr. Furuya says.

We pause to catch our breath, look down into the narrow valleys at the pinched villages that snake along the bottoms. "That's Yoshida town. The farmers down there used to have a miserable existence, barely scratching out a living by growing silkworms. Then came the citrus boom and now they're prosperous. More tangerines and summer oranges are grown there than any other place in Japan." I don't doubt it; citrus groves are planted right up to the tops of the mountains. "They have the climate for it," Mr. Furuya goes on. "That side of the mountain is one layer of clothing warmer than our side, but I wonder why people would want to live in such dark, closed-in little valleys."

He leads us up a bushy bank to a spring marked by a henro-stone. "Its name means 'clear water.' Henro always stopped here for a drink." The spring is clogged with dead leaves. Back on the path: "It was along here—a henro testified that along here he saw Kobo Daishi. He came down to our temple and donated a stone lantern to memorialize the miracle. It's in the garden." We enter the pass and find loquat trees bordering the path. "The farmers planted them so they'd have something to eat when they worked up here in the summer." Wild iris are in bloom—and appropriately, for today is Boys' Day and the iris is the flower of that old festival.

Then we top the summit. There are spectacular views of the strait, and masses of wild iris all about, and square in the pass named Long Tooth is the innermost sanctuary, the Hermitage of Hail and Farewell. It is a disappointment, though it cannot spoil the pleasure of being here: a plain little building of concrete block, and when we enter to say our prayers we find that someone has used charcoal to scrawl a nude on the wall behind the altar. "The old building burned a few years ago," Mr. Furuya tells us. "Henro used to sleep in it; some of them must have started a fire. This new chapel was built by the people of Yoshida town. Once there was a teahouse here. The old people of the village used to come up here to offer settai, and they kept the path clear. But now . . ." Now there is no traffic.

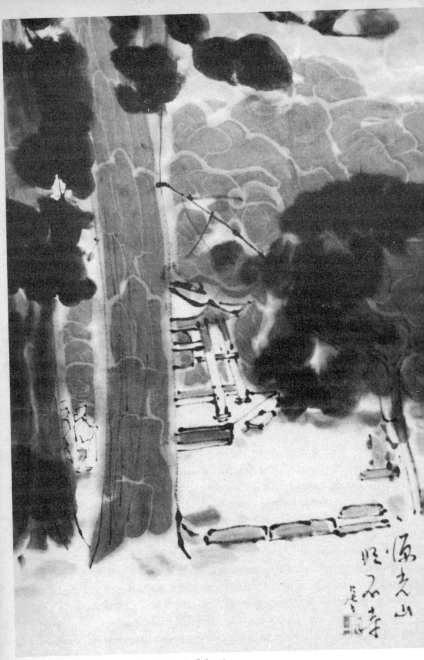

源光入山
照石寺
尾

Temple Forty-three *(a painting by Sakata)*

We thank Mr. Furuya and he starts home. We sit for a bit, drinking in the view. When we start down we discover that on this side of the mountain the henro-path is no one's concern. It turns into a narrow rut worn in rock, slick with moss and yesterday's rain. Lower it is blocked by trees felled across it. Finally it has been obliterated by loggers who have made it a chute to slide logs down the mountain. We can only slip and bump down a muddy slope. We come at last to a lane, which leads to a road, which brings us onto a prefectural highway, which we tramp for an hour.

Temple Forty-three stands not far from a town but aloof from it, on a heavily forested mountain. It is five o'clock when we approach a flight of stone steps under the trees, each step a single piece of granite five yards long. The main hall rises above, luminous in the gray light, with gilt and splendor such as we have not seen in some time. Worshiping before it, I remember that this temple has been a stronghold of Mountain Buddhism. Here before the mountain, in the hushed and dusky compound, ancient gods are surely present.

20

Most henro coming from the island of Kyushu have arrived at the port of Yawatahama on the west coast of Shikoku. Starting there, the first pilgrimage temple they hit was Number Forty-three. That was true of a young woman named Takamure Itsue who made the pilgrimage in 1918 at the age of twenty-four. Later, when she became prominent as a writer, she turned back in more than one essay to relive her experiences as a henro.

"To escape from a morass of depression, to try to find an answer to the problem of how to live, I undertook the pilgrimage. I planned to beg for my food and lodging but I needed cash for the fare to Shikoku; I offered to write a pilgrim's diary for the *Kyushu Daily News* and was paid ten yen.

"I made these resolves:

"1. To accept whatever happened, however unexpected, without anxiety.

"2. To ask for my needs in a straightforward manner.

"3. If my request for food or lodging was refused, to leave immediately.

"4. Not to cling to life tenaciously."

She had been lodging at a temple in the castle city of Kumamoto. "Wearing a pilgrim's robes and straw sandals given me by the priest, on my head a sedge hat with 'We Two—Pilgrims Together' written on it, holding a pilgrim's staff in my hand, I said good-bye to friends who came as far as the temple gate to see me off. Feeling as if in a dream I walked away. At the outskirts of Kumamoto I stopped at a store to buy a raincoat. As soon as the shopkeeper saw me he yelled, 'You won't get anything from us!' At that moment I knew I had become a mendicant pilgrim."

At the first house where she asked for lodging that evening she was refused, but they sent her to another where she was welcomed; she gave the family her book of Chinese poetry. She fared as well the second night; "I gave them my beloved flute. Now my pack was empty. All material things connected with the past had been given away."

She was crossing Kyushu from west coast to east over the island's volcanic mountains. Her fifth afternoon on the road, "while I was walking a narrow path that overlooked a deep gorge, an old man came out of a shack and invited me to spend the night, saying that beyond that point it was too mountainous to walk in the dark. There was just one room, furnished only with a Buddhist altar; it had been a hermitage enshrining Kannon." (Her parents had prayed to Kannon for a daughter; her mother had called her a child of Kannon and when she was a little girl that is what she thought herself to be.)

"The old man served me rice and soup in a cracked bowl. He was seventy-three years old, a practitioner of acupuncture and massage, deeply religious but very stubborn, greatly respected by the people. That night he dreamed that I was an incarnation of Kannon and he decided to accompany me on the pilgrimage. I felt that his dream was the result of self-hypnosis but nevertheless my independent travel ended there. It seemed fated to be and I let things take their course." She had resolved to accept whatever happened, and elsewhere she had written, "As a child I never wanted to be a leader, only a follower."

"I stayed there for more than a month, waiting for the old man to get ready. He borrowed some books for me to read from the Chinese scholar in the village and also an old broken zither for me to play. A curious rumor went around"—not so curious if the old man was telling people she was an incarnation of Kannon—"that illness could be cured by touching my staff. People flocked to the hut and, strangely, cures did occur: some who were carried there on the back of others were able to walk home. People came from miles away bringing offerings and so quite unexpectedly we were able to raise the money for the old man's travel expenses."

She had left Kumamoto on June 4. On July 18 she and the old man took the boat from Kyushu to Shikoku. They stayed the first night at a temple in the port city and early the next morning they set out for Temple Forty-three. Unfortunately someone showed them a shortcut that was a rough, steep mountain trail. When they finally tottered down to the henro-path again it was near sundown and they were both so exhausted they could go no farther. "We found shelter under a tree beneath crags, arranged three rocks to make a grate, and cooked rice in a small pot. We gathered edible grasses to put in our soup. This was our meal. Then, removing only sandals and gaiters, we each rolled in a blanket and slept. During the night I woke to find ants, lizards, and hairy caterpillars crawling on me. . . .

"There are two ways of doing the pilgrimage, the regular order and the reverse route. Doing it in reverse the hills are steeper and so it is considered more difficult and more meritorious. Thinking of the old man I suggested that we go the regular way but he chose the reverse order, saying it was more suitable for ascetic practice. I was forced to subjugate myself to the wishes of this obstinate old man.

"We resolved to walk the entire distance. It was an unwritten rule that henro ask alms at least once a day but we were determined to beg for all food and lodging and to sleep outdoors when necessary. All during the pilgrimage I was trying desperately to find myself. Agonizingly I struggled toward maturity. Undertaking dangerous travel without funds, I placed my life on the line."

She remembered her childhood as a fairy tale and everything after that as harsh. She idolized her parents, was proud that both could trace an ancient and distinguished lineage. Her father, coming of age in the expansive years following the Restoration, had wanted, like so many other bright young men, to go to Tokyo to seek his fortune. The poverty of his family prevented that and he became a dedicated teacher. He was an extraordinary man and not only for his time and his country: during the early years of marriage he hurried home after teaching both day and night school and, seated at a low desk opposite his young wife, he patiently taught her Chinese history and literature, Japanese poetry, and Western arithmetic. She was the daughter of a scholar-priest; though because she was a girl she had been denied the education her brothers received, she had absorbed much by observing their study and she was a grateful student. Her husband gave her an education as good as his own. "They did everything together: climbing over the mountains, gathering firewood, performing in village theatricals, attending magic lantern shows and parties. They always read together, newspapers, magazines, and books. I and my younger brothers and sister never viewed their lives as unusual but now as I look back I see that they were unique and I admire them deeply.

"My ideas on women's education are just like my father's. Yet my mother was never the 'female intellectual' type. She remained the gentle eternal virgin. And my parents always told me that I inherited exactly my mother's personality. In my novel the wife is modeled on my mother, a loving and inseparable companion to her husband. But in real life my husband was a materialist, having been infected by ego-centered Russian literature, so that our relationship was not as smooth as my parents'."

Takamure's problems began when she was sent to normal school for teacher training; she never fit in. From her parents' conversation she had learned of an orphanage and its needs. Out of her small monthly allowance she anonymously sent a little sum to the orphanage every month. A newspaper got wind of it and through postmarks and such was able to identify the giver; an article appeared commending her charity. In front of her class, school officials severely reprimanded her for seeking notoriety, though she had never given her name, and for usurping adult responsibilities. She was deeply hurt. She thought that if she had to be admonished it should have been in private and that it should have been acknowledged that her deed was good even while telling her to stop. Adult authority seemed ugly and hurtful.

From then on she became aware that her teachers looked on her with mistrust. She had entered the Literary Department, which was always regarded with suspicion because its members might be contaminated by dangerous humanist ideas contrary to the dogma that placed the nation's divine mission above all else. While others played outdoors she went to the library. Once she was found reading philosophy; she was told she was too young for such books, her library privileges were suspended, and again she was labeled an undesirable student. For the first time in her life she felt stress and this may have contributed to a severe illness during her summer holiday. When she returned she had difficulty moving about and sitting on the floor in classes like the tea ceremony, flower arrangement, and sewing; her grades suffered in those important courses.

When Japan annexed Korea in 1910 the principal assembled the entire school for an ethics lecture in which he justified strong countries' absorbing the weak (using Britain and its dominions as an example) and declared that a nation's morality was quite distinct from that of its citizens. She was not convinced and set down her doubts in her diary. When all of the students' written materials were swept up for censorship this was discovered. She was dismissed from the school. Her parents were shocked and though they supported her, her self-confidence was battered.

A term at another school, some months in a textile mill to help the family finances (her two brothers were now in higher school), a job as an assistant teacher—she was still troubled. At her father's insistence she wrote a short essay for an education magazine. It elicited a card from a young man who asked her to contribute to a magazine he was involved with. They became acquainted and found something in common: he too was teaching in a backwoods school because illness had kept him from completing normal school. They met and agreed to marry but she was so inexperienced with men and so unprepared for the physical side of marriage that the match seemed doomed. She left teaching and moved to Kumamoto to attempt a career in journalism. She failed at that.

It is no wonder that she found herself in "a morass of depression" and that she undertook the pilgrimage to try to find her way out of it. For an idea of what her pilgrimage was like, here is a pastiche from her accounts of it.

"By the time we left Temple Forty-three it was past noon. After the night of sleeping beside the road my legs were swollen. Struggling, I dragged them along. Up one mountain and down another, we got lost. I became slow of foot and the old man tried to cheer me by picking flowers for me. He seems stronger than most younger men; that would be because he is very religious."

A night at Temple Forty: "We spread a blanket on the veranda and licked raw sugar and salt. The moon cast a pale light and all creatures fell asleep. The old man prostrated himself before the memorial tablets of the deceased; I dozed with my back against a pillar. I feel desolate at night."

They took a little coastal boat between Forty and Thirty-nine, avoiding Pine Tree Ascent. "It was packed with passengers and very uncomfortable; I stayed on deck. Some men on the upper deck called, 'Miss, come up here,' and when I looked they stretched out their arms and lifted me up. I was so shy that one of them said, 'Let us see your pretty face,' and everyone about us burst into laughter.

"When we landed, a henro with reddish hair, long and wild, pushed his way through the crowds to stare at me. His face was hairy and his eyes sunken. It was frightening. In a town we rested under a tree, and there he was, staring with red eyes. Uneasy, I smiled at him. In the calm of Temple Thirty-nine he appeared again: when I pretended not to see him he came toward me; when

I looked at him he stopped. I waited, fearing what might happen but finally he turned away. If I want to free myself it is best to let matters take their course. If someone wants to kill me I deserve it. There is little in this life worth struggling to keep."

They spent the night at a henro-inn in front of Thirty-nine; it was crowded with nineteen pilgrims. "Since henro are human, they laugh and joke and make themselves at home. After dinner the men take a bath in order of arrival, then the women." Faced with a rainstorm, they and a few others decided to stay over the next day. "We relaxed and talked. An old lady said that after she made the pilgrimage all her chronic diseases disappeared, so she has decided to devote herself to the pilgrimage for the rest of her life. There was a blind man, very emaciated but eloquent in praising Buddha; he asserted that his being able to perform the pilgrimage all by himself, over mountains and across rivers, was the reward for his profound faith—a kind of vanity I recognize in myself. An old man sighed constantly that he hadn't enough to eat tomorrow; it became objectionable and the blind man told him roundly that his attitude was all wrong."

Later in the day, after the rain turned to drizzle, others arrived. "A bearded man accompanied a nun. His eyes were like stars: he was quite mad. And the nun was feeble-minded too. Coming close to me, she said, 'If you are retarded, do not get married. That is my advice to you. I was born retarded and my parents made me a nun because of that. But still a man got me in trouble. He fooled me easily.' Suddenly the man burst into loud laughter, startling everyone, and he and the nun moved into a corner together.

"At the other end of the room a girl whose head was covered with boils kept mumbling querulously. She wore a kimono that looked like a sack. When she scratched at the boils, blue-red pus oozed out and the stench was unbelievable. She knew nothing of her mother or her hometown. She was wandering with her father, a man with shrewd eyes and a thick short neck but a body that was as skinny and wrinkled as a twisted thread. He boasted that he had dared to beg at the police station; a policeman lectured him sternly but the inspector gave him two rice cakes so he was quite pleased at his success.

"A horrible old woman poked me, demanding that I write a letter for her. She dictated: 'If you don't send me money I'll curse you into the grave. Praise the Daishi! From sainted henro Okane.'"

A couple of days later, at the little chapel that Shinnen founded after he finished his guidebook: "There are many graves of henro. Scraping at the moss on one, I could barely read the name. We have so often seen lonely graves along the henro-path, many marked only by a staff or a sedge hat."

Again and again she writes of her loneliness on the pilgrimage but she was beginning to realize that she would be lonely all her life and she was coming to terms with that. A few times she speaks of a hospitable family, of caring for a baby or exchanging songs with a young girl, but underlying these brief encounters is the certainty that they are transient; she will never see these people again. She and the old man stopped to rest for ten days at the outskirts of Kochi City but she mentions meeting no one. Their inn was on the bay; once the ladies of the castle had rested there when they took boating excursions but nothing was left of its former elegance. Across the water at night she heard merry voices from the gay quarter; "they deepen a traveler's loneliness. . . .

"The old man considered himself to be my escort and guard and he always acted accordingly. He also took charge of our money, which he kept in a long cotton purse, once white but now grimy. Since his eyes were bad he would often drop coins and had difficulty paying for things, but though I worried I watched him fumble our money without a word.

"Whenever we came to a village or a town he never failed to ask alms. Leaving me to guard our packs at the roadside, he would stand before each house, ring his bell, and recite the sutra. In his role as my protector he felt he should be the one to beg, especially for lodging, so as to shield me from demeaning negotiations. He was a commanding figure but he looked so dirty that he was an unwelcome sight and was usually refused. Then I had to step in and smooth things over to get us lodging, though he resented my interference and said that those who treated him meanly were in the wrong.

"We each had a bag hanging from the neck in which we carried the handfuls of rice or barley we were given; if we gathered more than we needed to eat we could exchange it for coins at a henro-inn.

"People would go out of their way to bring settai to me. In one town we collected a large sum of money but I have a feeling it was because I went with him. People asked him whether I was his daughter or his mistress and so embarrassed me that I ran off by myself, homesick and thinking of the past. But I realized that human nature is the same everywhere, and all the time I was struggling to change myself. . . .

"We had to sleep on the beach some nights. The thunder of the Pacific breaking on the shore kept me awake but the old man slept soundly. . . .

"At a small henro-inn one of the others staying there said he was a descendant of one of the most powerful lords of old Japan and though he was a pilgrim he was also a medical doctor. A man who had been talking with him bowed as low as possible and said, 'Please oblige me by telling me what I can pay you for your help.'

" 'I am not a merchant,' was the lofty reply.

" 'Ah—then please accept this.'

" 'Oh? I cannot deny your request.'

"Then a young man approached with his mother, both bowing very low. The 'doctor' put his hands on the young man's head, turned and twisted it, and peered closely at his forehead. Then he wrote in his notebook and double-wrapped some powder, saying that no regular doctor could provide this medicine. 'I brought this back from the United States. You must take it at exactly twelve-fifteen p.m. with a prayer. You are in the first stage of brain congestion. No ordinary Japanese doctor could diagnose it.'

"The young man and his mother bowed so many times they almost hurt themselves. Then the young man said hesitantly, 'This is my mother. She has terrible pain in her legs. One doctor says she has rheumatism—'

" 'You don't have to tell me. A doctor like me can see what is wrong at a glance.' The two of them bowed flat and stayed motionless. The 'doctor' double-wrapped more powder for the mother.

" 'Please say how much.'

" 'I am not a merchant.'

" 'Then please take this.'

" 'I cannot refuse you.' I couldn't help laughing, thinking of those two taking their powders at twelve-fifteen exactly.

"The 'doctor' plunged into thought as though pondering some deep philosophical question. Suddenly he took up paper and brush and began to write. I inched around, expecting to see noble calligraphy. His writing was the worst I had ever seen. . . .

"While we were resting in the shade a group of young henro came by. 'Hey there, cutie!' they cried, and other such things. I paid no attention but they went on yelling until they were out of sight. . . .

"We had to stay in another dirty place, crawling with lice. We shared a room with a mother and her daughter of fourteen or fifteen. The girl wore a woman's hairdo with an artificial flower in it and her breasts were amazingly developed for one so young. The mother's hair was cut like a nun's but she was shamelessly talking with the girl about sex. . . .

"Again the loneliness of the journey bore in on me. . . . Shikoku is unbelievably beautiful in the autumn. I love it as much as I do my home. I want to come here again as a pilgrim, but alone. . . .

"On October 20 we returned to the port of Yawatahama, our pilgrimage completed. It had been more than four months since I started. I spent my last coins on a postcard, writing home to ask for money. We had to stay in an inn till it came. Our room was upstairs, with a low ceiling and dirty walls. Filthy old bedding piled in the corner made it smaller. Crowded in with us were a blind woman henro, a boy henro of fifteen or sixteen, a strolling comedian, and a fortuneteller with his wife, daughter, and baby. The comedian told his story with a laugh and a sigh. The fortuneteller was trying to persuade his daughter to become a prostitute but she was saying she wanted to work in a spinning mill.

"The old man and I were called down to be interrogated by two policemen, very haughty. 'Why did you leave home?' 'What is your name?' 'Say it again! Speak up!' 'Are you both henro?'

"The old man was enraged. 'Of course we are. People who make the pilgrimage to worship at the temples—all of them are henro, even if they come from good families.' The policemen went away laughing: 'We won't get anything interesting out of them.'

"Upstairs they were whispering that there must be a roundup of henro today. Perhaps so. The blind henro who went for a walk never came back."

Morikawa and I agree that the pilgrimage has become much tamer since then. Yet once in a while, an echo of those times. . . . We stop for lunch at an ordinary restaurant. As we are eating, the door clatters open and a scruffy old man in henro robe bursts in. Confronting the owner, who presides at the cash register, he asks alms. The owner eyes him coldly and refuses. The old man's voice rises. "I carry Kobo Daishi on my back! You must respect the Daishi!" The owner tells him to get out. The jabberer rages, repeats himself. The owner gets up, seizes his arm, and pushes him out as the storm continues: "—Kobo Daishi on my back! Respect the Daishi!" The door is banged shut. The voice continues a moment, then breaks. Through the frosted glass I watch an apparition sag, turn, and shuffle from view. The owner is already back into his newspaper.

Takamure never made another pilgrimage. She married the man—the "materialist"—who was part of what she was fleeing from, but marriage and a baby who died soon after birth only intensified her loneliness. She spent the last thirty-three years of her life, almost half of it, immured in their house in Tokyo, burying herself in her writing, never going out, never receiving visitors, in touch with the world only through her husband. Sixteen years after her pilgrimage, again facing a nervous breakdown, she decided to return to Shikoku—alone as she had promised herself she would; before she set out her health improved and she plunged back into her work on marriage customs and women's rights.

But being at Temple Forty-three reminds us of someone else

who did do the pilgrimage more than once, who performed it in 1918, the year that Takamure did; they certainly passed along the way, because he went in the usual direction. Probably they passed more than once: he must have made the pilgrimage five or six times that year. It was in 1918 that the total number of his pilgrimages climbed into the 260's.

His name was Nakatsuka Mohei and he was a latter-day holy man. Generations of henro have blessed Mohei, for he erected hundreds of stone guideposts at critical points along the henro-path. He put one below Temple Forty-three but not without running into problems, problems that are a matter of record since Mohei took up the matter with the police.

Yawatahama Police Headquarters
June 4, 1913

From: Officer Betsumiya
To: Nakatsuka Mohei

In answer to your request of April 27 this year regarding Hayashi Suehiro, stonemason of this town, we have reproved him and required him to make a written explanation, which we enclose.

The enclosure can be summarized:

Apology

About ten years ago, when I was a stonemason in Uno [the town below Temple Forty-three] I accepted an order from Nakatsuka Mohei to make a stone guidepost for the convenience of Shikoku henro, and I received a deposit.

Later I came to Yawatahama to succeed to the stonemason's shop of my late brother. At that time I planned to open a branch in Uno but I have not yet been able to do so. The stone for the guidepost is still in Uno.

However, when Mohei sent me the words to be engraved on the guidepost they were to cover four sides instead of three as originally ordered. This has also caused a delay, because naturally the fee must be increased to cover engraving four sides; I am considering this. But I will surely complete the work and deliver it within forty days.

Hayashi Suehiro
May 20, 1913

Mohei began his pilgrimages in the spring of 1865 when he was eighteen years old. It was not poverty that sent him to Shikoku: his family owned a sizable tract of land on one of the large islands in the Inland Sea; his father had been village headman. He had died when the boy was eleven; Mohei's brother, some fourteen years older, became head of the family. Perhaps the brothers did not get along. That would not have been unusual; younger sons were traditionally barred from inheritance so as not to divide the family property and they usually left home: commonly they were adopted and married into other families.

It was over marriage for Mohei that a bitter quarrel developed between the brothers. Mohei fell in love with a village girl, a match his brother would not permit; probably the girl's family was not considered worthy. Mohei turned to energetic dissipation, spending night and day in the town's red-light district. Just as suddenly—and we do not know who or what prompted him—he forsook those pleasures and headed for Shikoku to become a henro. He vowed he would never return home alive.

It was said in those days that anyone who made the pilgrimage once should do it at least three times. Mohei did. He turned himself into a firm believer. He chanted homage to the Daishi and homage to Amida Buddha, like the holy men of old. He also began to study with the priest of Temple Seventy-six, not far from the Daishi's birthplace and deeply associated with the Daishi's nephew. After twelve years of pilgrimage and study he was ordained a priest.

Clearly Mohei felt the power of the mountains. The next year, 1878, he briefly left Shikoku to practice austerities on Mount Fuji and on two of the peaks on the Kii Peninsula—among the mountains where Koya rises—which are most sacred to Mountain Buddhism. Four years later he took time out to perform the Pilgrimage to the Thirty-three Temples dedicated to Kannon that stretch from the Pacific to the Sea of Japan through Kyoto and Japan's ancient heartland.

In 1886 he completed his eighty-eighth pilgrimage of Shikoku. Eighty-eight pilgrimages had to be commemorated. It was then he resolved to erect stone guideposts to help henro find their way.

Five years and thirty-three pilgrimages later, he applied for and received from the headquarters temple in Kyoto certification as a priest of Mountain Buddhism. Now he was licensed to conduct the rituals to cure illness, to achieve well-being. As the count of his pilgrimages mounted toward two hundred he frequently performed such services. He used the offerings he received to help pay for his guideposts but he also received support from patrons, large amounts from some who were rich, small sums from many who were not. He had a long list of believers who regularly made contributions and who were happy to lodge him. He was welcomed all along the henro-path. People called him a living Buddha.

His diary for his last years shows that he was slowing down. He stopped for long rests at some homes and temples, so that he made the pilgrimage only two or three times a year, and he resorted to buses and trains. He was bothered by asthma and a cough; he frequently bought medicine, and sugar which he licked to ease his throat. (He also bought candy to give to children; they recognized him when they saw him coming and flocked to greet him.) "A good thing for a cough," he wrote, "is to eat for sixteen days a mixture of black beans, raw sugar, and codeine," and "Great medicine to ease itching skin is boric acid and nursery powder."

He completed 280 pilgrimages. In the course of his 281st he came in March, 1922, to a house in Takamatsu City where he had often stayed in the past, and there, on the twentieth, he died peacefully. Believers rushed to assemble and it was they who held the funeral service; the memorial gifts were large. As he had wished, his ashes were sent to his family. In death he came home.

Morikawa and I walk down the long sloping road from Temple Forty-three. At the bottom is the stone guidepost that Mohei succeeded in installing only after calling on the police for help. It is dated 1914: the stonemason did not keep his pledge to finish it within forty days but it was put up the following year. Perhaps the negotiations over engraving the fourth side took some time.

Mohei always had a good deal to say on his stones. This one gives directions and distances, the name of the man who gave the money for it, and the name of the man who introduced Mohei to him, and it states that this is the 286th henro-stone erected by Nakatsuka Mohei.

From here it is three days' walk to Temple Forty-four. We stop the first night at a bangai that celebrates one of the pilgrimage's deep-rooted legends. Kobo Daishi found himself at this place one winter's night. In a biting wind he made the rounds, asking at every house for lodging and being everywhere refused. He could only take shelter under the bridge; trying to sleep at the river's edge he composed a verse:

> *They will not help a traveler in trouble—*
> *This one night seems like ten.*

Since then the bridge here, though many times rebuilt, has been known as Ten-Nights Bridge. And so as not to disturb the Daishi's rest, every henro lifts his staff, never letting it tap on this or any other bridge he crosses. We climb down the bank to the altar beneath the bridge where a stone image of the Daishi lies, as the real Daishi did not, under thick comforters.

When I came here on my first visit to Shikoku the tottery old house nearby was a henro-inn where a pilgrim could sleep and eat supper and breakfast for the equivalent of twenty-eight cents if he brought his own rice or thirty-nine cents if he did not. Behind the house is a one-room building about twelve feet square that then was new; the charge to sleep in it was five and a half cents; no bedding was furnished but there was a mosquito net and outside was a shed with a simple hearth where henro could cook their own food. The two women who ran the inn told me that in spring and summer they averaged ten guests a night but that traffic was decreasing as fewer henro walked. Now the inn is out of business.

The next day we walk into the mountains again. In the afternoon our legs let us know that we are climbing. We are following the course of a clean, swift river through a ravine that deepens as

Roadside images

we go. The rock bluff at roadside is carved with Buddhist images. On the opposite bank masses of wisteria cascade over the river. The wild azaleas, which were faded in the valley below, are here fresh.

We mount one ridge after another, higher and higher, toward Shikoku's tallest mountains. We tire and our feet ache from walking on asphalt. If it is any comfort, I remind Morikawa, almost everyone who walks this road gets tired. Our friend Tosa did, and along here he and his companions were overtaken by dark, then rain, and finally snow. And that 1819 henro did: "The riverside upgrade was so difficult we felt we had walked fifty miles. Men were hunting deer and boar; we saw forty or fifty men with at least twenty dogs."

It is late afternoon when we reach a hamlet perched above a gorge where two streams rush together. The woman who runs the little inn is tending a patch of farm somewhere but a child is sent to call her and after a bit she appears and sets a fire for our bath. We are given the same room I slept in before; Tosa and his companions used it too, when at last they got here, wet and chilled. It has a student's desk and the walls are lined with photos clipped from fan magazines, youths with toothy smiles and electric guitars. Supper will be good country food. Through the night there will be the roar of the rivers. . . .

In the morning our hostess obliges with an early breakfast and we make a fast start. The air is crisp, the forested mountains exhilarating, our steps light. About midday we reach the spot where the old henro-path branches off from the road and up over the mountains. The path is neglected and deteriorating, some of it rough and hard work, but almost any path is better than a highway and this one rewards us with bursts of bloom—blue wisteria and azaleas in salmon, lavender-pink, and golden yellow. Violets crowd our footsteps.

From the pass at the summit the view sweeps as far as the sea and we sit for a while to take it in. In the distant haze is the city of Matsuyama; we can make out the hill on which the castle stands and Morikawa says he can see the castle walls. Matsuyama is home to both of us. Our pilgrimage will not end there but three nights from now we can sleep in our own beds.

Just below us, on a plateau sixteen hundred feet above sea level, is the town of Kuma, and on the mountainside just beyond it, deep among cedars and cypress, is Temple Forty-four. Kuma grew up at the gate of the temple, flourished as a lumbering center, and became a post town on the highway between Matsuyama and Kochi (it still is: even the express buses make a rest stop there).

Legend gives a different version of the town's beginnings. When Kobo Daishi came this way only one old woman lived here; she gave him lodging for the night. Grateful, he asked her what he could do to express his appreciation. Well, she answered, it was lonely living in such a solitary place: could he please make a town?

By his prayers the Daishi created a river and made the soil fertile; people moved in, and did the only decent thing—they named their town after the old woman, whose name was Kuma.

We plan to stay at the temple tonight but we could stay at a henro-inn; there used to be several along the lane leading up to the temple, and one that has operated for many generations is still in business. Tosa and his friends stayed there. They fell into luck, for their host fed them bountifully (he had received a cancellation from a party of skiers for whom he had laid in special food) and told them stories about innkeeping for henro. Before the war, he said, they would often nurse a sick henro for two or three months; it seemed that one no sooner recovered and left than another appeared. The arrival of parent and child henro would make the family wary: within the innkeeper's lifetime his family had raised three children who had been abandoned at the inn. "One of them still lives in the town, happily settled here and married."

From the high plateau below us to the city in the distance stretches the wide Matsuyama plain. Late tomorrow afternoon, if we can keep to our schedule, we will have visited Forty-four below us and Forty-five up a canyon to our right (that fantasy world of rocky cliffs sculpted by nature). Then we will descend the old path to the plain and the first of the six temples that lie along the road to the city. All of these temples are close to home and as familiar as old friends. And along that road to the city we will be walking among the fields that, as henro know, once belonged to Emon Saburo. Down there is where the legend of his redemption begins and ends.

At Temple Forty-six, the first on the plain, we will find a stone engraved with a haiku by Japan's greatest modern haiku poet, Masaoka Shiki, a native of Matsuyama. On a spring day (much like this one) in the 1880's he came to the temple, whose name is Joruri-ji, and sat beneath its two huge sandalwood trees, about a thousand years old.

How long the spring day is!
Remembering Emon Saburo
At Joruri-ji.

Temple Forty-eight *(a print by Kadowaki)*

A little farther along we will come to the spot where they say Emon Saburo's gate stood, where he dashed the Daishi's begging bowl to the ground. A bangai stands there now, and its priest recites the story, pointing to the illustrations above his head. Then, back from the road a couple of hundred yards, we will visit the eight lonely mounds marking the graves of Saburo's sons. That of the eldest is the largest, perhaps thirty feet square and twelve high; the others are somewhat smaller. On top of each is a tree and a stone image of Jizo, guardian of children.

All about them farmers cultivate rice. Farmers are notoriously unsentimental about land, yet these mounds remain inviolate. Archaeologists say that they do indeed date from twelve or thirteen centuries ago, the Daishi's time. That long they have resisted wind, rain, and man's encroachment.

It is a little way to another small bangai. This is said to be the site of the hermitage where the Daishi stayed; this is the first place that Emon Saburo came looking for him; this is where the long pilgrimage of the first pilgrim began.

When I began *my* first pilgrimage, and even when Morikawa and I began this pilgrimage, I was troubled that I knew so little Buddhist doctrine. How could I understand what I was doing? Morikawa too, though Buddhism is part of his heritage, confessed that he knew almost nothing of doctrine in general and nothing at all of Shingon doctrine and he worried that this would limit his ability to help me. (I confessed that I would be just as hard put to elucidate for him the doctrine of the Protestant Christianity that is my heritage.) But as we have walked together, as we have thought about the holy men who were the real founders of the pilgrimage and who were certainly not strong on doctrine, as we have talked with other henro at the temples where we stayed overnight, finding that most of them are not members of Shingon and hearing them reiterate that the pilgrimage is nonsectarian, that "you don't have to belong to Shingon to believe in Kobo Daishi," we have come to realize—we have been relieved to realize—that doctrine plays little part in this pilgrimage.

Emon Saburo personifies the religion of the pilgrimage—the common man's religion. He was a layman, not a priest. Salvation came to Emon Saburo not through study of doctrine but through hard practice. Morikawa and I have learned that the essence of the pilgrimage lies in treading a route that tradition says the Daishi trod, and in the conviction that, spiritually at least, one walks in the Daishi's company.

The henro puts his faith in the Daishi. Beyond that, doctrine is for priests.

The last of the six temples on the plain, Fifty-one, is well inside the city. Sightseeing buses and taxis will be crowding its parking lot and inevitably there will be a traffic jam at its entrance. It has always bustled there. In the old days a market, a fair, and a playhouse flourished; it was infested with beggars and pickpockets (a sign still warns against the latter). The poet Shiki came there often on his walks. His only haiku in which he used the word "henro" he wrote at Fifty-one. It is a reminder of what the pilgrimage was like when Takamure Itsue did it, when the word was in bad odor, when "henro" was a synonym for dirty, thieving, possibly leprous beggars. Mothers could quiet a naughty child by saying that henro would get him if he didn't behave. In his haiku Shiki clearly referred to disreputable characters because he used a vulgar word for "eat."

> In the spring breeze
> Henro gobble lunch
> Around the gate of the guardian deities.

For a long time after the temple was founded it bore a name that referred to Amida's Pure Land in the West. Then came the epilogue to Emon Saburo's story. It was in the nearby castle of the lord of Iyo that the baby was born with the clenched fist. It was the head priest of this temple whose prayers opened the little hand, revealing the stone that the Daishi had engraved "Emon Saburo reborn." It was the natural consequence of this miracle that the temple was renamed Ishite-ji, "Stone-Hand Temple." The temple displays the stone in its museum; we will take another look at it.

We have rested long enough. We rise, hoist our packs, and start down from the pass toward Kuma town and Temple Forty-four.

21 Leaving the last temple in Iyo we begin to climb an easy, gently rising path through a woods where the hush is broken only by our footsteps and the sounds of scurrying things in the grass. Gaining height, we cross and recross a motor road until our path disintegrates, then we walk the road the rest of the way up to Temple Sixty-six.

It is called the first temple in Sanuki—today's Kagawa Prefecture—but in fact we have climbed from Iyo into a corner of Awa, the province where we began our pilgrimage. The summit of the

Temple Fifty-one *(a painting by Kawabata)*

mountain marks the boundary of Sanuki and Awa but the temple stands in Awa. It bears a name that means "Temple Near the Clouds" and at about three thousand feet it is indeed the highest of the eighty-eight and another of those ancient places where holy

The ablution basin at Temple Fifty-two (*a print by Kadowaki*)

men have grappled the mountains for the secrets of their power.

It has been a key point militarily as well, for the crest commands on one side a view of Awa's mountains and valleys and, on the other, of the whole Sanuki plain. In the spring of 1577 that Tosa warlord Chosokabe Motochika, who very nearly conquered all of Shikoku, stood at the crest with the chief priest of the temple. The priest seized the occasion to rebuke him for his boundless ambition, indicating that he would better follow the will of heaven if he went home and looked after his own people. Motochika replied by comparing himself to "the lid of a teapot made by a master potter," implying that he intended to take and shield all Shikoku. The priest's retort: "That would be like trying to cover a water bucket with a teapot lid."

Motochika turned to his chief of staff and asked what he thought. "You should consult a priest about religious matters and

Awa's mountains from Temple Sixty-six *(a print by Kadowaki)*

a warrior about war," came the answer. "This priest is conceited and impudent and he knows nothing of strategy. We do. You have already gained half of Awa; subduing Sanuki and Iyo will be easy." Motochika followed his retainer's advice but when it went sour he probably remembered the testy priest. At any rate he seems to have respected frankness, for he did not burn the temple as he did many others that were strategically situated.

Today's priest fills us in on the temple's volatile history of prosperity and adversity and serves an excellent lunch. We learn that he is active in local affairs. He carries two kinds of name cards. Almost every character in the Japanese language can be read in two ways, each with a different sound and meaning; one of his cards gives the priestly reading of his given name, the other the civilian reading of the same characters. He uses the latter in politics, as chairman of the board of a construction company, and as an adviser to juveniles with problems (I think he must be good with youngsters).

Walking with us to the crest he pauses above a forested valley. "This is part of the temple lands. To encourage young men to stay in this locality instead of moving to the city, the temple will loan a chap twenty-five acres for forty-five years: he is to plant trees, care for them, harvest them in the forty-fifth year, and keep the proceeds." An admirable program and I do not doubt him when he says it is unique among the eighty-eight temples—few others have the resources.

We stand at the spot where Motochika and the priest stood, marveling at the view. "They say that Kobo Daishi climbed up here as a youth. Through the haze—there—you can see his birthplace." It is only about fifteen miles away; an active boy would have wanted to master this mountain.

He shows us the beginning of the path. A few steps down and we are in Sanuki. We turn and wave good-bye.

He had warned us that this path is in poor condition because so few use it. He understated; it is in terrible condition, as our friend Tosa found a few weeks ago: "Steep. Stones rolled under our feet; we often fell. 'Path of stumbling henro'—that old phrase describes it." But when was it an easy path? Not in 1819, when almost every pilgrim used it and that henro from Tosa wrote: "Fifty cho [about three and a half miles] downhill. Exhausting—nausea hit me. At the bottom I had to rest. I could eat no rice; I could only chew on a dried persimmon."

Descending a rugged path is always harder for me than ascending it. Down breakneck slopes washed out by the rains, slipping, falling, struggling to keep up with Morikawa who is much nimbler, but slowed by fear of a really serious fall, my knees paining as they always do on precipitous descents: three grueling hours until we reach the valley, a passable road, a stream flowing quietly, and land level enough to be farmed. Wheat is being harvested, cut with sickles and hung upside down from bamboo racks to dry before threshing.

Now we worry whether Temple Sixty-seven will take us in; we have no reservation. It is past five when we enter the gate and cross the compound to the inscription window where the priest sits. I am beat and I look it. He sees and smiles and I know it will be all right.

Soaking in the bath I think of the henro Tosa encountered here, a businessman from Osaka who exuberantly volunteered the reason for his pilgrimage: to give thanks to the Daishi for making him a great deal of money. Just before starting a pilgrimage last year he had bought some land; by the time he finished his pilgrimage and returned home, its value had multiplied ten times. "It was certainly due to Daishi-sama," he told Tosa, "so I am making this year's pilgrimage in gratitude." He was, of course, traveling by automobile.

I confess that I am impatient with motorized henro, those who are herded around by bus or who ride in cars and taxis. When I made my first pilgrimage, people joked about them, called them "instant henro." No more; there are so many of them and they spend so much money that no word of ridicule is heard. But to my mind, riding travesties the pilgrimage. If there is one thing Morikawa and I have learned it is that the Shikoku pilgrimage is not just a matter of visiting temples. The temples provide places of worship; they define the route; they are milestones of a sort. The temples punctuate the pilgrimage but they do not constitute it.

The pilgrimage is ascetic exercise for the layman. Its essence lies in the physical, mental, and spiritual demands made on the henro, and the physical, mental, and spiritual rewards that accrue. The legend of Emon Saburo epitomizes this.

I once tried a bus pilgrimage for three or four days to see what it was like. My fellow henro took what they were doing seriously; they were earnest in their prayers; they all denied that recreation was their primary reason for being there. But it was hard for me to believe that Kobo Daishi was traveling on that sense-numbing, sleep-inducing, dyspepsia-causing bus. Riding a bus is not ascetic exercise, and so the central meaning of the pilgrimage as it has existed through the centuries is lost.

Some of me hurts tonight and we are both tired but we are happy that we walked.

* * *

Rain dulls the light of early morning. We follow other henro along a covered passage to the morning service. Usually I have trouble following a priest's sermon and my thoughts wander. This morning I hear a familiar name and I strain to understand. The priest is talking about the visit to this temple of Ichikawa Danzo.

In April, 1966, the prominent Kabuki actor Ichikawa Danzo VIII formally retired from the stage in a series of gala performances. He was eighty-four years old but still vigorous, and retirement was not altogether traditional: many Kabuki actors die in harness. Almost at once he came to Shikoku, alone, and undertook the pilgrimage, a long-cherished dream. Finishing in late May he boarded an Inland Sea ferry but instead of crossing to Osaka he debarked at Shodo Island, which is encircled by a short replica of the Shikoku pilgrimage. He spent a few quiet days at an inn there, boarded a midnight ferry, and an hour later slipped over the stern in darkness to end his life. The press treated his death sensationally.

During the years I lived in Tokyo I saw all the Kabuki I could. Danzo was a familiar presence on stage; I liked watching him. I am still grateful for the pleasure he gave me, and again and again during our pilgrimage I have thought of him. After breakfast, when the other henro have departed in their bus, we ask the priest for all the details he can remember about Danzo's visit.

"It was just about this time, May 26 or 27, that he appeared. He came with bus pilgrims he had met at Sixty-five: they offered him a ride because they thought the climb to Sixty-six would be too difficult for him. The bus group was to spend the night here and I suggested that he stay also but he said he was afraid newspapermen would come and make trouble for the temple; he would go on.

"He complained about being harassed by reporters. Since on his white robe were written the names of those who had helped him during his long life, benefactors whom he was memorializing by pilgrimage, he was conspicuous and I suggested that he take off his robe and carry it wrapped so as to go unnoticed. His reaction was vehement: 'Rather than take off my robe, I would quit the pilgrimage and go home.'

"I still recall his dedication, his passionate refusal to give up his identification as a henro. I often tell the story to pilgrims as I did this morning. I think he knew no sutra; he just prayed from his heart. And he carried no inscription book, so the priests of most temples were unaware of his visit. But I was convinced of his sincerity."

We are nearing the birthplace of the pilgrimage now, for surely the Daishi's birthplace was the great magnet for worshipers. The five-storied pagoda of Temple Seventy-five calls to us across the plain. Biggest and busiest of the eighty-eight temples, the town it generated at its gate is the biggest and busiest of the temple towns. But its streets are no busier than the scene inside the gate. The long walkway is lined with stalls selling food, drink, souvenirs, toys, crockery, gewgaws; a few years ago there was an old man peddling pornographic photos—he seems to have disappeared. Big and popular temples and shrines usually have such a market at the gate. I was pleased to learn that each stallkeeper pays the temple a percentage of his take; I shrugged when I heard that he also pays protection to the underworld boss of the district—some things are universal. Before the war, beggar henro posted themselves here, observing the established financial procedures. They tell of one who did so well that he became a moneylender.

After the country temples we are used to, the precincts seem huge. The heart of the temple is a complex of impressive buildings where the family home stood; we are told that construction began in 861 after the Saeki family moved to the capital. We follow others up the broad steps and kneel to pray. At the far end of the hall, encased in cabinetry, is another of those statues of the Daishi carved by himself. The lavish altar glimmers; the smoke of incense rises; a priest intones a service. At our backs, worshipers tramp across the wooden floor, toss coins into the collection box, request

Calligraphy by the Daishi's mother, little Buddhas by the Daishi
(detail from a scroll of a sutra at Temple Seventy-five)

and pay for memorial services, while pigeons flutter in and out, scavenging offertory rice.

We browse through the temple's treasure house, its collection of ritual objects, imperial rescripts, paintings, and sculpture. What excites us most is one of the national treasures, a single scroll, part of a sutra, each line of text followed by a row of roseate little Buddhas on lotus pedestals; the calligraphy is thought to be by the Daishi's mother, the Buddhas by the Daishi. We linger in the temple gardens, return to pray again at the altar. We find it difficult to leave. Morikawa remarks that there is much to be said for beginning one's pilgrimage here, as Shinnen and Jakuhon directed in that first thorough guidebook.

But is it the Daishi's birthplace? On that score there is argument. About ten miles away, on the shore of the Inland Sea, is a bangai called Beach Temple that we will visit in a couple of days. There are many who believe that this is where Lady Tamayori, wife of Saeki Tagimi, gave birth to the Daishi.

According to ancient myths, childbirth, along with sexual intercourse and menstruation, caused ritual impurity. A temporary building was erected for a pregnant woman so that the dwelling house would not be defiled. In the Daishi's time there was also a custom, which has been observed in the West too, that a wife return to her parents' home to give birth. A short distance up the beach is another temple, said to stand on the site of Lady Tamayori's parents' home. Beach Temple is where they built the cottage for the birth.

There was a time when Seventy-five and Beach Temple were at each other's throats over this issue. In the early 1800's a lawsuit was carried to the shogun's commissioners for shrines and temples. The decision was in favor of Seventy-five, predictably, for in that period paternal links outweighed maternal. Beach Temple was permitted to call itself a sacred place of deep significance, "the first place related to him," but admonished not to promote itself so vehemently as his birthplace. Today it is not bashful about asserting its claim, but people don't get as exercised over the question as they used to. As the priest back at Sixty-seven put it, "Seventy-five's claim is legitimate because that was his family home. To honor Beach Temple would be as though we today were to honor the hospital where a baby was born." Though Seventy-five's eminence is secure, there is affection for Beach Temple.

But before we head toward the shore we must go in the opposite direction. We have from the beginning planned to visit the famed irrigation pond that the Daishi constructed, though few henro go there—few ever have—because it is a day's walk off the regular henro-path.

Moving across paddy lands toward the foothills shows us how much Sanuki depends on its ponds. Because rain can make a henro miserable we forget how farmers hope for it, how in the past emperors led solemn services to pray for it. We forget that the Daishi conducted such rituals and that Shingon had many prayers for rain. We forget the significance of all the legends about the Daishi's opening new springs and wells.

This plain has one of the lowest rainfalls in Japan. The summer monsoons, coming from the south off the warm Pacific, drop their rains against the mountains of Tosa and Awa. The winter monsoons, blowing out of Siberia, dump their snows on the mountains of the main island. The rain that falls here runs off quickly in Sanuki's short and "tailless" rivers. The underbed of granite stores little moisture. The province has a long history of struggle for water, of prayers for rain, and of building ponds to hold it when it fell. Today official reports count 18,620 irrigation ponds; they occupy more than a sixth of the area of the paddy lands. The pond we head for is the biggest of all.

They say a pond was first built there between 701 and 703. It was nowhere near as large as the Daishi made it later but it was big enough to cause havoc when its banks broke, which happened many times but with finality in 818, turning the land below it into a sea of mud. The imperial court sent its ranking builder of irrigation ponds; he worked two years without success. At that point, writes the Daishi's biographer, "the desperate governor of Sanuki requested that the court appoint Kukai [the priestly name the Daishi bore in his lifetime] as director. Here is part of the official letter sent by the governor to the court:

Since last year, the officers responsible for building the reservoir have been trying to repair it. The lake is large and the workers are few so that there is as yet no prospect of completing the work. Now the head of the county office tells me that the monk Kukai is a native of Tado County. He is a man of exemplary conduct and his fame . . . is unsurpassed. They say that, when he sits in meditation in the mountains, the birds build nests on him and animals grow tame. He studied abroad to seek the Way; he went empty-handed and returned fully equipped. Clergymen and laymen alike are delighted to receive his good influence, and the people look forward to seeing him. If he stays, a crowd of students assembles around him; if he goes, a multitude follows him. He has long been away from his native place and lives in the capital. Farmers yearn for him as they do for their parents. If they hear that the master is coming, they will run out in haste to welcome him. I sincerely request that he be appointed the director."

Hyperbole was called for in such a document, but after discounting that, the Daishi's prestige and magnetism are evident. Years of social work among the people had won their admiration and affection.

He arrived in the early summer of 821; the people rushed to him in such haste (says the chronicle of those years) that many slipped into their sandals wrong-foot-to. He began with a fire ceremony and prayers (an inlet in today's reservoir marks the spot). To the crowd assembled he explained that he had been given an imperial order to reconstruct the pond; he asked for their help. They gave it. The job was completed in less than three months.

This and other reservoirs that he was associated with demonstrate that he had an advanced knowledge of civil engineering. For instance, the dam is curved back against the impounded water; engineers today are often surprised to find that he knew that principle. The earthen dam that he built has never failed. Through carelessness and neglect, the wooden sluice gate has sometimes rotted out, but the dam, except that it has been raised somewhat during the past century, is as he built it.

We walk into the river valley and climb the dam. Even expecting bigness, I am surprised at the size of the lake that stretches far into the hills. The huge curving dam, wider than a highway on top, slopes gently into the water, its surface paved with stone. I feel a sense of exhilaration: after being asked so often to take on faith that he did this and that, it is tonic to stand before a certified achievement. This reservoir alone would account for the faith in the Daishi among farmers.

There is a statue of him overlooking the lake, and higher on the shore, a temple. We seek out the priest and he gives us some figures. This is the fourth-largest irrigation reservoir in Japan, the largest held by an earthen dam. The dam is more than 500 feet long, rises 105 feet from the valley floor. It is nearly 13 miles

around the edge of the lake, which irrigates almost 12,000 acres—
more than one-eighth of the Sanuki plain. It is named Manno-ike,
the "Pond for Ten Thousand Fields."

From Temple Eighty to Eighty-one the henro-path, as our old
guidebooks describe it, goes up and over a mountain. We ask the
priest at Eighty about it. It is impassable, he says; we must go
miles around by highway.

Eighty cannot lodge us so we spend the night at a little inn
nearby whose cheerful, talkative mistress quickly extracts a curriculum vitae from each of us. We ask her about the path. "Of course
it's passable," she declares. In the evening we scout the village.
Opinion is about evenly divided as to whether the path still exists,
but if it does we find where it starts.

Morning: we set out on a dirt road that aims for the mountain. Two or three villagers along the way are very doubtful that
we can get through, but at the last farmhouse on the road we find
a woman who says, "Of course you can; I do it myself," and she
points out the route up the mountain.

We follow the path up the lower slopes to where it ends at a
rock and dirt slide. Here there is a path that girdles the mountain.
After studying our map, Morikawa decides we should go to the left
(the map is Greek to me). We walk several hundred yards along
the face of the mountain to an irrigation pond and a rocky ravine.
We are struggling to get across when the woman hails us. She has
watched our progress from her home, seen that we took the wrong
way, and chased after us more than half a mile up the mountain to
set us right. We cannot go that way, she tells us; we must go
straight up the slide to where the path picks up again. She has
brought two big summer oranges to refresh us.

We dig our way up the washout, steep and not at all easy, but
as it ends we find traces that become more distinct, leading finally
into a continuation of the well-marked path we followed below.
We mount a ridge to a sere plateau, bare but for a few bushes and
scrub trees, slashed by gullies, a devastated landscape with a war
in progress: this is a training ground for the Self-Defense Forces.

We try to skirt their battle, scrambling over the rough terrain with the crack of their rifles and mortars in our ears, devoutly hoping that we are not between opposing forces and that if we are their ammunition is blank.

Across that dusty highway we might have had to walk we enter a forest and find the path to Eighty-one. We know we are nearing the temple when we come across old stone monuments directing us to dismount and proceed respectfully on foot.

It was in one of this temple's hermitages that the banished Emperor Sutoku was cloistered after his ill-fated little rebellion in 1156. It was at this temple that his ashes were interred after he was murdered in 1164. It was to this grave that his friend the poet and holy man Saigyo came to pray in 1168.

Fittingly, this is one of the beautiful temples of the pilgrimage: tall pines and cedars, swept gravel walks, white walls, impressive gates, handsome buildings. There is a hall dedicated to Sutoku, a structure of quiet elegance, roofed with reeds of miscanthus, draped with a white hanging bearing the imperial chrysanthemum in scarlet; it was dedicated in 1414 with most sincere prayers that his troubled and troubling spirit be soothed and swiftly achieve enlightenment. Behind this hall, at the top of a long flight of stone steps bordered by hedges, is his grave: two levels of raked pebbles bound by stone balusters, shaded by cedars. There are stone lanterns, a sacred *sakaki* tree with glistening leaves. There is quiet and peace.

At the outskirts of the city of Takamatsu is Number Eighty-three, plain and sprawling. But the Daishi Hall contains many plaster casts and crutches, evidence of faith in the temple even if it is not rich. "There are no treasures," the priest tells us. "A licentious priest ran away with them a few generations ago. But probably there wasn't much of value, for the temple was many times burned in war."

The temple's reason for being is only a gate away—Sanuki's Ichinomiya, its "Number One Shinto Shrine"; it is clear from old diaries that henro used to regard them as one institution. After we

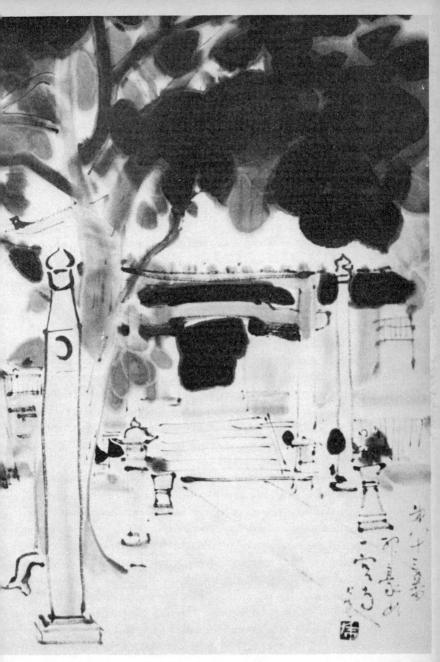

Temple Eighty-three *(a painting by Sakata)*

worship we walk through the gate; this is one of the few occasions when we have a chance to visit an adjacent Shinto shrine that is active and has a full-time priest. He welcomes us, seems pleased that we have called. "The pilgrimage grew out of popular belief, which was a mixture of Shinto and Buddhism, but nowadays henro do not visit shrines. This is contrary to custom. One reason may be that the guides provided by the bus companies have little knowledge and a very tight schedule." We demonstrate that our schedule is not tight by accepting another cup of tea.

The shipping lane between Takamatsu and Kobe curves around the broad island of Shodo. All over Japan and wherever the Japanese have emigrated there are miniature eighty-eight-temple pilgrimages; there are thousands of them, little models of the pilgrimage on Shikoku, eighty-eight stations that can be traversed in a few minutes or a few hours. Numbered altar by numbered altar, the worshiper bows before the same deity as at the corresponding temple on Shikoku; prayers are offered from afar. The longest and most famous of these replicas is on Shodo (although, because it was put together from existing temples, the deities of the temples do not correspond to those on Shikoku). Shodo's course takes about five days to walk and it is one I should investigate, but we are drawn there today because it is where actor Ichikawa Danzo, after finishing his Shikoku pilgrimage, spent the last days of his life. We speculate on why he stopped at Shodo. Certainly he was tired: rather than going straight home he wanted a quiet place to rest, to be private. Was it also because Shodo has its small counterpart of the long pilgrimage he had just completed?

It is raining steadily when we board the ferry at Takamatsu port. During the hour's passage I stare out the window into the rainblur, seeing him again: the long narrow oval of his face, the high cheekbones, the almost somber presence he brought to his roles. He was a stalwart, though not a star, of the Kabuki company I liked best. I saw him often in the 1950's, when he was in his seventies, and in the early 1960's, when he was turning eighty. He never faltered, never traded on his years, never asked in the ways some aged actors do for veneration as a monument. He had too much reserve, too much dignity for that. Some critics say he was too reserved, not showy enough, but his craftsmanship was sure; if he was not brilliant, he seemed indispensable.

He was born in 1882 and at the age of two first appeared on the stage ("I remember a photograph of myself in someone's arms," he told an interviewer) so that his retirement performances in April, 1966, were properly billed as a gala celebration of eighty-two years on the Kabuki stage. For almost a quarter of a century he had borne one of Kabuki's luminous names—he was the Eighth Danzo. Perhaps, as has been suggested, it was a burden to him: sometimes he seemed to imply that he was miscast as an actor. He never felt he measured up, specifically against his father, Danzo VII. The Seventh did have brilliance, the mystique of a star, but he seldom played with his famous contemporaries in the major theaters because of an almost continual sense of grievance against them: he had a gift for conflict as large as his gift for acting; he preferred to barnstorm the provinces. In this he embodied the prickliness that had characterized the name of Danzo from 1698, when a disciple of Danjuro I, the head of the house of Ichikawa (Danjuro is generally considered the greatest name in Kabuki), rebelled and as Danzo I established a tangential line.

The succession from Seventh to Eighth was from father to son, which is not all that usual with great names, in Kabuki or in other fields, ability being more important than blood. It was only the second time it had happened in the Danzo lineage (the Seventh was the son of a chef) and perhaps it increased the son's sense of inferiority. His father had been a merciless master: he several times pulled the young man from a part, not only before the opening but after it, and once he was so enraged by a performance that he tied the boy to a tree in the garden in midwinter and poured water on him (a scene right out of a Kabuki play) until a distressed disciple managed a rescue. Not the sort of tutelage to build confidence, but the son admired, respected, and defended his father all his life and wrote a biography of him that some call his most important contribution to Kabuki. He wrote it as methodically as he did all else, exactly three pages a day until he was finished. Then he took the manuscript to the Theater Museum at Waseda University to deposit it there, and was surprised when the director insisted on its being published because of its excellence.

He took the subway to the theater every morning and, after the Kabuki actor's usual twelve-hour day, home again at night. Unless you recognized him you would not take him for an actor. His colleagues respected him but his reserve kept them at a distance: they considered him solid, cautious, a little dull. Scandal never touched him, although his father had a certain notoriety as a womanizer. His hobby—listed as long ago as 1909 in a book about actors—was "travel to see historic relics and famous places." Returning from an engagement in another city, he would take a local train instead of an express as the rest of the company did (he would say he'd be back in time for rehearsals for the next month's bill and he always was) and then he'd get off at any stop that looked attractive. When he registered at an inn he never identified himself as an actor or requested special favors; he did ask about the local points of interest and he visited them alone. He was especially attracted to temples and shrines, where he worshiped with deep respect. He dreamed for a long time of making the Shikoku pilgrimage.

He had spoken of retirement as early as 1943, when the theater's business management pushed him into assuming the name of Danzo. It was the thirty-third anniversary of his father's death and the management liked to have the great names active—it was good box office. He protested but the pressures they applied were irresistible. Retirement certainly occurred to him in 1955 on the death of the head of the acting company, his intimate since their youth, and the last great surviving star of the prewar years, Kichiemon I. But the troupe continued, he still felt at home in it, and there was his sense of responsibility.

What he dreaded was "becoming unpresentable." He remembered that his father, playing a starring role when he was elderly, had while seated onstage dozed off during a long byplay, and had to be wakened and prompted. He was determined never to exhibit any sign of senility to an audience. That was the reason he gave when he announced his retirement. At eighty-four he was healthy and vigorous and that was the way he wanted to exit.

He had made arrangements concerning a successor, though none of his sons was qualified. A friend and colleague, Bando Yaenosuke, who was married to his wife's sister, and who had no sons, asked to adopt his first grandson. Danzo demurred, said the boy had no prospects. In his fourth grandson he saw something special and he approved the adoption. He kept his eye on the boy and when he was six he asked the foster father if he wanted to make him an actor. "I answered that I asked no more than a son," Yaenosuke told me, "but he said it would be all right to make him an actor. We had to invent a new name for him, because the names that have always marked the succession to Danzo were filled, although those who held them were going nowhere. We combined the *gin* of Danzo's real name, Ginzo, and the *nosuke* of my name and called him Ginnosuke."

I turn to Morikawa and tell him of what happened last February when I went to Tokyo specifically to conduct some interviews about Danzo. Before any of the appointments I went to Kabuki with a friend. We were both extraordinarily taken with the performance of a young man, in a minor role but with the magnetism that leaps across the stage to catch you by the throat. His part was not listed in our English program so we hurried to the lobby when that play was over to ask who he was. They told us he was Ginnosuke, Danzo's grandson and perhaps the future Danzo IX.

"Danzo left a written testament," said Yaenosuke. "If, when Ginnosuke matures, the four leading actors of the Ichikawa troupe agree that he is worthy, he may succeed to the name Danzo. The decision must be unanimous." Yaenosuke smiled. "Usually an actor has one mentor. Ginnosuke has five, including myself. It's an advantage, but there are more chances he will be scolded."

In Danzo's farewell performances he had his grandson, then fifteen, cast in one of the plays. Danzo made elaborate notes on the boy's script and personally coached him. "That was his legacy," Yaenosuke said. "During rehearsals he looked very worried but after the opening he said, 'Yes, I guess he'll do.'"

Danzo was as composed about his final performances as about any others. "On April 25, 1966, the curtain closed for the last time.

He walked toward his dressing room just as before, but in the wings he stopped, turned back to face the stage, and bowed very reverently. In his dressing room he folded his portable hand-mirror and, as a final gesture, locked it. Then he asked me, 'Do you think Ginnosuke will be able to use this?' I said yes, and he handed it to me for the boy."

He told a reporter, "I feel as if a heavy load had been lifted from my shoulders: it's a wonderful relief." And then he took the subway home.

He had told some of his colleagues of his intention to make the pilgrimage. His family raised no objection: he was eighty-four but hardy and alert. He bought a pilgrim's sleeveless robe and on the back his wife inscribed the names of the departed whose memory he wished to honor, patrons and members of the Kabuki world. Within a week after his retirement he appeared at Temple One in a dark blue suit. He took time to get into his pilgrim's garb—he knew what putting on a costume meant—and then he stood straight, grasping his staff. "Do I look like a henro?" he asked the priest. "Like quite a proper henro," the priest replied, and the man who had been Danzo smiled. "This has been my dream for twenty years. At last I am a henro."

The priest saw him off: "You will experience many difficulties. Please take care of yourself." The answer was very firm: "I would not be sorry to die. Living or dead, I will be with O-Daishi-sama." He knew of course that over the centuries countless henro had died on the pilgrimage, many of them elderly, most of them anonymously. Perhaps he envied their just slipping away. Years earlier he had composed a poem that is almost a paraphrase of the declaration henro used to have to make: "If I become ill and die, I ask that I be buried with no further trouble; there is no need to communicate with my home place."

> *When I die I don't want to be*
> *A trouble to anyone.*
> *I shall just say good-bye*
> *And go to hell.*

Ichikawa Danzo VIII
on his pilgrimage

Later he revised it to add, "Don't accept funeral gifts or hold a wake." He must have thought about death often on his pilgrimage. I am sure he knew the line from the fourteenth-century essayist Yoshida Kenko: "What shall it avail a man to drag out till he becomes decrepit and unsightly a life which some day needs must end?"

He moved rather swiftly, walking where the temples were close, taking a bus when it was convenient. On his third day he rested under the arbor of wisteria in full bloom at Temple Eleven. On his tenth day he reached Kochi City. He had had the experience of being hailed by an old woman and given a coin as settai: he knew he was convincing in the role of henro.

Reporters had begun to stalk him, caught up with him in Kochi. "Aren't you Danzo?" they asked, but he denied it. "Then aren't you Ichikawa Ginzo?" This he admitted. They dogged him most of the rest of the way.

At midday on May 30 he attained Temple Eighty-eight. That evening, in an inn at Tonosho port on Shodo Island, he wrote a postcard to his wife, telling her he had completed his pilgrimage. "Now I feel it was an advantage to have lived so long. I have finished memorial rites for the souls of Father and Mother and I have been able to say prayers for the souls of those with no surviving relatives."

He was tired, he wanted to rest, he wanted quiet, but Tonosho was not the place. Morikawa and I debark there and see why: it is noisy, gaudy, touristy. The next morning he asked the maid if she knew of something better. She suggested an inn called Tachibana-so, several miles down the coast. He took the bus.

When he arrived he heard the sound of a Buddhist service from the room off the lobby. "Do you take groups of pilgrims?" he asked as he removed his shoes. He was told it was the fiftieth-day memorial service for the father of the inn's mistress.

The Tachibana-so is built against a height overlooking the Inland Sea. One enters on the third floor. The maid guided him down to the first floor, to a small room, the Pine Room.

Morikawa and I take the bus to the inn, as he did, almost an hour's ride. We find the mistress of the inn very willing to talk—a pleasant, outgoing woman, chatty any day, I expect, but perhaps especially so today; without planning it we have come on the anniversary of Danzo's death.

"When my son went to Tonosho to see off our guests who had come for Father's memorial service, he saw Danzo's picture in a newspaper and recognized him. We asked him if he wasn't Danzo but he refused to admit it. He had registered as Ichikawa Hichizo." She gets the card he signed, which evidently is kept handy: age, seventy-five; occupation, none; and a Yokohama address where he once lived. "We said we'd like to move him to a better room, but he'd have none of it.

"At dinner the first evening he especially enjoyed the sashimi, the raw fish, and asked for more; after that we served extra portions. He didn't want to converse with the maids, so dinner was quiet. He drank two bottles of saké." (The bottles in which saké is served hold about three-fourths of a cup.)

"He said he was an early riser and asked to have his breakfast brought to him the evening before so that he could eat whenever he liked. Rice and pickles and a thermos of hot water for tea were left in his room; he made *ochazuke*." (Ochazuke is one of the simplest of Japanese meals: tea poured over boiled rice.)

"We thought he would stay just one night but he asked to stay another, and then another—three nights in all. Perhaps he went for a stroll in the morning—we don't know—but mostly he stayed in his room."

She takes us down to the Pine Room. It is just as it was when he was here. Its simplicity must have pleased him: rather like the dressing rooms in which he spent so much of his life, but with a view. One looks far down through the tops of pine trees to a sheltered little bay and the headlands that embrace it. He pulled the table over to the window so that he could sit there and look out. He had a couple of paperbound detective novels: he read, and watched the changing light on the Inland Sea, and napped; perhaps he thought back on his pilgrimage and his life. He rested. It was off-season: the inn was quiet, as it is now. He had found a peaceful place.

He left on the morning of June 3. When he was leaving this room he turned back for a long look. "He walked very briskly up the hill to the bus stop. We wanted to provide a car for him but he wouldn't let us."

He did not return to Tonosho but went to the nearer port of Sakate. Two boats a day stop there on the way to Osaka, one at noon, the other at midnight. He went to the pier and bought a first-class ticket on the noon boat. With a few hours to wait he went to a nearby inn, took a room, and asked the maid to wrap a parcel for mailing to Tokyo: his pilgrim's robe, souvenir towels from inns he had stayed at, extra socks. As she worked he looked out the window toward the mountains. She ventured to tell him that the temple on the hill in the foreground was Kannon-ji.

"Is it a pilgrimage temple?"

"Yes, sir."

"Then I must go to worship."

He mailed his parcel and walked to Kannon-ji, Number Three of the Shodo Island pilgrimage. Morikawa and I follow his trail there.

The temple is a modest one, quiet in the rain. There is no one at home but the monument we came to see is conspicuous in the garden. It is dedicated to Ikuta Shungetsu, a sentimental, nihilist poet of the twenties and a desperately unhappy man: in the words of the brochure in our hands, "he was one of those poets who could be called accursed." In May, 1930, he committed suicide by jumping from a ship into the Inland Sea. His body was found by fishermen and brought into Sakate port. Six years later this monument was unveiled on a hill commanding a view of the Inland Sea. In 1954, as the tourist fever flared, it was moved here, that being the condition set by the bus company for extending its tourist route into the town.

A rough-hewn slab of granite bearing a bronze plaque: we stand in the softly soaking rain to make out the quotation from Shungetsu engraved on it: "The sea chart hanging on the deck of the ship, the chart of the Inland Sea—as I gaze on it there gradually emerges a world new and unknown to me. On an ordinary map the sea is blank, but on this chart the land is blank, save for those mountain peaks which are seamarks, while, in contrast, colorful signs show the depth of the water and the configuration of the bottom. This chart seems to express what I now feel in my heart. The world in which I have lived till now becomes blank and the world hitherto unknown to me, into which I shall throw myself, is transparently revealed."

They say that Danzo gazed at this a long time, but I do not know that there were witnesses. What is known is that he came down from the temple to the pier and changed his ticket to the midnight boat, accepting special second class because first class was sold out. He went to the inn, took a long nap, ate dinner with his usual two bottles of saké, waited until the boat had docked, and then walked down the pier and boarded it. It was raining heavily.

The whirlpools of Naruto *(a print by Hiroshige)*

About an hour after sailing he undressed and folded his clothes neatly. In his underwear he went onto the deck, deserted because of the rain, moved to the stern, surmounted the rail, and entered the sea.

"He wanted to die quietly, forgotten," said Bando Yaenosuke, "but the next day there was a rumor of an airplane crash and the newspapers held space. The rumor proved false, then came word of Danzo's suicide, and they gave it spectacular coverage.

"The body was never recovered. At a spot about an hour from Shodo there is a dangerous current. Before that, a body would be washed up on Shodo; after it, on the Osaka shore; but in it one would be swept into the whirlpools of the Naruto vortex and lost. He had traveled so widely and absorbed so much local lore that I think he knew this."

In that respect he was spared: he was never seen unpresentable. His was an act not of desperation but of resolution. He walked out of life as he had walked off the stage, with composure. He never became a burden.

Morikawa and I are silent on the rainy ride back to Takamatsu.

22 Temple Eighty-six: we have stayed overnight in the town; in the early morning, through a soft, insistent rain, we walk to the temple. It stands on the shore of the Inland Sea and its compound is open to the beach and harbor. It seems to face, across the island-studded sea, the main island of Honshu.

The name of the temple is Shido-ji. Among the complicated charms of the Japanese language—the complications making it terribly difficult, even for those born to it, the charms making it nearly impossible for those same people to consider simplifying it— is the fact that almost every character with which it is written packs layers of meaning and allusion.

The priest back at Sixty-six could pronounce the characters of his name in two quite different ways, one for his priestly role, the other for his mundane duties in the community. Conversely, a name can be written with several different sets of characters, loaded with quite different connotations but pronounced in the same way.

So it has been with the name of this temple. The characters with which Shido-ji was written in ages past summoned the old feelings about the island of Shikoku: that it was remote, mysterious, even frightening; that to some minds the whole island had the character of its dark peaks—it was home to the spirits of the dead. And because this temple was regarded as a port of entry to the island, the characters with which its name used to be written meant "Bridge to Death." Sometime in the past that came to seem too forbidding; now the characters used to write Shido-ji mean "the will to achieve enlightenment."

(The word "henro" has undergone a similar transformation. It used to be written with characters that signified a journey to a remote, outlying place, a frontier. Now the characters simply indicate pilgrimage.)

A temple legend reflects the earlier meaning. An old temple, it has been several times renovated. These renovations are credited to the intervention of Emma-o, the king of the world of the dead, the judge at the gate to Buddha's land. When the necessity arose he would stop some rich man and turn him around, saying, "You must return to the land of the living and rebuild Shido-ji, for that is my native temple."

And it was the earlier connotation that a retired emperor had in mind when he wrote in the early 1100's: "Famous places of miraculous powers on Shikoku are the training sites of Muroto in Tosa and Shido in Sanuki."

In the rain and at this hour we are quite alone in the temple garden, walking its winding paths, tracing its devious stream. The garden is as big as most Japanese farms and set within it is a jewel of a rock-and-sand garden dating from the fifteenth century, as abstract in design as any modern work of art.

As we walk into the valley toward Eighty-seven we are very conscious that today we will reach Eighty-eight. That will not be the end of our pilgrimage: we must close the circle by returning to Number One. But will our pilgrimage—this pilgrimage that we began more than two months ago—end there?

There are pilgrimages all over the world. In most, one travels to a place or places hallowed by events that took place there. One goes; one reaches one's goal; one returns. There are pilgrimages in India that follow a spiral route, moving around a mountain in a narrowing circle, gradually approaching the summit, the goal. But this Shikoku pilgrimage is the only pilgrimage I know of that is essentially a circle. It has no beginning and no end. Like the quest for enlightenment, it is unending.

Things that I have read come back to me. "The important thing in Buddhism is not dogma but practice, not the goal—the mysterious and unascertainable Nirvana—but the Path. . . . The Path is not the means to an end: the Path is the goal itself." This might have been said about the pilgrimage.

The rain ends. We have been aware for two or three weeks that we were walking into the rainy season, though there have been sunny days to dry us out. The sun breaks through now, but still we walk in silence, each absorbed in his own thoughts.

Number Eighty-seven: the priest is away, training for a week; no chance to talk with him. But we temporize, dawdling over the monuments in the compound. I remember something the priest said when I was here before. "At this next-to-the-last temple many pilgrims suddenly relax. Their accumulated fatigue hits them and they are unable to continue. They find it necessary to return to the main altar and pray again that their impurities be removed. Then they can go on. Some call this a barrier gate." I suggest to Morikawa that we pray at the altar once more. Then we set out.

From the valley we walk into the mountains. It seems right that Eighty-eight should be a mountain temple. Every temple is in the religious sense a mountain—one of the names that every temple bears is the name of a mountain—but as the henro crosses the plains he finds himself focusing on the real peaks that rise beyond and on the temples that crown those peaks. He knows what the mountains will demand of him and what they will give in return: a lifting of the spirits at the summit, a sense of awe.

Along the slopes the last of the wild azaleas fade and fall. The ascent becomes steeper; the road is hemmed by rocky peaks with rough perpendicular faces. In the grass we see a worn old stone marking a henro's grave.

The poet Masaoka Shiki, whose haiku I quoted as we approached Matsuyama City, battled most of his life against, first, tuberculosis of the lungs and, then, of the spine. For the last seven years of his life he was bedridden but he never stopped working, pressing forward in his campaign to revitalize haiku, which, after the brilliance of the masters of the seventeenth and eighteenth centuries, had subsided into stagnation. This was the lifework he had set for himself while he was still a university student. Shiki's last years were tortured with pain. He considered suicide, and resisted it. He wrote: "Up till now I have been mistaken in my understanding of the word 'enlightenment.' I thought it meant the ability to confront death without flinching. I know now that it means the ability to face life without flinching, no matter what the circumstances."

A year or two before he died he wrote a story called "The Dog." Shiki never made the pilgrimage but he knew that for many, resolve has crumbled just short of the goal, and that graves are numerous along this road to Eighty-eight.

Once upon a time in ancient China there was a kingdom whose people and their king had a great love of dogs. One day in a brawl a man killed the favorite dog of the king. For this not only was he executed but in the next life he was reborn as a masterless dog in a cold province called Shinshu in a remote island country called Japan. Since this Shinshu was in the mountains there were no fish, and in order to eat, the dog was forced to go to Oak Mountain. [Oak Mountain is that legendary barren crag where the aged, no longer able to work for their keep, were carried by their relatives and left to die; because in legend as in life, women usually outlive men, most of those cast away were women.] There the dog eked out

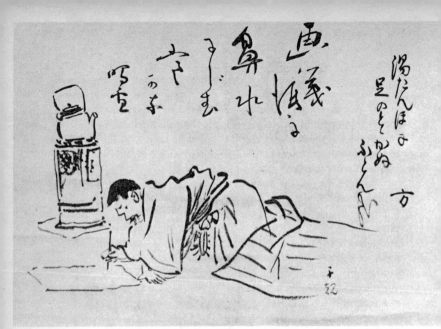

Shiki working from his bed on a wintry day *(a drawing by
Shiki's disciple Meisetsu with a haiku by Meisetsu and one by
Shihoda, another disciple)*

a miserable existence on that which was abandoned. It was after he
had eaten his eighty-eighth old woman that, glancing up, his eye
was caught by the first rays of the evening star and suddenly he
achieved enlightenment. He dashed to a temple where he confessed
all the crimes he had committed and prayed to be reborn as a
human being. Seven days and seven nights he remained under the
floor of the temple in unceasing prayer. On the seventh night sleep
came to him and in a dream Amida Buddha appeared and told him
that by virtue of his earnest supplication his wish would eventually
be granted. "In the meantime, exert yourself unceasingly and en-
gage in constant prayer. Thus even a beast may attain salvation.
What a miraculous thing this is!"

At these words the dog awoke and, greatly heartened, con-
ceived of furthering his goal by pilgrimage. Eventually he crossed to
the island of Shikoku, where there are eighty-eight sacred places. It
struck the dog that visiting one temple would atone for eating one

human being and worship at two would expiate two of his crimes, so barking "Namu Daishi Henjo Kongo" he dashed from one sacred place to the next. He had safely offered his devotions at eighty-seven sacred places when suddenly—probably from relaxation at the thought that he had only one place left—he collapsed just before the gate of the last temple. Gasping for breath he weakly lifted his head to find in front of him a stone statue of Jizo with a broken nose. [It is Jizo who saves souls from hell, guiding them to salvation.]

At once the dog offered a prayer to Jizo-sama, saying, "Please, will you show me the path I should take at the six crossroads so that I may reach the world of human beings? If you grant me this, I promise that I will give you a red bib after I am reborn." And the Jizo answered, "Your desire will be granted. You will realize your great wish." On hearing these words the dog was overjoyed: he growled three times, turned around, and died.

From somewhere a flock of eighty-eight crows appeared and swarmed over him, tearing at his belly and face and devouring him so ferociously that a passing monk took pity and buried his corpse. Then the Jizo spoke up: "The eighty-eight crows were the avenging spirits of the eighty-eight women. Had they been allowed to eat his flesh, his sins would all have been atoned for. Burying his corpse seemed like an act of mercy but really it was not. However, this is what fate decreed and it cannot be helped. He will be reborn as a human being but he will suffer from sickness and poverty all his life: his chance of becoming a worthy man is slim indeed."

. . . There was a dog like this and it could very well be that he was reborn into this world as me. I cannot stand upon my legs. I can just manage to crawl like a dog.

Echoing in the mountain we hear the temple bell. We round the last curve. Opposite the temple is a campsite, proclaimed by a Coca-Cola sign. There are parked cars and a Sunday crowd of picnickers; this has become a tourist spot. We feel on exhibition as we walk past food, drink, and souvenir shops toward steps that rise against the mountain. At their base is a stone pillar deeply engraved: THE PLACE OF FULFILLMENT OF THE VOW. Self-conscious or not, we take each other's picture beside it before we climb.

The walls of the main hall are hung with crutches, braces, plaster casts, cloth breasts; suspended from the ceiling is a

Temple Eighty-eight *(a painting by Sakata)*

two-wheeled cripple's cart; each is signed or tagged: name, age, address—specifics evoking the nameless who have thronged the pilgrimage over all the years seeking to be healed.

The priest attending the altar, having leafed through our albums to confirm that we came all the way around from Number One, asks us to kneel. Murmuring a benediction, he touches us with a priest's staff. Then he inscribes our albums with a vermilion stamp reading, like the stone pillar below, "The Place of Fulfillment of the Vow."

He shows us the staff with which he blessed us. It is of forged metal about as big around as a finger, surmounted by a metal finial shaped into two loops, each holding three metal rings. It was the Daishi's, he tells us, given to him by his master in China, left here by him when he completed his pilgrimage.

In front of the hall a group of women are chanting a short sutra over and over again. Before the Daishi Hall a worn old woman is repeating, "Namu Daishi Henjo Kongo," and an expression of gratitude that pours out of her: "This is more than I deserve. . . . This gift is too good for me. . . . I am unworthy of your kindness."

Following what they believe to be the Daishi's example, many henro who have completed their pilgrimage leave their staff here. The Daishi Hall and the veranda around it are crowded with staffs and sedge hats. The priest tells us that the temple annually holds an out-of-door fire ceremony toward the end of summer to burn the year's accumulation.

I ask him about Ichikawa Danzo. "He came here on May 30. He ate his lunch surrounded by reporters; there were many waiting here for him. We opened the sliding doors to make one big room so as to accommodate them all. The temple served tea and the newsmen ordered noodles for everyone from the shops on the road below. Since then, on the anniversary of that date the shops serve noodles as settai, saying they do it for the peace of his soul."

The night before he had stayed at an inn up on the mountain near Temple Eighty-four. When he came down the mountain in the morning he was met by reporters but they did not upset him.

His attitude had changed: he was not pleased to be an object of public interest but he was resigned. He was willing to permit photographs of the names written on his robe. He had concluded that letting the public know about his pilgrimage was perhaps a way of honoring the memories of those for whom he was praying. He accepted as settai the reporters' offer of a ride to the last four temples. He talked freely along the way and here at Eighty-eight.

"For twenty years I have dreamed of making a pilgrimage to the Eighty-eight Sacred Places. During my childhood I was delicate but after I grew up I was strong. During my entire career sickness kept me off the stage only three days, so I was quite able to undertake the pilgrimage. Walking in the company of the Daishi I was never lonely, nor did I worry about death.

"I came determined to detach myself from the secular world. I wanted to rinse every impurity from my guts.

"Now I have finished praying for the souls of the departed. I wish only to spend the rest of my days in a quiet place."

In the morning we ask the priest about the henro graves that cluster at this temple and he says he will guide us to them. After morning service and breakfast we shoulder our packs and he leads us down the steps, across the road, and down again into a ravine cut by a swift stream. "The old henro-path runs below the present road," he tells us, "and below the henro-path are dozens of graves. This came to be called the Valley of Amida's Pure Land." We plunge into a tangle of rank weeds and scrub, searching for stones. Of those we find, most are marked simply HENRO; a few bear a posthumous Buddhist name and a date. Morikawa finds one, still decipherable, from 1845.

Some were old. Some were ill or diseased. Some were outcasts, paupers, or beggars. Some had no home to return to: they had committed a transgression, or they wanted to lift a burden from their family, or their family had suggested they go on pilgrimage and not come back. Whatever their stories, they finished their pilgrimage.

"We have planted cedars and someday their shade will eliminate this thicket but so far they barely show above it. This used to be a bamboo grove; a blight killed it." It must have been lovely then: the deep shade, the ground clean of grass and weeds, the whisper of the wind through the bamboo.

We climb back to the old path, say good-bye, and set out. We still have walking to do, and we have the kind of path that makes portions of the pilgrimage a joy, old and well worn but clear and clean. There are henro-stones to mark the distances and images of Jizo to watch over it. It reminds me that there have always been happy henro who went home grateful and at peace.

Morikawa takes the lead here. His pack is as usual a little askew—our maps bulge at one side—but it rides easily on shoulders two months toughened. There is a bond between us now, a bond forged of shared delights and discomforts, of mutual dependency, of search and discovery, each into himself and together into a new landscape. They say a henro carries the baggage of his life: true, and the pilgrimage gives him time to sort out some of it.

We are headed back to Number One but I know now that my pilgrimage will not end there. When I started from Mount Koya on my first pilgrimage, the abbot of my temple sent me off by saying, "You will see all aspects of man, some pure, some impure. You should see both without misunderstanding." Pure and impure: I have seen both aspects, in myself. He also said, "If you are earnest, you will to some degree be transformed." This I know to be true. Anyone who performs the pilgrimage seriously must be to some degree transformed. But in my own case, to what degree? Of one thing I am certain: the transformation I yearn for is incomplete. I do not know whether I am any closer to enlightenment—I do not really expect to achieve it—but I know that the attempt is worth the effort.

The pilgrimage is addictive, as a henro we met some time back remarked. This circuit around Shikoku will pull me back to try again. And again. It is a striving, and that goes on. What is important is not the destination but the act of getting there, not the goal but the going. "The Path is the goal itself." Morikawa, dropping back to walk beside me, breaks the silence: "Someday I want to make the pilgrimage again."

It is growing dark and it is raining when we enter the gate of Temple Number One. Morikawa rings the temple bell.

Namu Daishi Henjo Kongo!

Two henro *(a print by Mutsu)*

THE PILGRIMAGE TEMPLES

This summary list gives each temple's number (B indicates a bangai, unnumbered), its most commonly used name (familiar names used locally are in parentheses), the deity or deities enshrined at its principal altar, and its sect. However, it should be noted that most temples bear three names; for instance, Number Thirty-eight is formally Ashizuri-san Fudaraku-in Kongōfuku-ji.

NUMBER	NAME	DEITY	SECT
		Awa	
B	Tōrin-in	Yakushi	Shingon
1	Ryōzen-ji	Shakuson (the historical Buddha)	Shingon
2	Gokuraku-ji	Amida	Shingon
3	Konsen-ji	Shakuson	Shingon
B	Aizen-in	Fudō	Shingon
4	Dainichi-ji	Dainichi	Shingon
B	Jizō-ji Okunoin (innermost sanctuary)	Shakuson	Shingon
5	Jizō-ji	Jizō	Shingon
6	Anraku-ji	Yakushi	Shingon
7	Jūraku-ji	Amida	Shingon
8	Kumadani-ji	Kannon	Shingon
9	Hōrin-ji	Shakuson	Shingon
B	Shōnen-ji	Amida	Jōdo
10	Kirihata-ji	Kannon	Shingon
11	Fujii-dera	Yakushi	Zen
B	Chōdo-an	Kōbō Daishi	Shingon

NUMBER	NAME	DEITY	SECT
		Awa	
B	Yanagi-no-mizu-an	Kōbō Daishi	Shingon
B	Ipponsugi-an	Amida	Shingon
12	Shōsan-ji	Kokūzō	Shingon
B	Shōsan-ji Okunoin	En no Gyōja (En the Ascetic)	Shingon
B	Joshin-an (Emon Saburō's grave)	Jizō	Shingon
B	Konchi-ji	Zao-gongen	Shingon
B	Dōgaku-ji	Yakushi	Shingon
13	Dainichi-ji (Ichinomiya-san)	Dainichi, Kannon	Shingon
14	Jōraku-ji	Miroku	Shingon
B	Koyasu-an	Kannon	Shingon
15	Kokubun-ji	Yakushi	Zen
16	Kannon-ji	Kannon	Shingon
17	Ido-ji	Yakushi	Shingon
18	Onzan-ji	Yakushi	Shingon
19	Tatsue-ji	Jizō	Shingon
B	Jigan-ji	Kannon	Shingon
20	Kakurin-ji	Jizō	Shingon
21	Tairyū-ji	Kokūzō	Shingon
22	Byōdō-ji	Yakushi	Shingon
B	Tsukiyo O-Mizu Daishi	Yakushi	Shingon
23	Yakuō-ji	Yakushi	Shingon
B	Taisen-ji	Kannon	Shingon
B	Saba Daishi Yasaka-ji	Kōbō Daishi	Shingon
		Tosa	
24	Hotsumisaki-ji (Higashi-dera, "East Temple")	Kokūzō	Shingon

NUMBER	NAME	DEITY	SECT
		Tosa	
25	Shinshō-ji (Tsu-dera, "Port Temple")	Jizō	Shingon
26	Kongōchō-ji (Nishi-dera, "West Temple")	Yakushi	Shingon
27	Kōnomine-ji	Kannon	Shingon
28	Dainichi-ji	Dainichi	Shingon
29	Kokubun-ji	Kannon	Shingon
B	Zenraku-ji	Amida	Shingon
30	Anraku-ji	Amida	Shingon
31	Chikurin-ji	Monju	Shingon
32	Zenjibu-ji	Kannon	Shingon
33	Sekkei-ji	Yakushi	Zen
B	Kōya-ji	Kōbō Daishi	Shingon
34	Tanema-ji	Yakushi	Shingon
35	Kiyotaki-ji	Yakushi	Shingon
36	Shōryū-ji	Fudō	Shingon
B	Hotokezaka Iwanofudō-son Kōmyōbu-ji	Fudō, Jizō	Shingon
B	Kannon-ji	Kannon	Shingon
B	Kōya-san Daizen-ji (Futatsu Iwa Daishi-dō)	Kōbō Daishi	Shingon
37	Iwamoto-ji	Fudō, Kannon, Yakushi, Amida, Jizō	Shingon
B	Shinnen-an	Kōbō Daishi	Shingon
38	Kongōfuku-ji	Kannon	Shingon
B	Tsukiyama Jinja	Getsuei no Reiseki	(Shintō)
39	Enkō-ji (Terayama)	Kannon	Shingon

NUMBER	NAME	DEITY	SECT
		Iyo	
B	Kōya-san Butsugan-in	Kōbō Daishi, Yakushi	Shingon
40	Kanjizai-ji	Yakushi	Shingon
B	Kankikō-ji	Yakushi, Kannon	Zen
B	Sasayama Jinja	Four Shintō deities	(Shintō)
B	Ryūkō-in	Kannon	Shingon
B	Ganjō-ji (Kujira Daishi)	Amida	Zen
41	Ryūkō-ji	Kannon	Shingon
42	Butsumoku-ji	Dainichi	Shingon
43	Ageshi-ji	Kannon	Tendai
B	Fudakake Daishi	Kōbō Daishi	Shingon
B	Toyogahashi Eitoku-ji	Kōbō Daishi	Shingon
44	Daihō-ji	Kannon	Shingon
45	Iwaya-ji	Fudō	Shingon
46	Jōruri-ji	Yakushi	Shingon
47	Yasaka-ji	Amida	Shingon
B	Tokusei-ji Monju-in	Kōbō Daishi, Jizō	Shingon
B	Fudahajime	Kōbō Daishi	Shingon
48	Sairin-ji	Kannon	Shingon
49	Jōdo-ji	Shakuson	Shingon
50	Hanta-ji	Yakushi	Shingon
51	Ishite-ji	Yakushi	Shingon
B	Gian-ji	Yakushi	Zen
52	Taisan-ji	Kannon	Shingon
53	Enmyō-ji	Amida	Shingon
B	Tsue Daishi	Kongō	Shingon
B	Kama Daishi	Kōbō Daishi	Shingon
B	Henjō-in	Yakushi	Shingon
B	Aoki Mizu Daishi	Kannon	Shingon
B	Enpuku-ji	Kannon, Jizō	Shingon
54	Enmei-ji	Fudō	Shingon
55	Nankō-bō	Daitsūchishō	Shingon

NUMBER	NAME	DEITY	SECT
		Iyo	
B	Kōya-san Imabari Betsu-in	Kōbō Daishi	Shingon
56	Taisan-ji	Jizō	Shingon
57	Eifuku-ji	Amida	Shingon
58	Senyū-ji	Kannon	Shingon
59	Kokubun-ji	Yakushi	Shingon
B	Dōan-ji	Yakushi	Shingon
B	Shōzen-ji (Ikiki-zan)	Yakushi, Jizō	Shingon
60	Yokomine-ji	Dainichi	Shingon
B	Kōon-ji Okunoin	Fudō	Shingon
61	Kōon-ji	Dainichi	Shingon
62	Hōju-in	Kannon	Shingon
63	Kichijō-ji	Bishamonten	Shingon
64	Maegami-ji	Amida	Shingon
B	Izarimatsu Emmei-ji	Jizō	Shingon
65	Sankaku-ji	Kannon	Shingon
B	Senryū-ji	Kōbō Daishi	Shingon
B	Jōfuku-ji (Tsubaki-dō)	Jizō	Shingon
		Sanuki	
66	Unpen-ji	Kannon	Shingon
67	Daikō-ji (Komatsuo-ji)	Yakushi	Shingon
68	Jinne-in*	Amida	Shingon
69	Kannon-ji*	Kannon	Shingon
70	Motoyama-ji	Kannon	Shingon
71	Iyadani-ji	Kannon	Shingon
B	Hichibutsu-ji (Chichi Yakushi)	Yakushi	Shingon

*Kannon-ji and Jinne-in now occupy the same compound; they constitute one temple but two Sacred Places.

NUMBER	NAME	DEITY	SECT
		Sanuki	
72	Mandara-ji	Dainichi	Shingon
73	Shusshaka-ji	Shakuson	Shingon
74	Kōyama-ji	Yakushi	Shingon
B	Senyūgahara Jizō-dō	Jizō, Child Daishi	Shingon
75	Zentsū-ji	Yakushi	Shingon
B	Jinnō-ji (Mannō-ike)	Yakushi	Shingon
76	Konzō-ji	Yakushi	Tendai
77	Dōryū-ji	Yakushi	Shingon
B	Kaigan-ji	Kannon	Shingon
78	Gōshō-ji	Amida	Ji
79	Tennō-ji (Kōshō-in)	Kannon	Shingon
80	Kokubun-ji	Kannon	Shingon
81	Shiramine-ji	Kannon	Shingon
82	Negoro-ji	Kannon	Tendai
83	Ichinomiya-ji	Kannon	Shingon
B	Kōya-san Sanuki Betsu-in	Kōbō Daishi	Shingon
B	Honen-ji	Amida	Jōdo
84	Yashima-ji	Kannon	Shingon
85	Yakuri-ji	Kannon	Shingon
86	Shido-ji	Kannon	Shingon
87	Nagao-ji	Kannon	Tendai
88	Ōkubo-ji	Yakushi	Shingon
B	Yoda-ji	Yakushi	Shingon

POSTSCRIPT

When I decided that I wanted to write this book I turned to Professor Joseph M. Kitagawa of the Divinity School, University of Chicago. His counsel and enthusiasm gave me the start I needed and through the years since then he has educated and encouraged me. He read my long first draft and the present one and gave me invaluable advice. Without him the whole pleasant task would have been much more difficult. This book is affectionately dedicated to him.

One of his first acts was to introduce me to Shingon priest and scholar Shozui M. Toganoo; * he too has been a support and he introduced me to the Reverend Keiryo Mizuno, who in 1968 guided me on my first pilgrimage. The accounts of my own pilgrimages are based chiefly on that one and on my second all the way around, with Nobuo Morikawa in 1971. I am indebted to both Mizuno and Morikawa for their companionship and their help. Morikawa has been a fast friend ever since and has aided me in many ways at many times. I am grateful also to the friends who accompanied me on other, shorter pilgrimages along sections of the route; I cannot name them all but there is something of every one of them in this book.

When I made my first pilgrimage I already had a circle of friends on Shikoku. I visited that lovely island initially in 1961, armed with introductions. Mr. Saburo Takeda took me to Zentsu-ji, the Daishi's family home, to nearby temples and henro-inns, and finally—as described in Chapter 12—to the Haiku Teahouse and Temple Seventy-one; later he introduced me to his brother,

---

* Japanese names in this Postscript are given in Western style, surname last.

Mr. Akira Takeda, the author of several useful books on Shikoku and the pilgrimage.

At Matsuyama I was lucky to have Professor Masaaki Nagata and Mr. Jun'ichiro Kitagawa as my guides; Mr. Kitagawa shared all his lore about pilgrimage in the past and capped his kindness with an essay on pilgrims in the old days, a gift to me as I set out on my 1971 pilgrimage. Professor Nagata's broad knowledge was always at my disposal and it was through him that I met many other scholars; when I returned to Matsuyama in 1969 to live there for two years he introduced me to Professor Kametaro Yagi, then president of Matsuyama University of Commerce, who became both mentor and close friend. In Matsuyama I am also grateful to Mrs. Hideko Ogura and Mr. Kiyoshi Shioiri, and I wish I could list all of the students who made my life there brighter.

In the city of Kochi I fell into the best possible hands: Professor Michio Hirao was, as I have described him in the text, a Tosa historian with a national reputation and a delight to be with. He introduced me to generous Kochi scholars and to Mr. Fumio Tosa, whose pilgrimage in 1971 just preceded Morikawa's and mine and whose accounts of it in the *Kochi Shimbun* were collected into the book from which he has given me permission to quote.

In the city of Tokushima I am grateful to have known historian Shoichiro Miyoshi and the Reverend Ninsho Miyazaki, priest of the temple Hannya-en. Although Hannya-en is not a pilgrimage temple, Reverend Miyazaki is noted as a scholar of Shingon and the pilgrimage and I came back to him again and again for the light he could throw on issues troubling me.

I always looked forward to visiting Takamatsu because of Mr. Kiyoshi Murayama, genial, knowledgeable, and always helpful. He introduced me to Mr. Takashi Sogo, who was a gracious and able guide, and to Professor Shoichi Matsuura, who freely shared his knowledge of Sanuki's history and legends.

And finally, I feel privileged that on Mount Koya I have been welcomed by Abbot Zenkyo Nakagawa of Shinno-in, "the temple I call mine." He has been an inspiration as well as a source of insight into Shingon.

This book is an attempt to fathom the meaning of the

Shikoku pilgrimage. It is not an exposition of Buddhism in general or Shingon in particular, but because faith in Kobo Daishi is central to the pilgrimage I have tried in the first section, "Master," to illuminate the founder of Shingon in Japan, the man who lived from 774 to 835. My basic source was Professor Yoshito S. Hakeda's *Kukai: Major Works Translated, With an Account of His Life and a Study of His Thought* (New York: Columbia University Press, 1972), from which I have frequently quoted. I have used Professor Joseph M. Kitagawa's papers "Master and Saviour" in *Studies of Esoteric Buddhism and Tantrism* (Koyasan, Japan: Koyasan University, 1965)—the essay that suggested the structure of this book—and "Three Types of Pilgrimage in Japan" in *Studies in Mysticism and Religion* (Jerusalem: presented to Gershom G. Scholem, 1967); also his unpublished University of Chicago dissertation, *Kobo Daishi and Shingon Buddhism* (1951), and his books *Religion in Japanese History* (New York: Columbia University Press, 1966) and *Religions of the East* (Philadelphia: Westminster Press, 1960); the quotation concerning the Path on page 320 is from the latter. The description of the Daishi's ascetic practice in invoking Kokuzo is based on Dr. M. W. DeVisser's *The Bodhisattva Akasagarbha (Kokuzo) in China and Japan* (Amsterdam: Uitgave Van De Koninklijke Akademie Van Wetenschappen Te Amsterdam, 1931). The account of Kukai's voyage to China is drawn from Professor Robert Borgen's paper "The Japanese Mission to China, 804–806" in *Monumenta Nipponica,* spring, 1982. Information about En the Ascetic came from H. Byron Earhart's paper "Shugendo, The Traditions of En no Gyoja, and Mikkyo Influence," in the same Koyasan University volume as Kitagawa's "Master and Saviour."

The second section, "Savior," attempts to show how the historical figure, Kukai, was transformed into the saint and the deity worshiped as Kobo Daishi, a process largely brought about by the holy men *(hijiri)* of Koya. My basic source has been *Koya Hijiri* by Professor Shigeru Gorai (Tokyo: Kadokawa Shoten, 1965), but I have dramatized the stories of historical figures such as Joyo, Chogen, Butsugen, Gyosho, and Saigyo, and based on Gorai's work I have created fictional characters to represent the hundreds of anonymous holy men; however, the burial mounds of a holy man who suffered toothache and of one who prayed for rain do exist, in the neighborhood of Temple Fifty. Chapter 9 about Saigyo relies on Professor William R. LaFleur's unpublished University of Chicago dissertation *Saigyo the Priest and His Poetry of Seclusion: A Buddhist Valorization of Nature in Twelfth-Century Japan* (1973) and his translations of Saigyo's poems and headnotes in *Mirror for the Moon* (New York: New Directions, 1978); Professor LaFleur has further helped me by reading this chapter. In writing of Ashizuri in Chapter 12 I have used Professor Yoshihiru Kondo's *Shikoku Henro* (Tokyo: Ofusha, 1971). Throughout this section I have been guided by Professor Ichiro Hori's *Folk Religion in Japan* (Chicago: University of Chicago Press, 1968).

The translation of Kuya's songs is from Tsunoda, de Bary, and Keene, *Sources of the Japanese Tradition* (New York: Columbia University Press, 1958). Chogen's description of Mount Koya and the stories of Shunkan, the Saint of Koya, Kumagai, and the imperial messengers to the Daishi's tomb are all drawn from *Heike Monogatari* as translated by A. L. Sadler (Tokyo: *Transactions of the Asiatic Society of Japan,* 1918 and 1921). The poetry on page 138 is from Arthur Waley's translation of the No play *Shunkan* in *The No Plays of Japan* (London: George Allen and Unwin, 1921). The fictional account of Saigyo's visit to the tomb of Emperor Sutoku is from Leon Zolbrod's translation of Akinari Ueda's *Ugetsu Monogatari* (Vancouver: University of British Columbia Press, 1974); other quotations in this episode are from William R. Wilson's translation of *Hogen Monogatari,* a *Monumenta Nipponica* monograph (Tokyo: Sophia University, 1971). The account of how Cape Ashizuri was named is from Karen Brazell's translation of *The Confessions of Lady Nijo* (Garden City: Anchor Press/Doubleday, 1973). The song on page 151 is D. L. Philippi's translation in "Songs on the Buddha's Foot-prints" from *Nihonbunka-Kenkyujo-Kiyo* No. 2 (Tokyo: Kokugakuin University, 1958). Fumio Tosa has graciously given me permission to draw on his account of his own pilgrimage, *Dogyo Ninin* (Kochi: Kochi Shimbun, 1972), and I have done so at several points. The translation of the four-line poem on the henro's hat is by Edward G. Seidensticker from his translation of Junichiro

Tanizaki's novel *Some Prefer Nettles* (New York: Alfred A. Knopf, 1955).

In the third section, "Pilgrims," I drew on Professor Kiyoshi Hiroe's compilation of Tosa materials relating to henro, *Kinsei Tosa Henro Shiryo* (Kochi, Japan: Tosa Minzoku Gakkai, 1966); on the papers of Frederick Starr in the Regenstein Library, University of Chicago; on several essays by Itsue Takamure about her pilgrimage (found in her collected works and translated for me by Mrs. Sachiko Kanai), and here let me thank Professor Eiki Hoshino for bringing Takamure to my attention; on Matsuichi Tsurumura's study of Mohei Nakatsuka's life and diaries, translated for me by Nobuo Morikawa; and on Alfred Bohner's *Wallfahrt zu Zweien* (Tokyo: German Society for the Study of the Countries and Peoples of East Asia, 1931) in an unpublished translation by Katharine Merrill Skog (1941); Danzo's story is based on interviews and magazine articles.

I have of course referred to standard histories of Japan in English, such as Sir George Sansom's, and to several works on pilgrimage by Japanese scholars, notably: Tsunezo Shinjo, *Shaji Sakei no Shakai-Keizai-shi Teki Kenkyu* (Tokyo: Hakkosho, 1964); Takashi Maeda, *Junrei no Shakaigaku* (Osaka: Kansai University, 1971); and Kondo's book mentioned earlier. Old guidebooks to the pilgrimage have proved valuable.

I want to thank those who made works in Japanese accessible to me: my friends Mr. Sadao Nakano and Mr. Hiroshi Ueno of the National Diet Library, Tokyo, and Professor Madoka Kanai of the Historiographical Institute, University of Tokyo; and those who translated hundreds of pages for me, especially Mrs. May Hashimoto Flood-Murphy, Mr. Tanejiro Kamei, Mrs. Mariko Sato, and Mr. Takashi Nonin. Professor Ineko Suehiro of the University of Hawaii has helped me often. Charles Mitchell of Tokyo gave me the delightful volumes *Shikoku Reigen Kio Ki* from which I have drawn illustrations.

All reference works notwithstanding, my education would be woefully incomplete without the understanding that has come from uncounted conversations. I have talked at length with the priest of almost every temple, with other henro, with persons along the way, and with scholars and enthusiasts who have studied one or another aspect of the pilgrimage. It would take a long chapter to list all those who have contributed to this book. It would include my students: in 1977 I was invited to be a visiting professor of Asian Studies at the University of Hawaii at Manoa, where I taught a seminar on the pilgrimage. The lively intelligence of the participants helped me to sharpen and clarify my ideas; I hope that they were equally rewarded.

Readers may notice that I have not mentioned many of the pilgrimage temples. I do have favorites among the temples—each has its own personality—but some of my favorites were omitted; I focused on those temples that fit the structure of my narrative.

I owe much to the friends who read my manuscript and gave me the benefit of their opinions: in addition to those already mentioned, Professor Hakeda and Kenneth and Priscilla Hecht read the first draft, and the present version was read by Colonel Jesse Doyle, Professor Windsor G. Hackler, Jeffrey Hackler, and Professor James Brandon; special thanks go to Damaris A. Kirchhofer for her close reading and detailed comments.

A Guggenheim Fellowship enabled me to undertake this book and a University of Hawaii Center for Asian and Pacific Studies Scholar-in-Residence Fellowship made it possible for me to finish it. I am deeply grateful for both.

OLIVER STATLER
January, 1983

Honolulu

INDEX

(Page numbers in italics refer to illustrations)

341